RED CACTUS

RED CACTUS:
THE LIFE OF ANNA KINGSFORD

Alan Pert

GenNext Publication

First Published, 2018

Published by

GenNext Publication
5, Ansari Road
Daryaganj, New Delhi-110002
Phone: 9811692060
E-mail: gennextpublication@hotmail.com

Printed at: G. Print Process, Delhi.

Cataloging in Publication Data—DK
Courtesy: D.K. Agencies (P) Ltd. <docinfo@dkagencies.com>

Pert, Alan, author.
Red cactus : the life of Anna Kingsford / Alan Pert.
pages cm
Includes bibliographical references and index.
ISBN 9789380223124

1. Kingsford, Anna Bonus, 1846-1888. 2. Physicians—Great Britain—Biography. 3. Women physicians—Great Britain—Biography. 4. Hermetism. I. Title.

R489.K56P47 2017 DDC 610.92 23

Contents

Chronology of the Life of Anna Kingsford 7
Acknowledgements 9
Introduction 11

1. Early Years 13
2. A Young Woman 25
3. Marriage 31
4. Anna's Own Paper 43
5. Anna at Home 51
6. Medical Studies 61
7. Anna's Mystical Illuminations 75
8. New Friends and Medical Graduation 83
9. Back in England 89
10. A Public Figure 99
11. President of the British Theosophical Society 113
12. Controversy in Theosophy 133
13. The Hermetic Society 145
14. Multifarious Activities 153
15. A Busy Life Takes Its Toll 163
16. Dying is a Very Slow Process 175
17. After Anna 193
18. Maitland's Biography of Anna in Question 203

Appendix - 1

Some features of Anna's character as revealed in her horoscope **223**

Appendix - 2

Some features of Maitland's horoscope **227**

Appendix - 3

The fate of Eadith Kingsford **229**

Bibliography **231**

Index **241**

Chronology of the Life of Anna Kingsford

1846 : Anna is born on 16 September at Stratford, Essex, England. Her maiden name was Annie Bonus; later she chose Anna for her first name.

1851 : The Bonus family are living at Blackheath.

1863 : Publication of her first book *Beatrice, aTale of the Early* Christians.

1863-64 : Anna attends finishing school at Brighton,

1864 : Family moves to St Leonards on Sea, Sussex.

1865 : Anna's father John Bonus dies.

1866 : Her poems *River-Reeds* are published.

1867 : Anna active for women's rights. Marries Algernon Kingsford at St Leonards on Sea, 31 December.

1868 : Algernon Kingsford studies at the Lichfield Theological College, Staffordshire. Birth of Anna's daughter Eadith 24 September at St Leonards. Anna writes stories and a long pamphlet on women's suffrage.

1869 : Algernon becames curate at Atcham, Shropshire.

1870 : Anna is baptised in the Roman Catholic Church to avoid the duties of a clergyman's wife.

1872 : Anna acquires the *Lady's Own Paper* in London in October.

1873 : Anna meets Florence Fenwick Miller, then Edward Maitland. Algernon becomes a rector at Pontesbury, Shropshire. Anna begins to study medicine in London.

1874 : Commences to use 'Anna' as her first name. Begins her medical course at the Ecole de Médecine, Paris in April.

1875 : Anna's stories *Rosamunda the Princess* are published. Theosophy Society founded in America by Helena Blavatsky and Henry Olcott.

1877 : Anna active against vivisection. She receives illuminative dreams which continue for ten years. Maitland visits mediums, writes *England and Islam* and *The Soul and How It Found Me.* Anna makes him withdraw the latter from circulation.

1878 : British Theosophical Society formed.

1879 : Anna's friend Lady Caithness settles in Paris.

1880 : Anna graduates as a doctor of medicine. Maitland makes many visits to mediums and séances.

1881 : Anna and Maitland study Hermetic works at the British Museum. Anna's thesis *The Perfect Way in Diet* is published. They deliver 'The Perfect Way' lectures in London.

1882 : *The Perfect Way, or the Finding of Christ* is published. Algernon Kingsford becomes vicar of Atcham.

1883 : Anna is appointed president of the British Theosophical Society. She lectures for vegetarianism and against vivisection in Switzerland and later in Scotland. Disagreement with A.P. Sinnett over reliance on the Eastern masters in his *Esoteric Buddhism* and the direction of the Theosophical Society.

1884 : Anna meets Helena Blavatsky in London. In May, Anna and Maitland resign from office in the Theosophical Society to form the Hermetic Society. Anna undertakes lecture tour against vivisection in England in December.

1885 : Anna and Maitland deliver Hermetic Society lectures in the Summer in London. Anna gives lecture tours in England.

1886 : The last Hermetic Society session is held. Anna's *Health, Beauty and the Toilet* is published. Anna drenched on an abortive visit to Pasteur's Institute in Paris 17 November, activating her disposition to consumption.

1887 : Anna and Maitland travel to the French Riviera and Italy in a vain attempt to restore her health. In July she moves to her final home, 15 Wynnstay Gardens, Kensington.

1888 : Anna dies on 22 February, aged 41 years, 5 months. Mother dies on 17 March.The Hermetic Order of the Golden Dawn is established. Anna's *Dreams and Dream Stories* published.

1889 : Publication of *Clothed With the Sun*, Anna's mystical illuminations.

1896 : *Anna Kingsford: Her Life, Letters, Diary and Work* by Maitland published in January.

1897 : Edward Maitland dies 2 October at Tonbridge, Kent.

1913 : Algernon Kingsford dies 10 August at Petworth, Sussex.

Acknowledgements

Various people and institutions have helped me to produce this book. Mary Greer lit a spark when she suggested I write a biography of Anna Kingsford. I thank Gareth Knight for his interest. Naomi and Cai Blumensaadt of the Campbell Research Library, Theosophical Society of Australia, Sydney gave invaluable assistance, as did Dai Trandang of the said Society. Rob Alexander, the Surrey genealogist, provided inestimable help. Cameron Moffett, Helena Wojtczak, Gill Burton and Sue and Brian Poulson of England gave great support. The Shropshire Records and Research Centre was an enormous help. Thanks to Fiona Bartlett of Scotland for the picture of Anna with a headband, and to Nancy Bonus of Canada. Jane Stanley and Alison Duncan of Australia provided hard to get resources when overseas. Libraries which provided vital material were the British Library, the Wellcome Library in London, the University of Harvard Library, the Stanford University Library, the Australian National Library, Fisher Library of the University of Sydney, the State and Mitchell Libraries of New South Wales, and the University of Queensland Library. Many thanks to Richard Charteris and Sarah Penicka for editorial assistance .

Introduction

The English born Anna Kingsford (1846-1888) was a most remarkable woman. Everyone who met her said so. With destiny bestowing the mantle of greatness upon her, she stood out from the crowd. She possessed flawless beauty, a brilliant mind, and mystical insight of a rare order.

Anna accomplished much in her life, tragically cut short by consumption (TB). She wrote on a variety of subjects, beginning at a young age with poetry and a novel on religious themes. After inheriting a comfortable income from her ship-owning father, Anna married a theological student, Algernon Kingsford. He agreed to her condition of marriage that she be free to follow her own career. By choice, she had only one child, called Eadith, and began to apply her considerable intelligence and talents to social causes that were dear to her heart. During Anna's early married years she wrote on women's rights, short stories, and owned *The Lady's Own Paper* in London in 1872.

In 1874 Anna commenced medical studies at the Medical School in Paris. Not only was she interested in health, she wanted credentials for her campaign against vivisection and in the promotion of vegetarianism. Her husband supported Anna in her studies and career, although he stayed in the background. Anna met the writer, Edward Maitland, who became her co-worker in her causes, and often traveled with her. She obtained her medical degree in 1880, having the distinction of not performing any vivisection during her course.

From 1877 onwards Anna received mystical illuminations which formed the basis of *The Perfect Way, or the Finding of Christ,* published in 1882. This is a major work on Hermetic philosophy, also called esoteric Christianity. Other pilgrims on the mystical path recognized her stature, and appointed Anna president of the British Theosophical Society in 1883. Due to factionalism in the Society, she did not stand for president in 1884.

In response Anna formed the pivotal Hermetic Society, which influenced among others, the poet William Butler Yeats, and Samuel MacGregor Mathers, a founder of the legendary occult society, the Hermetic Order of the Golden Dawn. Despite suffering from asthma, Anna led a very busy life, lecturing widely on vegetarianism and against vivisection in addition to her medical practice. In November 1886 Anna received a drenching in a Paris downpour which triggered consumption. Travel to the Riviera and Italy did not improve her condition. In June 1887 she settled in London, and died there in February 1888.

As a mystic, Anna Kingsford is on a par with Meister Eckhart and William Blake. Significant people have been influenced by her works. Mahatma Gandhi was impressed with her spiritual teachings, and sold her mystical books in South Africa in the 1890s. Mary Greer called her the magical mother of the Golden Dawn. The leading twentieth century occultist Dion Fortune recommended Anna's mystical works, as did the scholar of esoteric spirituality, Antoine Faivre. Countless theosophists, mystics, and other seekers of enlightenment have found inspiration in her works. Anna also holds an honoured place in the histories of vegetarianism and animal rights. Over recent years her life and works have received increasing attention from the women's movement and spiritual studies.

The only other biography of Anna Kingsford, by Edward Maitland, was published in 1896. I have discovered this work is full of errors. Also, it omits much personal information about Anna, and her relationships with her family and friends. When Maitland finished writing Anna's biography, he burnt all the papers, diaries and letters which she had bequeathed to him, forever losing priceless information about her life.

However, I have located significant new information about her, and in the last chapter I expose the errors of Maitland which have tarnished her reputation.

Despite her impressive accomplishments, some strange and disturbing things have been written about Anna Kingsford. Did she really kill two French vivisectors with black magic? Did she once offer herself to be vivisected? In past lives was she Mary Magdalen, Joan of Arc, and Anne Boleyn? Did a black magician take over her mind to make her his slave? For the first time, the answers are given in this book.

Chapter - 1

Early Years

Annie Bonus was born at Maryland Point, Stratford, Essex , England at 5.00 p.m. on Thursday, 16 September 1846. Though she was christened Annie, she used various first names until she settled on Anna at the commencement of her medical career. Her father, John Bonus JP (1794-1865), born at Stepney, Middlesex, was a wealthy ship owner and agent. His family, of Italian descent, had lived in London for several generations. Her mother, Elizabeth Ann (1805-1888) (née Schroder), of Irish and German descent, was born at St Georges East in Middlesex, and married John on 3 January 1826 in the parish of Walthamstow. Members of the Bonus family were in the Merchant Taylors Guild as far back as the late 1500s. The Family crest was a wild dog. Their motto was 'In medio tutissimus ibis', which loosely means 'In the middle of things, you will go most safe '.

Anna had seven older brothers, and four sisters, three of whom died before Anna was born. Ann (1827-1844), the first child in the family, died from consumption. In his biography of Anna, Edward Maitland would write that she had golden hair like her deceased sister. He said that although Mrs Bonus did not believe in spiritualism and had not heard of reincarnation, the two daughters were so alike as to make her think Ann had come back as Anna. Because Mrs Bonus was 41 when Anna was born, it suggests she was her parents' last attempt to replace their lost daughter, a view which is reinforced by the similarity of their names.

John Bonus (1828-1909), the eldest son, matriculated to Wadham College, Oxford on 27 January 1847. Annie 's next brother was Henry (1830-1903), then Albert (1831-1884), who both went into their father's shipping business. Mary was born in 1833 and died when two months old.

Edward (1834-1908) attended Felsted School in Essex and later became rector of Hulcott in Buckinghamshire. Next was Joseph (1836- 1926) who attended the George Monoux School at Walthamstow, Essex. He achieved recognition in the army and rose to the rank of major general. Her last two brothers were Schroder (b.1837) and Charles (1839-1883). Anna's only surviving sister was Emily Louisa (1841-1912) who, like Anna, was a Virgo. Alice Kate Bonus (1842-1844) had an all too brief life.

The name Stratford, meaning road by the ford, was first recorded in the 11th century. In about 1110 the building of the Bow Bridge by Queen Matilda over the River Lea was a decisive step in Stratford's growth. The Maryland Point area contained substantial houses with large gardens for the well-to-do. The first house in this area was built by Richard Lee (d.1664), a rich merchant who had returned from Maryland in America. He also built Stratford House, the seat of Lord Henniker. Norman White described the industrialization of Stratford as follows:

> Whereas the metropolitan area of London was being protected in various ways from some of the worst effects of industrialisation, the Stratford area was just outside London's eastern boundary of the River Lea, and had to receive various kinds of refugees and rejects from the city. The Metropolitan Buildings Act in 1844 began heavy restrictions on offensive trades in London. As a result soap works, boneboilers, varnish makers, vitriol manufacturers, and chemical manure works set up in the Stratford district...Fields, the typical marshy pastures, and market gardens were rapidly being replaced by building developments to house immigrant workers.[1]

In 1846, the year of Anna's birth, Britain was well on the path of industrialisation and imperialistic expansion. Queen Victoria had been on the throne for nine years. The Corn Law had been abolished, resulting in cheaper bread, and the Whigs were in power. In Ireland the potato famine was devastating the population. In India Britain took thePunjab in the First Anglo-Sikh War. The American dentist William T. Morton performed the first successful tooth extraction under ether. Was it a portent that just six days after Anna was born the German astronomer Johann Galle discovered Neptune, the planet of mysticism? The British astronomer William Lasell soon followed with the discovery of Triton, a moon of Neptune. In the world of music, French composer Hector Berlioz completed his dramatic cantata *The Damnation of Faust*, and Felix Mendelssohn's oratorio *Elijah* was premiered in Birmingham. In France the anarchist Pierre-Joseph Proudhon published *The Philosophy of Poverty.* In Europe revolution was in the air, leading to various political upheavals in 1848, the year of *The Communist Manifesto* by Karl Marx and Frederick Engels.

On the day Anna was born the main domestic news item in *Thev Times* concerned an investigation into conditions at the St Pancras workhouse. This article arose from the inquest into the death of the seventeen year old Mary Anne Jones, who had left the job she had been sent to from the workhouse. Poor Mary drowned herself in a canal to avoid being locked up in cramped, unhygienic quarters, and fed poor quality food, as was the customary punishment in the workhouse. A classified advertisement in the same paper announced 'Mr Dickens's new work, Dealings with the Firm of Dombey and Son.' On this day *Romeo and Juliet* was playing at the Theatre Royal, while *King Lear* was at the Royal Surrey Theatre.

As a child Anna spent many happy hours in the large garden surrounding her home, conversing with the flowers and leaving notes among them she had written for the fairies. Anna always had a strong imagination, dressing her many dolls in special costumes and creating plays for them. She also told her dolls fabulous stories about 'fairies and princesses, knights and castles and dragons, gods and goddesses.' Anna had the free run of her father's library and devoured the classics, especially liking the *Metamorphoses* of Ovid and other mythologies.

When Anna was still young the family moved to Blackheath, south of the river Thames. The 1851 census shows the Bonus family was living in The Grove, Blackheath, parish of Greenwich. Mr and Mrs Bonus, Henry, Albert, Edward, Emily, Anna and five servants comprised the household. Henry and Albert were clerks to their father. Edward was a scholar, and Emily and Anna were described as 'at home.' Among the servants was the single 'nurse ' Mary Woodley, thirty years of age, who no doubt looked after young Anna.

Blackheath had a long and colourful history. Situated an easy distance from London and on the road to Canterbury and Dover, Blackheath was a chosen site for military gatherings and state receptions. In June 1381 Wat Tyler camped his peasants there before pressing on to London to protest against high taxes. The Heath was notorious for highwaymen until the late 18th century when a residential suburb was developed. With the coming of the railway in 1849 Blackheath became an attractive place to live, especially for people like Anna's father who commuted to London.

The 1861 census shows the Bonus family living in Point House, The Grove, Blackheath. It was a large, nondescript three story square house, now converted into flats. By 1861 Anna and Emily Louisa were the only Bonus children living at home. Owning a profitable shipping business, Anna's father could well afford a large house and servants. The household included a coachman, a footman, and four women domestics: a cook, a servant and two housemaids. Anna's brothers were moving on in the world. John was living in Ivy House, a property owned by his father at Turnham Green in the parish of Chiswick. John, now a Roman Catholic priest at St Mary's, Turnham Green, ran a small school for boys in his home. Boarding with him was Kate Wilson, a widow aged 36 years, and three male teenage 'scholars.' Albert Bonus was living at Kidbrooke, Kent, with his wife and two small sons. Edward Bonus, as yet unmarried, was curate of Buckley and boarded with a schoolmaster and his family at Tring, Herfordshire.

We have scant information from Anna herself about her childhood. The following extract from her book *Health, Beauty and the Toilet* (1886) relates one of her memories, indicating the family took regular holidays at the seaside:

> …the odour of sweet peas invariably recalls to me the parlour of a little seaside cottage in which, when a child, I spent many very happy days. Certainly I have smelt sweet peas since then in hundreds of various gardens and houses, yet none of these is recalled to mind by the aroma in question, but only and always that one particular place, of which I am never reminded in any other way. And these memories are not mere indefinite recollections. They are vivid, sharp, distinct with life. They spring up in the mind like actual revivals of the past, with all the accessories of minute detail and personal feeling associated with them years and years ago. As the magic odour floats over our nervous surfaces, the heart throbs again with emotions and hopes of which we have long ceased to have experience. Time rolls back, the atmosphere around us is changed – we are young, we are sanguine, we believe in love! But, in a moment, the curtain falls again; the perfume is dissipated or spent in the air, and no effort voluntarily made can continue or revive the charm. Memory sinks once more to her ordinary level of generalities, the living moment has passed, and we are back again in the existence and scenes of the present hour.

Anna was a born writer, and at an early age she excelled in poetry and prose. Her first book, *Beatrice, a Tale of the Early Christians,* was published in her seventeenth year. Maitland informs us she wrote it at thirteen years of age, a remarkable achievement for one so young. Anna submitted it to the *Churchman's Companion*, but the publisher Joseph Masters thought it worthy to come out in a separate volume. '"And I accordingly," she said, when recounting her early history to me [Maitland], "received two guineas, for they knew I was but a child. I afterwards wrote a quantity of poetry for the *Churchman's Companion*, which I do not consider composed by myself, as it came to me readymade, and I had but to write it down." '

Beatrice, a Tale of the Early Christians is a novel of 114 pages, amounting to approximately 25,000 words. It opens in Rome in the year 303AD, when the Roman emperor Diocletian (245-313) was persecuting Christians. If Christians refused to burn incense to the gods they could be tortured and killed by the authorities. In Anna's story the Christian brothers Simplicius and Faustinus were on trial in the Forum, observed by their eighteen year old sister Beatrice. Her 'appearance, though her dress was of the plainest kind, denoted high birth. Her beautiful face was calm, but colourless as the white marble pillars around her, and in her eyes, like wells in their depth and darkness, lay almost hidden a sad sweet look, which told at once of keen mental suffering and of holy trust.' After the brothers were sentenced to death, Beatrice joined some Christians hiding in the catacombs. She was otherworldly and longed for a pure life, eventually finding fulfilment in Christian martyrdom. Beatrice was captured, tried and strangled. Her body was unceremoniously tossed into the river where she floated Ophelia-like, her countenance wearing 'a sweet expression of perfect unbroken peace.' At the end of the book Beatrice has achieved her ideal:

> Meanwhile, she sleeps patiently in her quiet cell among the blessed dead, her pale white hands resting peacefully on her breast, and her dark blue eyes closed for ever upon the pains and sorrows of this troublesome world, and her works do follow her.

The following extracts show Anna's youthful piety, and an unusual depth of religious thought and feeling for a young girl:

> Christianity is especially opposed to selfishness, its sublime teaching is all directed to the abasement of self, and love of others...

> Selfishness is peculiarly the sin of man, perhaps because he is accustomed to supremacy and sway over the weaker sex.

Even at this tender age, Anna showed a glimpse of disquiet at the subordination of women. After mentioning Adam's punishment in the *Bible*, she continued, '...Eve was also condemned to suffer many sorrows and greater bodily pain than her husband, besides being required to yield entire obedience to his will, a commandment by no means easy to observe.' In order to 'finish' her education Anna was sent to a fashionable school at the popular seaside town of Brighton, Sussex. Maitland gave no details of Anna's school, and no information about it has come to light. However, we can glean something of Anna's schooling through information on other schools from the era. In 1857 there were 132 schools for 'ladies' at Brighton. A representative girl's school from the 1861 census was in Sussex Square, a few streets from the beach at the eastern end of Brighton. It was run in the family home by two unmarried sisters, Clementia and Mary Grantly. There were twenty eight pupils, ranging in age from ten to seventeen. The most common age group was fifteen to sixteen, comprising twelve girls. We do not know when Anna attended school or for how long, but most likely it was in her mid teen years.

The only words we have from Anna about her school days is this amusing extract from her book *Health, Beauty and the Toilet* (1886):

> The bane of all uncultured girls consists in the propensities to giggle, to grimace, and to gabble, especially whenever anything methodical or serious is demanded of them. When I was at school, a certain gentleman who professed literature at one of our Universities used to come occasionally to read Shakespeare with us. The members of the class, composed of girls between the ages of fourteen and eighteen, read aloud in turn, and if by chance one of them, momentarily moved by the sentiment of the lines, suffered her voice to be betrayed into tones less rapid and meaningless than the usual wont, the suppressed tittering of her companions speedily covered her face with the blush of confusion, and against their mirth the encouragement of the Professor went for nothing. It was considered the correct thing to gabble, and we each gabbled accordingly, else the rest were sure to giggle. 'Alas,' as Walter Besant's French Professor would pathetically exclaim, 'alas for Girl, gaunt, ungainly, and ungracious Girl!'[2]

According to Maitland, Anna had a strong will, an independent mind, and was 'heedless of persons when principles were concerned.' At school Anna always won first prize for English composition, but she would get into trouble for persistently demanding explanations for the religious doctrine that was taught. She was very high minded from a young age, as shown by this extract from an essay she wrote on Ambition while at school:

> For to be ambitious is not only to desire and hope for, but to aim at and to purpose. And, year after year, the ambitious soul mounts higher and

> higher up that vast mountain whose top no mortal in this life has ever yet attained, and of which we shall never know whether there is any top; so huge and great is Wisdom; so unlimited and untried the human intellect. And even while man mounts and toils and struggles, higher and higher yet, there comes to him one day a bright angel, and carries him away to the Highest, Sublimest place of all, where all shall be known and understood – that is, God – and where at last there is peace.

Some notable women have written about their schooling at Brighton. Frances Power Cobbe (1822-1904), a feminist activist on various issues, who became associated with Anna in fighting vivisection, attended a 'ladies' school' at Brighton from 1836-38. At this time, ladies' or girls' schools in Brighton were highly esteemed, and school fees could be astronomical: Cobbe's fees were £1,000 for two years. Her school had seven teachers plus a 'considerable staff of responsible servants' to look after twenty five or six young ladies aged from nine to nineteen. Expensive does not necessarily mean good. Cobbe wrote with critical amusement about the defects of her schooling, which she remedied, like Anna, by her own wide reading. Isabella M.S. Tod, an advocate of positive education for girls, stated the prevailing attitude to girls: 'So far as the majority of parents have any standard of results for daughters, it is only that their manners shall be pleasing, that they shall have such command of "accomplishments" as may please others, and that they shall have so much surface knowledge as may guard against a display of gross ignorance in society.'[3]

Elizabeth Wordsworth (1840-1932) left us an account of her impressions of school at Brighton. Her father, Christopher Wordsworth, was headmaster at Harrow School and later Bishop of Lincoln. William Wordsworth the poet was her great uncle. Elizabeth attended a Brighton boarding school in 1857, and wrote about the lack of exercise there:

> All the exercise we got was an occasional dancing lesson, from 'Madame Adelaide' (Michaud), and a very clever woman she was in her way; rides on the Brighton downs for the favoured few, and 'crocodile ' walks on the King's Road and elsewhere, not unfrequently enlivened by a visit to the pastrycook's. There was a good deal of silly nonsense about dress, flirtations and the like, which centred round an Italian singing master, who was the idol of a certain set of girls. I often think that if some of this enthusiasm could have been expended on a tennis or hockey match, it would have been better, for both mind and body; and a good deal of my readiness to encourage games, in later years, at Lady Margaret Hall, is traceable to my Brighton experiences.

Elizabeth Wordsworth refers here to the new women's college at Oxford, where she was head from 1878 to 1909. Thus, inadequate educational experiences spurred some women to improve education for girls.

Like many towns of the period, Brighton underwent rapid growth: from 40,600 inhabitants in 1831 to 90,000 in 1871.The coming of the railway in 1841 not only boosted the population, but made this seaside town much more accessible for the pleasure-bent thousands of day-trippers. In his essay 'Sunny Brighton' Richard Jeffries (1848-1887) painted a lively and appealing picture of the town. In particular he liked 'those glorious beams of sunlight which fall at Brighton,' and 'the wind coming up the cliff seems to bring with it whole armfuls of sunshine, and to throw the warmth and light against you as you linger.' Jeffries thought 'there are more handsome women in Brighton than anywhere else in the world...Every morning the girls' schools go for their constitutional walks; there seem no end of these schools—the place has a garrison of girls, and the same thing is noticeable in their ranks. Too young to have developed actual loveliness, some in each band distinctly promise future success.'

Edward Carpenter (1844-1929), writer, social reformer and antivivisectionist, grew up in Brighton. He especially liked the 'two Natureelements in it—and these two singularly wild and untamed – the Sea and the Downs.'As a child, on stormy nights he felt 'grisly joy' while groping across the stony beach to the sound of a booming wind and crashing breakers. He spent marvelous times curled up in some secluded hollow in the Downs behind Brighton. Here he would read, think and daydream, looking at the sky and the grasses and the occasional butterfly. Girls at school were strictly controlled, but if Anna had the chance she surely would have enjoyed these 'Nature-elements' of Brighton.

Anna wrote many poems from a young age, some being published in *River Reeds* (1866). A remarkable feature in poems by one of such tender years is the aplomb with which Anna tackled major themes such as loss, the soul, and the after-life.

The first poem in the collection shows young Anna's burgeoning poetic sensibility:

River Reeds

Reeds in the river! reeds in the river!
All the long day through they tremble and shiver!
Men that go past, brush them down with their feet,

But the breeze that comes soft from the westerly sky,
Stirs them to melodies tender and sweet,
May be low laughter, or may be a sigh.
Reeds in the river! reeds in the river!
My thoughts and my rhymes are like reeds in the river!
Some that go past tread them down in disdain,
But the wind's of God's heaven that over them blow

Shall presently wake them to music again,
May be of gladness, or may be of woe!
Reeds from the river! reeds from the river!
O I bring you a bundle of reeds from the river!
Fresh smelling reeds, newly gathered and green:
I bring you a bundle of fancies and rhymes,
Though I know that my gift is but lowly and mean,
And fair are the flowers that bloom in our times!

Reeds in the river! Reeds in the river!
O deep in my heart like the reeds in the river,
My thoughts grow in darkness, far down out of my sight,
And over my life passes shadow and light,
Like sunshine and cloud on the breast of the stream;
But I sit by the banks of my river and dream,
For day after day they grow silent and strong,
The reeds of my Syrinx, the reeds of my song.

There are deep thoughts from a girl in this extract from a long poem:

Doubting

Thou sayest all things fade and die,
Thou holdest faith an idle boast,
And weak, the souls that love to trust
A far-off immortality.

Why then the strife with moral wrong?
The love of moral good? And why,

If all we love must wholly die,
Should human passion be so strong?

Shall all the love I bear to thee,
My buried darling! pass away?
Nor rather dawn in fuller day
Upon some fair eternity?

I know not; only this I know,
This, that thou art no longer here,
And day by day, and year by year,
The clouds above me seem to grow.

Anna was strongly attracted to nature:

Hymn

See how the blessed Angels light the silver lamps on high,
And draw the purple curtains close o'er all the silent sky;
Hark, how the evening wind awakes, and round the shore it sings,
And creeps among the creviced rocks, with soft low murmurings—
O what if it should be the breath of angels' waving wings?

The drowsy mists are creeping o'er the bosom of the sea,
And the sleepy surges ripple on in sweet tranquility;
And from her purple tent on high, where daylight scarce hath died,
Comes slowly forth the gracious moon, like some fair eastern bride,
And lightens with her brilliant eyes, the dark and dreamy tide.

Lord! Let no harm this night approach, Thy children to molest,
But let Thine holy angels lull us in their arms to rest,
And let them watch us around our beds, through all the quiet night,
And shield us with their unseen wings, till darkness melts to light!

A Round Of Days

I sang to my heart in the sunshine of May,
And the garrulous bird on the sycamore spray
Said to his mate in the nest;

'Sweetheart, daffodil blooms on the lea,
The blossoms are thick upon bramble and tree,
And all through the long merry year we will be
Treu und Fest, Treu und Fest.'

I sang to my heart in the burning July,
And the yellow-haired sun in a sapphire sky
Uplifted his fiery crest;
And the thousand-tongued land was melodious with song,
'O the fields shall be golden, the days shall be long,
And Love in the sunshine is valiant and strong—
Treu und Fest, Treu und Fest.'

I sang to my heart in the wane of the year,
And the glare of the sunset hung lurid and drear
Far down in the sorrowful west;
The nest was forsaken, the sparrow had fled,
The music was hushed and the blossoms were dead—
But a voice through the silence and solitude said,
'Treu und Fest, Treu und Fest.'

And still clings that voice in the wind and the snow,
'There is light after darkness, and joy after woe,
And the love that is tried is the best;
I care not though tempest be black in the sky,
Though the bird may be fickle, and blossoms may die,
What matter? – my darling shall find me for aye
Treu und Fest, Treu und Fest.'

River Reeds was favourably reviewed in *The Athenaeum*4, one of the leading literary journals of the day:

> This little volume of poems, by a lady, is named after the first, but not the best, of the series. The author has a pretty knack of versification; her lines are polished, her language is well chosen, and she has some power of thought; producing some work of greater pretension than the present. The collection before us consists of short poems, chiefly of a religious or contemplative

character. Those entitled 'A Vision of Philosophy' and 'A Round of Days' are perhaps (each in its way) among the most promising. It is refreshing to be able to notice for once a new book of poems without having to enter our usual protest against bad rhyme, slipshod metre, and ungrammatical English.

Notes

1. The poet-priest Gerard Manley Hopkins (1844-1889) was born in Stratford, Essex. His family moved to Hampstead in 1852. He died from typhoid. Norman White, 'The Parents of Gerard Hopkins,' *Hopkins Quarterly* 20, no. 3-4 (1993): 95.
2. Kingsford 1886, 137-38. Anna gives here the gist of the attitude of Hector Philipson, the French Master who hated his girl pupils in Walter Besant's novel *All In a Garden Fair* (1883).
3. Spender, 231.
4. *The Athenaeum* (20 February 1875): 258.

Chapter - 2

A Young Woman

Anna's family moved to 56 Warrior Square, St Leonards on Sea, Sussex in 1864, where Anna joined them on leaving school. St Leonards was founded in 1828 as the 'New Hastings' by the well known architects James Burton (1761-1837) and his son Decimus (1800-1881). It was designed as a high-class district for the well-to-do, situated at a distance from the hustle and bustle of the fishing quarter in Hastings. It is a unique example of regency town planning and garden landscaping. St Leonards received royal recognition when Princess Victoria (1819-1901) stayed there from 3 November 1834 to 29 January 1835. She recorded her impressions of the place in her diary:

> For some reasons I am sorry we have left St Leonards, which are, the nice walks, the absence of fogs, and looking out of my window and seeing the people walk on the esplanade, and seeing the sun rise and set, which was quite beautiful. The rising began by the sky being quite pink and blending softly into a bright blue, and the sun rose by degrees from a little red streak to a ball of red copper. The setting began by the whole horizon being orange, crimson, and blue, and the sun sunk down a ball of fiery gold dyeing the sands crimson. But then again my reasons for not being sorry to go are, my not sleeping there, my *not* having been well, and the roaring of the sea.

Like many well bred young ladies of the era, Anna tried her hand at archery. The Society of St Leonards Archers was co-founded in 1833 by the Mackay ladies (the widow Lucy and her three spinster daughters). James Burton donated land for the archery grounds, and they were improved upon by the Mackay ladies until they ranked with the best in the country.

Queen Victoria became patron of the society and it was renamed 'The Queen's St Leonards Archers' on her ascension to the throne in 1837. The Bonus family occasionally attended archery meetings but were not members. Anna won a bouquet for 'best shot in the gold.'[1] Archery clubs were very select, and offered young women and men an opportunity to meet under approved circumstances. In her novel *Daniel Deronda* (1876) George Eliot describes a typical archery meeting where Gwendolen, the heroine, wins a gold star to pin on her breast. In this novel, a dinner and ball are held after the meeting to facilitate further social intercourse between the sexes.

Anna's father, John Bonus, died on 10 July 1865 at St Leonards. His death certificate states the cause of death as 'Chronic bronchitis, Decay of Nature.' His will was drawn up on 29 May and proved on 8 August 1865. He was a rich man and distributed his wealth generously among his family. Probate stated his assets at £160,000, which was worth £7,509,651 in 2001. His 'beloved' wife Elizabeth Ann was executrix and the executors were his son Henry and Mr Bonus's friend Peter Rolt of St Michael's House, London. On his decease Elizabeth received £200 and a handsome yearly income of £1,400. Son John inherited Ivy House, Turnham Green, Middlesex. Margaret and Jane Bonus, sisters of John senior, received £100 each on his death and a yearly income of £350 between them.

John Bonus took particular care to look after the interests of his daughters. He gave them £5,000 each plus an equal share of the residue. Their money was to be put into trust funds for them. In his will he made it explicit their husbands, if any, could not have any power over the interest they received from their trust funds. Anna's support of married women's property rights was obviously influenced by her own situation, and advice from her father. The residue of her father's estate was divided equally between all nine children. Maitland stated Anna's inheritance provided her with £700 per year. Florence Fenwick Miller, later Anna's friend, wrote Anna's inheritance brought in £800 to £900 per year. John Bonus stipulated his daughters' money be invested in government securities by the executors. Such securities were popular in the nineteenth century and gave a return of around five per cent per annum. Anna's share would have been around £17,777, and at five percent her annual income would have been about £888, proving Florence Miller correct.

In the light of Perkins' figures on middle class incomes of the late 1860s, the Bonus family were well-off:

> At the top were a small group of wealthy businessmen, lawyers and government servant who had incomes of £1,000 or more a year and

lived as stylishly as the upper class. By 1867 roughly 10 per cent of middle class families earned over £300 a year, 41 percent earned between £100 and £300 (lower professions and smaller businessman), and 49 per cent earned under £100 (small shopkeepers, clerks, schoolteachers). By comparison, highly skilled workmen earned between £50 and £73 a year.[2]

Around 1866 Anna had first hand experience regarding the prevailing social attitude towards middle class women who wished to take up employment. Maitland wrote she applied to a local solicitor for a clerkship, not for the pay but for 'occupation.' The solicitor 'listened with mingled interest and amusement, and then, to her great delight, seated her at a desk and gave her some copying to do; but as his next step was to call at her home and report the incident, her hopes in this direction were soon extinguished.' No doubt this personal experience of sex discrimination had a formative influence on her subsequent activities for the promotion of women's rights.

At this time employment opportunities for women were severely limited. In 1861 thirty percent of women were in paid employment, the majority in domestic service and textiles. Agriculture was taking a decreasing share of the female labour market. The only occupations deemed suitable for middle class women were those conforming to the feminine ideal of selfless service: nursing, teaching and mission work. Josephine Butler estimated that in the 1860's about 1,000 women in the whole country earned over 100 pounds per year.3 Anna was indeed fortunate to have independent means which enabled her to pursue her interests.

As she grew up, Anna became aware of political and social matters, and her innate activism manifested. In 1867 she gathered signatures in her neighbourhood on a petition for the right of women to control their property when they married. It was a brave thing for young women to take around these petitions at the time. The following incident of 1867, related by the feminist Millicent Garrett Fawcett (1847-1929), shows the entrenched opposition to married women's property rights:

> At a Liberal meeting at my father's house in Suffolk I had taken round a petition asking Parliament to pass the Married Women's Property Bill then before it. Those present were mostly Suffolk farmers; I explained my petition and asked for signatures but obtained very few. One old farmer voiced the feelings of the majority. 'Am I to understand you ma'am, that if this Bill becomes law and my wife had a matter of

a hundred pound left her, I should have to arst her for it?' Of course I was obliged to confess that he would have to suffer this humiliation, and then I got no more signatures.

As the law stood, on marriage the personal property of a woman (including money, stocks and shares and personal belongings) was passed over into the control of the husband. She also lost her legal identity on marriage. In 1855 Married Women's Property Committees were set up to fight this injustice. In 1870-72 activists issued 35,000 pamphlets and sent 212 petitions containing over 100,000 signatures to parliament. The Married Women's Property Act 1870 was a token gesture as it designated only certain categories of property exclusively to the wife. A second Act in 1882 redressed these issues, giving married women a separate legal identity.

After leaving school Anna wrote short stories which were published in a number of magazines. They were collected and published early in 1875 under the title *Rosamunda the Princess, an Historical Romance of the Sixth Century; and Other Tales*. The volume includes twenty four black and white drawings (not done by Anna). In her short preface Anna stated all the stories except 'Rosamunda' had first seen the light of day in the following magazines: *Macmillan's Magazine, London Society, The Churchman's Companion*, and the *Penny Post.*

The stories shed light on Anna's character and interests at the time of writing. Most of the tales are of a pious religious nature. All but one are set in the past, showing Anna's love of historical romance. Anna must have read widely to acquire inspiration for these stories. Periods embraced by the stories include ancient Greece, second century Gaul, India in the 14th century, Venice in the 15th century, and England in the time of Charles II.

In 'The Painter of Venice,' Anna shows her appreciation of allegory in fairy stories, which was later to develop into her allegorical explorations of scripture:

> We cold-blooded, dull-hearted denizens of unspeculative England, can but dimly comprehend the deep mysterious meanings that lie hidden beneath the simple wording of those Italian and German fairy stories – we read, and smile, or even weep perhaps, over the poetic visions pictured in their fascinating pages, but we miss the philosophic thought, the daring guesses at truth, the wonderful powerful idea that underlies their baby-language, and points every adventure and utterance of their imaginary heroes and heroines. But farther south, where a brighter sun

enlightens the eyes and souls of men by day, and where the skies are so pure and clear that at night one can see the stars down to the very edge of the earth, and water all round the horizon – there, too, the hearts and understandings of the people lie nearer their lips and ears than they do among themselves, so that they speak in allegory of things we do not dare to dream about, and hear with reverend looks and grave countenance certain histories and fables that we are wont to profane with jests.

Anna put her love of nature into the words of the youth Angelo:

'Uncle,' said Angelo, stretching out his hands towards the purpling landscape before him, 'how is it that, when I look upon all this beauty in such calm moments as these, I feel that it is not enough to look at it? I seem to want other mode of apprehending and enjoying it – some other sense than mere sight, or even touch. I want to lose myself in it, to embrace it, to drink it, to take it all to my soul, and become identified with its perfect peace and loveliness!'

Fra Giuseppe, his uncle, replies:

'...For I believe that thou wilt only know what new sense it is thou so vainly desirest, when thou shalt have put aside the senses of thy body, and art become a pure spirit full of eyes, in the perfect light of God...That vague desire that fills thy heart in beholding the beauty of the natural earth and sea, is a yearning to drink of the eternal waters of Wisdom, a longing for perfect rest upon the bosom of divine Love.'

A minstrel-painter also echoes Anna's thoughts on nature:

Nature is ever seeking to assimilate earth to heaven; if we do but suffer our ears to hear her voice, and our eyes to dwell upon her beauty, she will infallibly recall us to pristine tenderness and peace.

Anna's life was dedicated against the forces of materialism, and in this story there is an early indication of her views:

So surely does every fresh discovery and application of the strength of the Orgre Mechanism become the means of filching occupation and existence from thousands; and while disseminating knowledge and luxury among the poor and rich, still realizes the old nursery legend of its devouring kin, and ever as the years roll on, continues to ply with ceaseless hand its iron mill, and grinds the bones of Art to make its bread.

A footnote in 'The Painter of Venice ' mentions two books which were the source of Anna's story, Vasari's *Vite dei Pittori* and Baldinucci's *Notizie dei Professori del Disegno.* Anna gives the titles in Italian, showing a likely proficiency with that language. Other footnotes throughout the book show that Anna had done a certain amount of reading. Names mentioned are Gibbon, Steele, Montaigne, Pliny, Epicurus, Juvenal, Martial, Leigh Hunt, Dijon, Langres, and Saulien.

Notes

1. Communication from Helena Wojtczak of Hastings, Sussex.
2. Perkin, 86.
3. Turner, 153.

Chapter - 3

Marriage

Anna's independent streak manifested in her choice of husband. Florence Fenwick Miller, who would become Anna's close friend in 1873, gave an account of Anna's engagement and marriage in her autobiography:

> As she was beautiful, gifted and well-dowered, her mother naturally anticipated that she would 'make a good match,' and wealthy suitors presented themselves. But the lovely girl chose for herself – Algernon Kingsford. He was about her own age, a nice fellow, but with no money and no better position that of a junior Civil Service Clerk. But he loved her devotedly, and one of his greatest attractions, she told me, was that he promised not to interfere with any career she wished to adopt, and to leave her absolute freedom, while the wealthy older men would naturally have expected her to just manage a big house and possibly rear a large family. But her mother emphatically refused her consent to this detrimental match and sent her to Switzerland, in company with some other young girls, in care with an elder relative, to get her away from her young lover. Hereupon she made up her audacious mind to elope with 'Algie.' They went off accordingly for a fortnight's trip with each other. It was perfectly virtuous expedition, she assured me; but after this adventure her mother was convinced that the marriage must be sanctioned, and it took place immediately after Annie came of age.

Algernon Godfrey Kingsford was born on 7 April 1845 in Millbank Penitentiary, London and educated at St Edmund's School, Canterbury, Kent. His father, Godfrey Kingsford (1819-1852) gained his BA at Cambridge in 1841 and was ordained a deacon (Rochester) in 1842. He was assistant chaplain at the Millbank Penitentiary from 1844 to 1846, then chaplain to the Convict Station at Gibraltar until 1852. Algernon's mother died on 31 September 1846, possibly during one of the frequent epidemics that ravaged the colony. Godfrey Kingsford then married Emma Louise Burrow on 10 October 1848. They had a daughter, Catherine Anna Kingsford, who was born on 19 August 1850. Godfrey's life ended in tragic circumstances: 'In a fit of delirium from fever he cut his throat.'1 He was described as 'a zealous preacher and much esteemed by all classes at Gibraltar.' Algernon's parents were buried in the Sandpits Cemetery, Gibraltar. In 1861 Algernon was living at Wandsworth with his grandmother Elizabeth Baldock Kingsford (1793-1878), a 'landowner.' Algernon's stepmother and stepsister lived at Honiton, Devon with Emma Kingsford's parents.

Algernon was admitted to the Lichfield Theological College, Staffordshire, in Michaelmas (third term) in 1867. He had been living with his stepmother in the lace-making town of Honiton. Lichfield, in Staffordshire, is seventeen miles north of Birmingham. Dr Samuel Johnson was born in Lichfield in 1709, and in 1776 he took his friend James Boswell there to show him 'genuine civilised life in an English provincial town.' Lichfield possesses a most imposing and ancient cathedral. It 'is one of the smaller English cathedrals (371 ft), but it has two features which single it out from all others: its three spires and the Minster Pool and Stowe Pool assuring it of a picturesqueness of setting which none can emulate. Moreover it has a Close more complete than most and more intimate than any.'[2]

Usually the parson of the parish was a Cambridge or Oxford man. Due to the rising population, especially in the second half of the century, there was a pressing need to train more clergy. Colleges were set up to train non-graduates, and in some cases to provide specialised training for graduates. Some people did not like this turn of events. In his book on clergymen the novelist Anthony Trollope argued the colleges could not produce the 'gentlemen' parsons who were necessary to gain the respect of their parishioners.

Algernon was distantly related to Anna by marriage. Her brother Henry Bonus married Emily Kingsford (b. 1835) who was a first cousin of Algernon's father, Godfrey Kingsford. Emily was therefore Algernon's first cousin, once removed. In those days respectable young women like Anna were closely chaperoned to ensure they did not marry the 'wrong' man, so it is most likely Anna and Algernon met due to this family connection.

It is not surprising that Mrs Bonus was opposed to Anna's marriage. Algernon was not well-off, and his prospects were none too promising.

As a chaplain to prisoners, Algernon's father's position held little prestige, and his suicide was a blot on his copybook. However, Anna was a resourceful young woman when her mind was made up, and she usually got her own way. Anna's elopement resolved the issue, giving her family little choice but to concede to her wishes. On the last day of 1867 Anna and Algernon were married in St Mary Magdalen, Church of England, St Margaret's Road, St Leonards, just around the corner from where Anna lived.[3]

Anna's marriage was noted in *The Times*, Thursday January 2, 1868 as follows:

> On New Year's-Eve at St Mary Magdalene, [sic] St Leonard's-on-Sea by the Rev. Edward Bonus, rector of Hulcott, assisted by the Rev. Septimus Kingsford, ALGERNON GODFREY, son of the late Rev. GODFREY KINGSFORD, chaplain of Gibralter, to ANNIE, younger daughter of the late JOHN BONUS, Esq., formerly of Point House, Blackheath. No cards.

Anna's marriage certificate states Algernon was 22 years of age and living at Lichfield. Anna's age was 21 years. They were 'Married in the parish Church according to the Rites and ceremonies of the Established Church after Banns.' The witnesses were Peter Rolt, a London merchant and family friend, and Anna's sister Emily Louisa Bonus. The Rev. Septimus Kingsford (1836-1913) was a distant cousin of Algernon.

Anna and Algernon went to Brighton for what Maitland called their 'wedding-trip,' but he gave no further details. Brighton was a popular destination for honeymooners. Novelist Thomas Hardy, who was to MARRIAGE 25 meet Anna in 1886, sojourned in Brighton with his wife Emma in September 1874 after their wedding in London. The Hardys visited the aquarium, the pier and the Pavilion, which offered concerts and various amusements. On Sunday 20 September they went twice to church and on Monday Hardy swam in the rough sea. The same evening they took a boat to France. According to Maitland the day after her marriage Anna suffered a severe asthma attack and returned to her mother at St Leonards.

Anna's only child, Eadith Bonus Kingsford, was born on 24 September 1868 at St Leonards. Maitland wrote Anna bestowed this name 'in indulgence of some early English prepossessions.' It is likely Anna was thinking of Edith or Eadgyth (c. 1020-1075), the daughter of Earl Godwine of Wessex and his Danish wife Gytha, who married Edward the Confessor in 1045. 'Ead' was an Anglo-Saxon prefix meaning wealth, prosperity, success.

After her marriage and probably during her confinement, Anna busied herself writing a novel called *For Richer, For Poorer.* Only six chapters were ever published, but they throw interesting light on Anna and Algernon. It was published in *The Amateur Author's Magazine* over three issues in late 1868, with the name 'Mrs Ninon Kingsford.'

Anna's story is slight, but nevertheless interesting because of certain autobiographical elements. The beautiful twenty one year old Scottish heiress Lucy Adair and Algie Goodfellow, a Naval sub-lieutenant, are in love. Courtenay Harcourt, man about town and dedicated cad, makes a wager with his fast friends he can marry Lucy within one year. He befriends the innocent Algie and lures him into a life of gambling, drinking, music halls and vice. The hapless Algie is rapidly ensnared in a life of dissipation, much to the pity and sorrow of his beloved Lucy. One evening at Lucy's home Algie confesses his sins to her and begs forgiveness. The compassionate Lucy extracts from him a promise never to see Harcourt again. A distraught Algie returns to his own place, pondering his predicament. This is the outline of all that was published, and we can assume that Anna never troubled herself to finish the story.

In many aspects Anna based Lucy on herself. Lucy was tall and slender, with hair that 'was very soft and fine indeed, of a hue that inartistic and envious people call red, but that poets knew for true gold.' Photographs of Anna show us Lucy's eyes were much like her creator's, being 'very deep-set, wakeful, steadfast, meaning eyes, that looked out from beneath their high overshadowing brows like two good warders from their turret windows, keeping guard over the household within.' Like Anna, Lucy was 'a very clever and a very headstrong girl, with keen intellectual tastes and feelings.' She had many books and was an avid reader. 'Every morning the Latin and Greek were taken out as usual, and Lucy's eyes conned the glorious verses again and again.' I suspect Anna was thinking of her own character when she wrote that Lucy 'was a wise woman as well as a good girl, and she had no fine ladyism in her character – no extra polish of delicacy, no fear of looking ugly things in the face.' However, I could not imagine a neat and elegant Virgo such as Anna wearing her hair like Lucy, 'in a hundred different fashions, all of them charming, because all of them were peculiar, and all untidy.'

Anna must have been thinking of herself when she penned these words about Lucy:

> She was a 'blue-stocking,' too, and knew a good deal of Grecian philosophy, studied Ovid, Horace and Virgil untranslated, and wrote

> odes in sapphics and hendecasyllabecs. People whispered besides that she talked rationalistically, occasionally wore spectacles, and approved of lady doctors; in addition to which enormities, it was known for certain that she utterly discarded crinoline, an article of womanly attire just then in its zenith of glory among ladies and dressmakers.

Algie Goodfellow resembled what we know of Anna's own Algernon:

> The face of this young waif was very different from Lucy's, for the most observable feature in his physiognomy was a pair of large open blue eyes, softened by long fringes of eyelash, and as unclouded by any species of serious thought as a child's. The rest of his face was ordinarily good-looking and honest, and the abundant crop of curly brown hair that crowned his temples added effect to the general innocence and youthful appearance which pervaded his whole exterior. He was two years older than Lucy, but his simplicity of mind and speech would have made him seem many years younger if the tokens of manhood had not been apparent on his cheek and lip…he was one of those boyish, frank-faced, easy young fellows whose name one involuntarily shortens into a diminutive.

Algie Goodfellow, inherited 'gentle blood and simple, generous manners' from his parents. Lucy loved him 'first of all for pity's sake, because he was poor and desolate and orphaned, and afterwards because she found him so simple-hearted that it was a pleasant office to her to act as his guide and director.' Here is another resemblance to real life, for Algernon too was an orphan, and not financially well endowed.

Ever the teacher, Anna exhorted young men to desist from sin:

> And count the cost, boys, before you sow those seeds of mischief and bitterness which the world lightly enough calls 'wild oats.' Bethink you that the price of your evil pleasures must be paid in the shame and sin of human beings like yourselves, and that though you may have been hardly tempted, you are not for that the less responsible for your share in the downfall of others…keep your souls clear and your hands clean of those youthful sins, for to all of you they are surely sin; because they make human hearts desolate, and human lives sickly and loathsome and vile.

After Algie Goodfellow confessed his wayward ways to Lucy, Anna contemplated the eternal theme of the ideal versus the real:

> There is no bitterness of regret so keen to a good soul as the knowledge that its best beloved has fallen. There is no mortification so extreme to

a pure-hearted woman as the evidence of her hero's disgrace. And, to Lucy Adair, philosopher and poet though she was, simple Algie Goodfellow had been both best-beloved and hero. And now she knew that, after all, it was her own ideal that she worshipped, and not the living, breathing creature of flesh and blood – the lover as she would have had him, not the lover as he actually was. This is what all women do until they have lived long enough to find out their mistake for themselves, and have learned the A, B, C lesson of real life through the spectacles of experience.

For women, of whatever sort they may happen to be, when they fall in love for the first time, are vastly apt to bedeck their bachelor with all manner of imaginary virtues, and to attribute to him a wondrous capability for all kinds of heroic actions, much in the same way as religious devotees adorn the effigy of some favourite deity or saint with tinselled garments and golden trinkets. But then comes a day when the god they have invested with this fictitious divinity, and arrayed in these fair bright robes of their own fancies, tumbles ignominiously from his pedestal, and breaks himself to pieces on his own shrine; and, behold! He is only quite a common clay idol after all!

Anna was fully committed to the rights of women. 1868 saw the publication of her pamphlet, *An Essay on the Admission of Women to the Parliamentary Franchise,* which 'received a measure of publicity.'4 The work shows that even at this young age Anna had an incisive mind and the ability to express her ideas logically and with conviction. She saw votes for women not as an end in itself, but as a means to raise women from their inferior position, created by men, 'to the position they ought to occupy, of citizens and responsible beings.' Girls lacked the ambition of boys because they were not given a challenging education. Showing her interest in health matters, Anna deplored the fact that girls are denied a range of physical activities. 'No races, no football, no chase, no merry rompings in the playground, because, forsooth, such games are not fit for young ladies!' Anna was way ahead of her time when it came to sport for girls: 'Where are the cricket clubs for girls? Where are the boxing-gloves, the foot-races, the fencing matches, the paper chase, the gymnasiums, and the hundred brave and health giving games that boys enjoy?'

Anna favoured a classical education. 'Why should not girls be taught Latin and Greek as boys are? What resources would such knowledge open to them! In what grand studies and enjoyments might they take part! But now the writings of the old poets, the historians, the philosophers of past times, with all their sublime thoughts, their noble conceptions, their glorious imageries, are sealed volumes to them. They are to them as if they were not; they hear them as beasts hear sweet music, understanding none of its beauty and meaning.'

Referring to the exclusion of women from the professions, Anna mentioned the first woman in England to receive male sanction as a doctor, Elizabeth Garrett (later Mrs Anderson):

> We all know – to cite an incident very lately under our notice, and already quoted in the House by Mr Mill – with what strenuous opposition and ridicule Miss Garrett has met, in her pursuit of the science she loves – the noble science of medicine. I do not know whether I am at liberty to mention some circumstances connected with her medical career, which came within the sphere of my own immediate knowledge – but this at least I will say, that the difficulties and obstacles purposely set in her way, were more than enough to dishearten and disgust any woman less nobly determined than Miss Garrett proved herself to be. And now, as Mr Mill told us – no second Miss Garrett may pass the wicket – it is shut henceforth upon all aspiring women.
>
> But what a grave mistake is this! – even setting aside the injustice of the act itself! How can the grand science of medicine be fully developed and appreciated by the human race, unless both sexes study it alike?...Men for men and women for women; for there is in fact no study, no profession so fitted for women as this of medicine.

Anna then argued women physicians were necessary in order to study and treat female diseases.

Anna had little time for many of the magazines and newspapers aimed at women. 'These publications treat of the caprices of female dress, the details of "fashionable intelligence" (whatever that may be), and instructions on embroidery and pin-work, while the remaining sheets are stuffed with senseless verses, impossible love tales, and unnatural sentiment.' In reply to the argument that this was what ladies wanted, Anna wrote this was a direct 'consequence of illiberal and insufficient education.'

In the next section of the essay Anna wrote about the importance of education to women in their later years. She eloquently displayed considerable worldly wisdom:

> But, unhappily, the world, like Paris of old, always gives the apple – the fatal apple of preference – to Venus. Her shrine is crowded with

> worshippers; Minerva's temple stands empty. 'Beauty and love,' say the poets of society, 'are women's empire; there she reigns supreme.' Yes, but all women are not such empresses; and most of the sex, unlike Ninon de l'Enclos, have an unfortunate knack of growing old long before eighty. Love, too, when it is a mere tribute paid to beauty, is scarcely worth having, and is certainly never constant long. Many new loves, on the other hand, are wearisome, if there be nothing else more substantial than gallantry to fill the intervals of passion. And where, then, is Lady Venus, unless Minerva, or some charitable dispenser of intellectual tasks and pleasures, come to her assistance?

Anna advised women not to 'sit in idleness' and wait for men to improve their lot. 'From what we know and have seen until now of men's nature, we cannot expect that they should work for women. They mind their own affairs generally, and are very sharp and cute in minding them to the great disadvantage of the rival sex.' Woman was regarded 'as an inferior sort of man, not as the parallel of man.' Women must not succumb to a slave mentality, but realise they need to strive for their independence. Anna recommended the writings of Mrs. Bodichon, Mrs. Stuart Mill and Miss Helen Taylor for further reading on the subject.

Anna mentioned *The Elements of Social Science* by a 'Graduate of Medicine.' This book, she contended, 'contains what is more precious than gold – brave, honest truth. For the sake, then, of reason and of common sense, I earnestly advise – I entreat – my readers to study that book well.' *The Elements of Social Science* was first published anonymously in December 1854. It was written by George Drysdale (1825-1904), a physician and dedicated social reformer who wrote various pamphlets, and articles for the secularist press. The *Elements* was 'one of the most notorious books of the century.'5 The Victorian era was sexually repressive, resulting in widespread prostitution, disease, and various psychological complexes. Drysdale wanted to attack the root cause of these problems, advocating a liberal approach to sexual matters. In the book he wrote about male and female sexual diseases, criticised celibacy, and advocated contraception. His views were too radical for even some of his fellow Secularists, and caused a split in their ranks. He supported women's rights in all areas of life and thought it was best for women to be treated by women doctors. In her youthful enthusiasm Anna naively advocated Drysdale 's book. Though always a libertarian at heart, the years brought Anna the discretion to restrain her views on such controversial matters.

In her essay Anna wrote she looked forward to a time when 'society in general will no longer be scandalised when it hears of strong minded and self reliant Mary Walkers.' This indicates the latter was a woman of inspiration for Anna. Mary Edwards Walker (1832-1919) was born in Oswego, New York. In 1855 she received her physician's certificate from the Syracuse Medical College. She set up a practice with, and married, fellow medical student Albert Miller, but when he proved MARRIAGE 31 unfaithful and they separated. During the Civil War (1861-1865) she spent a short period as an assistant surgeon. Sex discrimination thwarted her many attempts to become a surgeon for the Union cause. She undertook various voluntary projects and built up a reputation as a woman dedicated to the welfare of ordinary folk. Resolute against much ridicule, she wore trousers under her frock to make a statement for more comfortable women's clothing.

To conclude the essay, Anna made mention of the National Society for Women's Suffrage, stating that she was a member, and a new petition to the House was available from Mrs. P.A. Taylor of Notting Hill, London, or herself at Leamonsley, Lichfield, Staffordshire. The Mrs P.A. Taylor mentioned by Anna as a contact for more petition papers was Clementia Taylor (1810-1908), wife of Peter Taylor, a businessman and M.P. From 1860 to 1875 the Taylors lived in the grand Aubrey House, Kensington, which became a centre for radical movements. In her long life Clementia Taylor was active in the promotion of various women's issues.

A law report and some letters in *The Times* in August 1869 inform us of a salutary incident in Anna's life. In September 1868 she corresponded with an Eleanor Born to discuss the formation of a Ladies' Secular Club. Their aim was to bring together women who supported Freethought, discuss issues, and promote the interests of women through parliamentary and social action. Eleanor produced a circular with a list of ten women supporters. On the list was Emily Faithfull, a publisher and prominent women's activist. James Grant, a journalist and fervid Evangelical, saw a report on the proposed club in the *London Review*. He wrote a scathing attack on secularism, equating it with atheism, and implying Miss Faithfull was an atheist. As a committed member of the Church of England and the daughter of a clergyman, Miss Faithfull was seriously affronted by this slur, and successfully sued Grant for libel. *The Times* of 9 August 1869 gave extensive coverage to the court case.

Letters by Miss Faithfull, Anna and Eleanor referring to the case were published in *The Times* on 11 August 1869. Eleanor blamed Anna for the inclusion of Miss Faithfull's name. She wrote she asked Anna if she thought

Miss Faithfull would support them. She claimed Anna wrote back, 'Use Miss Faithfull's name with mine.' Most likely Anna meant, 'If you get her permission, use Miss Faithfull's name.' As Eleanor was the compiler of the list, it was her responsibility to ask the women involved for their agreement, and not shift the onus onto Anna. Eleanor sent a copy of the circular to Miss Faithfull, who immediately asked to be 'disconnected' from the club. Eleanor went to see her, regretted that she had been 'misled,' and promised 'to make any public explanation if she [Miss Faithfull] thought it necessary.' Eleanor's letter shows she did not accept responsibility for her actions, and took no steps to redress her mistake. She heard nothing and was very surprised to be subpoenaed by Miss Faithfull's solicitor on 5 August 1869.

In her letter to *The Times* of 11 August 1869 Anna wrote that as her name was mentioned in court, she wished it be known that she and Miss Faithfull withdrew their names from the list at the same time. She stated she was no longer connected with the club. Anna signed herself 'Ninon Kingsford' and gave her address as Warrior Square, St Leonards. On the list of club supporters, Anna's name was followed by 'Lichfield' in brackets, indicating this was her home residence with Algernon in 1868.

This incident gives us some insight into Anna's life at this juncture. At the time of Eadith's birth, 24 September 1868, Anna was thinking of social activism, for it was second nature for her to be in the public arena discussing and promoting her ideas. It was the intention that she be president of the club, with the first meeting on 2 November 1868. However, Eleanor Born stated in her letter to *The Times* that Anna did not attend the meeting for health reasons, and on her doctor's advice 'withdrew from public action.' It is likely Anna's family were concerned about her involvement with the proposed club. They may have pointed out to her that as a new wife and mother her first duty was to Algernon and Eadith. They would not have been happy with her espousal of Freethought, for Mrs Bradlaugh, wife of the egregious atheist Charles Bradlaugh, was on the list of supporters. The reputations of Anna and Algernon could have been harmed by Anna's involvement. The actions of James Grant showed how certain zealots were only too ready to attack those associated with Freethought. Further, Anna probably realised that collaboration with the unreliable Eleanor would not be a wise or productive enterprise.

Notes

1. Venn, Part II, vol.iv, 48. Dates for Godfrey Kingsford and his family are from the database operated by Orman Lewis Speed from Orangevale, California.

Algernon's family has been traced back to John Kingsford of Kent, born c.1510 and died September 1558. See http://freepages.genealogy.rootsweb.com/~speedo/kingsford/d1.htm#i6376.

2. Pevsner 1974, 174.
3. Annie Besant (1847-1933), who much later became head of the Theosophical Society, was married in Anna's church on 21 December 1867. Her mother moved from Harrow to live in Warrior Square, St Leonards in the Spring of 1867. Annie Besant was less fortunate than Anna in her choice of husband, marrying a violent clergyman whom she had to leave in the sixth year of her marriage when she lost her faith.
4. Crawford, 352.
5. Benn, 23.

Chapter - 4

Anna's Own Paper

In 1869 Algernon became curate of Atcham, Shropshire, a village some four miles south east of Shrewsbury. The county of Shropshire is in the west of England, bordering on Wales. Shrewsbury, the administrative centre, is 140 miles northwest of London. Atcham's earliest recorded name, Atingeham, dates from 1086. Atcham means 'land in a river-bend belonging to the followers of Eata.' The church of St Eata, situated on the banks of the River Severn,[1] is the only one in England dedicated to this saint. St Eata is remembered as one of the twelve English boys received by St Aidan, as Bede tells us, and he grew up to be the first Abbot of Melrose, the teacher of St Cuthbert, and Bishop of Hexham, where he died in 686. He was finally laid to rest in Durham Cathedral. An old rhyme sung by children in Shropshire, 'The Bells of Shropshire,' includes the lines 'Pitch 'em and patch 'em say the bells of Old Atcham.'[2]

The vicar of Atcham was Henry Burton, aged 67 and born in Atcham. His wife, the Hon. Charlotte B. Burton, was 66 years of age. No children are mentioned in the census. The Rev. Burton must have been reasonably well off, for the vicarage had the services of a butler, a coachman, a lady's maid, a housemaid, and a 'dairy and kitchen maid,' and he also farmed thirty one acres.

Anna was baptized in the Roman Catholic Church on 14 September 1870, adopting the names Mary Magdalen. On 9 June, 1872 Anna was confirmed by Archbishop Manning, 'who admonished her to utilise her attractions in making converts.'3 She received the additional names of Maria Johanna. 'Maria' was chosen by the Archbishop, and Anna chose the latter as her father and eldest brother were called John.

In 1873 Anna told her friend Florence Miller why she joined the Catholic Church, as explained by Florence in her unpublished autobiography:

> With the almost cynical frankness with which she always spoke to me about herself, she told me that the chief reason why she openly joined the Roman Catholic Church was that she meant to avoid the ordinary routine of 'the Vicar's wife.' As a Catholic she never went to service at her husband's Church, or visited in the Parish with Testaments and tracts, jellies and baby clothes, or organised bazaars, or performed any of the rest of the duties expected of the Vicar's wife.

There was logic in Anna becoming a Catholic, because 'Roman Catholics had little role to play in the villages, for they were rarely found in country districts, save where the resident squire was himself a Catholic.'4 Although Florence saw an image of the 'Blessed Virgin clad in her blue robes' in Anna's 'own sanctum,' she told Florence 'that she had no director, and never "practised," as the faithful put it.' In her later esoteric studies Anna learnt that Catholicism still retained the vestiges of the ancient Mysteries. She never opposed Christianity *in toto.* Her ultimate mission was to restore the true Mysteries, as shared by (early) Christianity and the Classical world.

Anna could have been influenced in part to join the Catholic Church by John Bonus, the brother with whom she had the most affinity. He was caught up in the Oxford Movement of the 1840s when certain Anglicans became interested in Roman Catholicism, with some, like John, switching sides. He took 'a notable part in stormy controversies at Oxford,' but left without taking a degree. He was a man 'who refused in an age of narrowness and prejudice to accept conventional standards of thought.'5 John Bonus gained his Bachelor of Divinity at the Roman Catholic University of Louvain in Belgium. From 1852 to 1862 he was a Catholic priest, living mostly at Ivy House, Turnham Green, Middlesex. We have no details as to why he left the priesthood. In 1856 he published himself some of his 'moral discourses' under the title Shadows of the Rood: or, Types of Our Suffering Redeemer Jesus Christ *Occurring in the Book of Genesis.* In 1857 he took his degree as Doctor of Philosophy and Literature at the University of Louvain. He became a friend of the sexologist and writer Havelock Ellis (1859-1939) who, in his autobiography, called him 'a remarkable person.' In 1870 Anna became a vegetarian, inspired by the example her brother John.

The 1871 British census was conducted on the night of 2 April 1871. It shows Anna, Algernon and Eadith lived in Atcham House, a dwelling near the vicarage. Anna's age is given as 23 years, but she was really 24. This is rather strange, for in the 1881 census Anna's age is given as 33, when she was actually 34. We do not know why Anna reduced her age by one year for the census. Margaret Willner, aged 30, was their cook, born at Lichfield. Eadith's nurse was the 18 year old Lucy Cruttenden who was born at Bexhill, Sussex. Their groom was a 17 year old youth called Phillip Ball, born in Buckland, Bucks. Also living in Atcham House at the time was a malster William Machin and his wife Hannah, both aged 40 years. They had three daughters and two sons, the eldest child being William aged 12 years.

Anna's passion for reform could not be satisfied in a small country village. She needed a larger stage from which to express her views and talents. To further her aims, Anna acquired the weekly *Lady's Own Paper* in London and assumed editorship in October 1872. This was a conventional woman's paper which had been running since 26 November 1866 with the descriptive subtitle, *Weekly Journal of Fashion, Fiction, Music, Literature, the Drama, & Domestic Economy.* Its content was fashion, gossip, hints for young mothers, sewing, gardening, theatrical amusements, a serial story; the typical fare considered suitable for middle class women. In 1872 the editor was Georgina Charlotte Clark. In her last issue as editor, 28 September, Clark announced the paper was changing to reflect the progressive views 'of the most eminent ladies.' She stated the next issue would be in the hands of 'Mrs Algernon Kingsford, whose talent and labours are too well known to require laudatory comment.'

After producing only four issues of her paper, from 5 to 26 October 1872, Anna relinquished the venture. Both Edward Maitland and Florence Fenwick Miller gave conflicting and inaccurate data about the paper. Maitland said that it ran for two years. In her autobiography Florence wrote that it ran for three months. Maitland said that Anna lost 'several hundred pounds' because she did not take advertisements that were counter to her principles, and Florence stated she had no advertisements at all. The reality was Anna adhered to her principles by not taking advertisements for corsets or leather products. She had on average four pages of advertisements per issue, the same number as before, with many of the advertisements being carried over.

The regular readers of the *Lady's Own Paper* must have received a shock when they opened the first issue by Anna. She made no attempt to ease readers into the new regime with a mix of articles; the usual domestic, fashion and gossip features were gone for good. Earnest articles on serious issues such as temperance, women's rights and vivisection became the order of the day. Anna's new subtitle indicated the paper's new direction: *A Journal of Taste, Progress, and Thought.* She incorporated a quotation from Rousseau into the masthead: 'The world is the book of women.' Anna's 'Address' to the reader expressed her high aims for the paper:

> Advocates of progress and reform in politics, education, and social manners, are apt, in their zeal for the serious and useful, to ignore the aesthetic; and by the vehemence of their crusade against frivolity, have, in the minds of many among the conservative party, identified the ethics of the liberal school with Vandalism and insensibility. There has come lately into the world of women a vast and wide-spread reaction, which, like most revulsions of thought, whether national or individual, is disposed to be extreme or intolerant. Some years ago we were exclusively domestic; now we are inclined to be exclusively politic. Once we were all for the feminine monopolies of the Bona Dea; now we will have nothing but Minerva and her manlike paraphernalia. This is a state of affairs which is doing a good cause great harm outside the charmed circle of the Amazonian camp. Home-keeping wives and women of idealistic tendencies imagine us to be a hard unlovely crew, with no interests beyond polling-booths and school-boards, contemners of art and taste, barbarous, implacable Gorgons, in whose vicinity no fair or graceful thing can endure, but whose very aspect freezes into stone all living forms that heaven given beauty which ought to be 'a joy for ever.'
>
> The Editor of the Journal feels, therefore, that time is ripe for the establishment of a new and aesthetic school among 'political women' – a school which shall aim at uniting the worship of the Graces with the pursuit of liberty, the members of which, while claiming and asserting their rightful dignity and individual freedom, shall, none the less, uphold and preserve the distinctive charm and gentleness of true womanhood.
>
> But while we hope to make our future programme inclusive of articles and correspondence on the subjects already indicated, there is yet another branch of progress and thought which we should indeed be sorry to forget – the all important interest of Hygiene. No reform can be achieved, intellectually or socially, no permanent advance can be assured in national education or custom, if we neglect to study the proper adjustment of those things which are inseparably connected with all mental growth and being. Earnestly, therefore, we invite discussion in our columns, as well as on hygienic and physiologic topics

> as on other matters more generally interesting to thoughtful and enlightened women. In conclusion, we hope to make it clearly understood that while careful to guard this Journal from becoming the organ of any clique or party, we shall be always willing to give each a fair hearing; and though we cannot be personally responsible for the opinions of our contributors, we shall yet withhold space from none of them, on the ground that we happen to differ on one point from their expressed views and theories.

Each issue of Anna's paper comprised sixteen pages of two columns each. In those days it was usual for articles to appear unsigned. However, under the title of the paper it was stated in capital letters, 'Edited by Mrs Algernon Kingsford,' and most articles carried the author's name. The very first article was 'Coffee-Houses or Gin-Palaces' by Alice Bell Le Geyt of The Cottage, Corston, near Bristol. Miss Le Geyt advocated the establishment of coffee houses to counter the evils of strong drink. She wished to open a coffee house herself, and asked for donations to be sent to her address.

The next article, 'One Fine Art in Dress' by M. Jane Ronniger, contended women should be educated in 'the principles of art' to enable them to dress, and adorn their home, in a tasteful fashion. Mrs Ronniger lectured on woman's suffrage around the country for the London National Society between 1871 and 1874. From 1876 to 1879 she was editor of the *Aesthetic Review*. The third article in Anna's paper was 'The Educational Agitation' by Emma Wallington. Using the pen name 'Colossa,' Anna reviewed *England, Russia and Persia: a Sketch, Historical, Political and Prophetic* by J. Bertrand Payne. The first six chapters of Anna's novel *In My Lady's Chamber: a Story of Her Deceased Husband's Brother* were published in the four issues of the paper.

The second issue, dated 12 October 1872, began with an article against vivisection written by Henry J. Bigelow, Professor of Surgery at Harvard University. This article was 'communicated by Miss Frances Power Cobbe.' In 1846 Bigelow (1818-1891) published the first paper on the use of ether in a surgical operation. He held that vivisection was therapeutically useless and morally corrupting. Cobbe also wrote a letter against vivisection for this issue. In her review of some current magazines Anna commended the article 'Female M.P.s' in *Tinsley's Magazine.* She wrote that *The Women's Suffrage Journal,* edited by Miss Lydia Becker, 'is never anything else but good, and is, of course, composed only of such matter as is specially interesting to thoughtful and earnest women.'

The third issue, 19 October, opened with an article on vivisection by Anna which she concluded with a call to draw up a petition to parliament to ban the practice. Anna's independent approach to matters is exemplified by these verses she published concerning the votes for women campaign:

* A New Arrangement Of An Old Ditty

O who will on the boards so free?
O who the chair will fill?
O who will up and follow me
To pass a little bill?

The Ministry has locked the door,
The Premier keeps the key,
But neither bolt nor bar shall part
My right to Vote and me!
I know the journals of the day
Abuse us sharp and sore,

But there shall come a time when they
Shall rant at us no more!
Fierce Bouverie shall silence keep
And Scourfield cease to quote,
For Ladies then as well as Men
Shall have a Right to vote!

We 've promises from Jacob Bright
With members brave and true,
A gallant band to lend a hand
And drag the measure through!

To win next year we do not doubt,
Although we're waiting still,
And ere the next new Session's out
We 'll pass that little Bill!

The 'Bouverie' in Anna's verse was Edward Pleydell Bouverie (1818-1889), a Liberal MP for Kilmarnock who belonged to the old whig school. Anna singled him out because he was the leader of a group of MPs who vehemently opposed women's suffrage. In a debate on the Women's Disabilities Bill he put forward the usual arguments that most women didn't want the vote, and their place was in the home, not in 'rough competition with men.' He was afraid that if women had the vote it would lead to them acquiring a share in legislative, judicial, and administrative power. He feared 'the very foundation of society' was under attack.6 John Henry Scourfield (1808-1876), Liberal-Conservative member for Pembrokeshire, also spoke in the debate. He simply poured ridicule on the issue, stating everyone who signed a petition for women's suffrage should have their photograph taken, because 'he could not help suspecting that many of the signatories were not women, but men in women's clothing. (Laughter.)'[7]

The supportive Jacob Bright (1821-1899) was a Quaker and Radical Liberal MP for Manchester. During his parliamentary career he proposed a number of bills for women's suffrage. His wife, Ursula Bright (1835-1915) was also active in the women's movement. Jacob was the brother of the prominent MP John Bright. Anna was not alone in her approval of Jacob Bright. Lydia Becker wrote to Helen Taylor in 1867, 'Of Mr Jacob Bright's services to our cause, it is impossible to speak too highly. He deserves the hearty thanks of every one interested in it. His influence in Manchester is great, and he freely devotes it to our service.'[8]

In the last two issues of her paper Anna expressed her outrage at wife beatings that occurred at Wandsworth, Brighton and St Leonards. The last issue has an article entitled 'Public Schools for Girls,' by Mrs Henry Kingsley, wife of the novelist. While living in Edinburgh in 1870-72 she was for a time secretary of the committee supporting Sophia Jex-Blake and other women in their efforts to gain a medical education. Others who wrote for the paper were the novelist Anne Beale (1831-1900) and George Browning (1812-1878) author and secretary of the Society for Promoting Fine Arts. Florence Miller wrote that Sophia Jex-Blake had an article in the paper, but this was not the case.

In her paper Anna showed a high regard for Princess Louise (1848-1939), the sixth of Queen Victoria's nine children. The issue of 12 October carried a news item stating the Princess had become the patroness of the National Society for the Protection of Young Girls. In the next issue Anna mentioned 'the good Princess Louise, who seems always ready to help in wise and benevolent movements,' was present at the forty eighth annual meeting of the Royal Society for the Prevention of Cruelty to Animals.

The day to day realities of owning a paper soon doused the flames of Anna's initial enthusiasm, for she ceased publication after four issues.

It would take Anna more time until she found her true vocation. However, the exercise gave her valuable experience, as it was her most significant venture into the world at large to date. Through the paper she made contact with a range of people, some of whom would subsequently play a role in her life.

Notes

1. Geoffrey of Monmouth in his mythical *The History of the Kings of Britain* c.1136 designated the Severn, the Thames and the Humber as 'the three noble rivers' of Britain. Sabrina was the goddess of the Severn.
2. Briggs, 124.
3. Maitland 1905, 9.
4. Horn, 174.
5. Biographical note by B. Lindsay in Bonus, 1914, 82.
6. Lewis, 63.
7. Ibid., 65.
8. Crawford, 79.

Chapter - 5

Anna at Home

After closing down her paper, Anna finished her novel and renamed it In My Lady's Chamber: a Speculative Romance, Touching a Few Questions *of the Day*. It was published under the pseudonym 'Colossa' in the Spring of 1873. In this novel Anna gives intriguing insights into her married life and her ideas. Two central characters, Cora Bell and her husband the Reverend Archibald (Archie) Bell, are in some ways based on herself and Algernon. Anna blended fact and fancy in this extract:

> Mrs Archibald Bell, the wife of a country curate, whose name was never heard but in connexion with the sayings and flittings of his eccentric spouse, and who plodded soberly on from month to month among the backwoods and primitive lanes of Littlebog-cum-Mudbury, a sequestered parish somewhere up by the Welsh borders, in blissful innocence of his fair Cora's metropolitan experiences. For Cora was popularly supposed to be afflicted with delicate health, the rigorous inconveniences of which were only to be mitigated by frequent visits to the West End, and it was an actual fact incontrovertibly established by many salient proofs, that the air of the country in general, and of Littlebog in particular, was certainly in her case inconducive to a condition of physical salubrity.
>
> Cora had a large circle of friends dotted round and about the Babylonish city, most of them aunts and uncles on her husband's side, who, because their nephew was not particularly sagacious, and had been penniless before his marriage, were the more prone to consider the pretty wife, who had brought him four hundred a year, a prodigy of wit and learning, whom it was an honour to entertain whenever she pleased to bestow the joys of her society upon their respective establishments.

> Cora's father had been an actor in his youth, in his manhood a prosperous merchant, and at his death a wealthy testator; but his sons were seven and their debts were many; and it came to pass that by the end of five years after the old gentleman's demise there was not much of the original property remaining in the family. In this respect, Cora was the best off among the survivors, for she was an only daughter and the youngest of the brood, in virtue of which pleasing accident the testator aforesaid had bequeathed her an extra five thousand, and had caused the same to be settled upon her for separate use, so that she had an independent income, and wrote her own cheques upon the 'London and County.' And, in fact, both Cora's parents – they had been good old people in their way – had so spoiled and petted and indulged their youngest darling, that if their tenderness had not actually created that deplorable delicacy of her constitution, at least it had greatly fostered and encouraged it; and could they only have lived, poor souls, to witness the foolish and undesirable marriage that Cora was pleased to make two years after the death of her widowed father, their last moments would not have passed away in that peace and serenity of mind which had edified their children so notably.

Cora obtains her husband's permission to spend time in London with Vane Vaurien, but he does not know they are lovers. When Archie is thrown from his horse, Cora returns to him, as she considers 'the sowing of her wild oats legitimately accomplished.'

Anna describes Cora's marriage as being 'foolish and undesirable.' We may ponder whether Anna was thinking about her own marriage when she wrote these words. With her head full of ideals and ambition, Anna may at times have wondered how she came to live in a remote country vicarage. Like her other works of fiction, Anna interposes some of her social ideas in the novel. One female character criticises the inferior position of women in marriage and their lack of rights, while another supports rights for women, including the vote, in a discussion with her brother that covers ten pages. The artist Tristan advocates a meatless diet with a list of famous vegetarians, and to reinforce the point Anna adds another fourteen names in a footnote.

The Examiner of 26 April 1873 listed *In My Lady's Chamber* among twenty eight 'Books of the Week' which were given short reviews. The reviewer had mixed feelings about Anna's novel:

> Why a novel in many respects so well written as *In My Lady's Chamber* should, in addition to literary crudities, be so full of gross and

unpardonable misprints, mis-spellings, and typographical errors that there is scarcely a page free from them, we are at a loss to conceive. Anyone, however, who does not mind encountering these annoying blunders will find the story in many ways superior to its class. A frequent use of German, French, and Latin words, not seldom misspelt, is one of many drawbacks, as is also the following passage, of whose artistic merits we leave our readers to judge:

'The pose…was one of perfect confidence and interesting agitation, the rippling crispy braids drooping over Miss Brabazon's supporting arm, the blushing face hidden upon the pillowy shoulder of that fair politician, the two heaving bosoms pressed together in the close embrace of feminine friendship. It was like a picture by Millais – like a full-page illustration in the *Cornhill Magazine.*'

The reviewer was correct about the inordinate number of misprints in the novel. However, he or she missed the fun elements in the work. Anna included some frisky expressions in this light-hearted novel: the 'red-eyed engine with a scream like an ogre in a fit;' the 'hothouse of a theological college;' Diana Brabazon has a 'pillowy bosom;' Vane Vaurien the 'bipedal fox' has 'faultlessly trousered legs;' and Cora is a 'pretty painted parsoness.'

Florence Fenwick Miller (1854-1935) became a close friend to Anna and wrote about her in her autobiography. Florence wished to study medicine at Edinburgh University, but was not allowed to sit for the matriculation exams in October 1871. At the same time, Sophia Jex-Blake and her pioneering group of women lost a bitter legal battle to continue their medical studies at Edinburgh. Florence then enrolled at the Medical College for Women in London and qualified as a midwife in April 1873.1 It was here she met Dr Charles Drysdale, brother of Dr George Drysdale.[2]

Florence was a reader of the *Lady's Own Paper* and after it closed down she wrote to Anna 'to thank her and assure her how I should miss the paper. She told me later that mine was almost the only letter of thanks and loving appreciation of her effort that she received, all through her editorship; while she had had "dozens blaming, and advising alterations, and generally tearing me to pieces."' Florence continued:

She replied to me in a cordial letter, dated from her mother's house 5 Jan. 1873. She says:

'Such sympathy as that you give me is all the more valuable to me because it comes from one who has never seen my face. Would I had met with but ten other friends such as yourself! My life then might not have been what I now sometimes fear it must be. Ever since I had wit to think for myself, or to act with any independence, I have striven hard against an adverse tide of indifference, open opposition, and even bitter enmity. What little I have been able to do for the Right, I have done in the teeth of the World's opinion, looking for no reward that men will give me. And hitherto, I have failed, I think. Will it seem impertinent to you if I ask you to write to me again and to tell me something of yourself ?'

She concluded by hoping that we might one day meet, 'for as you are interested in those social questions which affect women, we may have some mutual friends, and may be both present on some occasion when I am in London.'

Florence told of her first meeting with Anna:

As I knew that dear Mrs Sims was acquainted with Mrs Kingsford, I read this letter to her, and she immediately arranged an introduction. I was charmed with the beauty, the vivacity and originality of my new acquaintance, and forthwith asked my mother to invite her to lunch with us; and she accepted. Knowing her to be a vegetarian, we made the family meal that she was to share on that line. I consulted a young man I knew, an enthusiast for 'pure diet,' who subsequently gave up his other business to found one of the most successful of London's vegetarian restaurants. He suggested lentil omelette served with grilled mushrooms, macaroni cheese, and stewed apples and cream. My brothers enjoyed this vegetarian luncheon hugely, but our guest partook very sparingly of each course. She really enjoyed the dessert, some grapes and other fruit, for, she announced, she had recently come to the conclusion that the proper and natural food for man was uncooked, therefore mainly fruit and nuts.

Like everyone else, Florence was captivated by Anna's beauty, describing her thus:

Though many other lovely creatures of my own sex have passed before my eyes since that date, I still think that she was the most beautiful woman I have ever seen. She was tall, slender and graceful in figure, crowned with an aureole of golden hair, falling in little curls on a broad brow; her features were of classical mould, with a short upper lip shaped like a cupid's bow,

Florence also remarked on the qualities, which, in her opinion, made Anna a unique woman:

> ...she united to her beauty of person not only an exceptionally fine and active intellect, but also the strength and 'staying power' required to cultivate highly her mental gifts in the direction of scientific knowledge as well as aesthetically. In this combination, she differed from any other woman I have known, or heard of in my own time, although tradition ascribes a similar efflorescence of mind and person to several of the famous women of past ages. Cleopatra, Queen of Egypt, is recorded to have spoken to the Ambassadors of eight foreign States successively, each in his own tongue. Ninon de l'Enclos, Madame Pompadour, Mary Queen of Scots, Hypatia the Martyr, and Aspasia the friend and counsellor of Pericles, are only some of those who are reported to have combined a cultivated mind and beauty of person.

After her first meeting with Anna Florence wrote:

> I have always gloried in, stimulated and celebrated, as far as lay in my power, any gifts, graces, or achievements of other women, and I was delighted with my new friend, who had such charms and talents and placed them all at the service of the woman's cause. We met fairly frequently, and when she was going down to her country home, she wrote to me:
>
> '2 Horbury Crescent, W. 15 May 1873
>
> This is a Parthian shaft sent after you to renew very urgently the request I made to you last night. Pray let me find you at Euston Station to-morrow at 11-30! I am sure you want some country air. Our part of the world is preeminently beautiful, and your spirit would be etherealised by the mere sight of our hills and vales. My husband is the most charming of men – I only fear you will fall in love with him! All the work you have in town you will, I am certain, take up with fresher and keener zest for having had a week in our pure, sunny atmosphere.'

Florence was too busy to accept Anna's invitation at the time, but it was left open until she was free. In August Florence spent a week at Anna's home, Hinton Hall, Shropshire, near Pontesbury, where Algernon had recently become a rector. As Algernon drove Florence to Hinton Hall from the station in his dog-cart she took a nostalgic view of a threatened country custom:

> ...I was amused to note the reverences paid by the country people, one and all, to my host; not because they knew him, but because he was

'one of the gentry,' and it was still the fashion then in rural circles to acknowledge class distinction as a matter of good manners. The men and boys touched their hats or pulled their forelocks, the women and the school-girls half paused in their walk for a brief 'bob;' and my host scrupulously acknowledged with the regulation flourish of his whip the greeting of the smallest and the humblest. Is the rural world any happier for the decay of such friendly notice between passers-by under democratic equality?

When she arrived at the vicarage, Florence discovered 'It was not quite an ordinary household in which I found myself.' She noted Anna's asthma and hay-fever, and the fact that 'her nervous organisation suffered, too, from the dulness of the country-side and the narrowness of its society.' Florence wrote Anna had already told her that she and Algernon had agreed to live as brother and sister, but it was not because of Anna's health. Unfortunately, Florence does not reveal to us Anna's reason. Florence went on to comment, 'there seemed perfect concord and mutual admiration' between Anna and Algernon.

Florence noted the role reversal which prevailed in the household:

> Mr Kingsford, assisted by a buxom and capable young woman (who was called, I think, Belinda) as cook-housekeeper, did the housekeeping; he ordered the meals, and arranged all the details of the daily life. On the other hand, as we sat at dinner on the evening of my arrival, and my hostess was planning what we should do the next day, Mr Kingsford quite simply said – 'You know, Nina, to-morrow is Saturday, and that sermon is not altered yet.'
>
> Meekly, and as a matter understood, she replied – 'Very well, Algie, I will not forget about it.'
>
> No doubt, the parish pulpit and the domestic arrangements both gained by this division of duties between the spouses behind the scenes, in accordance with their respective talents!

Florence was not, however, very impressed by Anna's pet:

> Her own special animal pets were, oddly enough, guinea-pigs. The favourite, a big, reddish-brown, male specimen, whom she named Rufus, was very frequently in her arms during my visit to Hinton Hall, and he afterwards travelled with her, in a specially built basket, wherever she went. It exasperated me to see the blandishments this lovely being lavished upon such an absolutely insensible rodent, and now and then

I would puff into Rufus's silly face in order to give him a moment's apparent animation by shaking his offended head.

As Maitland provided scant details about Eadith, we can be thankful to Florence for providing glimpses into her life:

> When Belinda, the maid, brought me my hot water on my arrival, and helped me to unpack, there came at her skirts little Eadith, aged five, 'sole daughter of the house and home.' She and I soon got on good terms, and presently, Belinda being gone, I was amusing the little one by trying on her the four or five hats and bonnets that I had with me, and fluffing out or smoothing down her hair to suit each one, as she stood before the glass. She was not at all a pretty child, totally unlike her beautiful mamma; rather of the practical, stodgy order, indeed – I daresay she exemplified the ancient Egyptian theory of heredity and resembled her grandfather, the successful shipowner. Anyhow, she was much enjoying the changes of headgear and coiffure, when her mamma, hearing our chat and laughter, looked in at the door to say coldly –
>
> 'Don't take much notice of that child! If you encourage her, she will be bothering you all the time.'

Florence related further anecdotes concerning Eadith:

> Next day there was some question of a length of blue satin ribbon which Eadith had made free, and which her mamma had wanted. The poor mite was not allowed to explain or defend herself; her look of misery as she stood silenced behind her mother's chair touched my heart – having so recently been an unpetted and snubbed child, with a temperament antagonistic to that of the person whom blood nevertheless gave power over my feelings.
>
> There was one matter at least in which little Eadith was personally looked after by her Mamma. When the Vicar came home from service on Sunday morning he announced – 'I have brought an invitation for the little girl to spend the day on Tuesday at Mrs Norton's.' Eadith looked soberly pleased at the prospect of a day's play with a family of other children, and no more was said. On Tuesday morning, as Nina and I sat in her boudoir, the door opened sufficiently to admit Eadith in a pretty white frock with a pink sash and pink ribbons in her carefully done hair. She stood to be surveyed, while Belinda, outside, held the open a few inches to hear any criticisms of her handiwork.

'Yes, child,' said Mamma, 'you look very nice, but I can't imagine why you are togged out like that at this time of day.

'Going to Mrs Norton's, ma'am,' said the voice of Belinda.

'Oh, yes, I had quite forgotten. Now, how am I to tell them that this child must not have any meat to eat? Baby, will you tell them you are not to have any meat, and if they still give you some, say "Mamma does not like me to have it," and do not eat it ?'

Of course Eadith obediently replied, 'Yes, Mamma,' and went off without further parley.

Anna keenly felt the pressures on women regarding family duties versus career aspirations, which she expressed in a letter to Florence written in late March 1887:

> I think of all your papers I liked best those in which you showed by the examples of Mendelssohn's sister and Merschel's what women might be if they were not everlastingly suppressed and bullied into silence. When idiots like Romanes tell us women have never been great, that they have been tried and found wanting, and so forth, these little biographies are pathetically eloquent. My heart aches when I read these things, and feel all the pangs of disappointed hope and ambition that poor women must have suffered. It is the Bible and child-bearing that quenches us all and dries up the flame in our spirits. What is to be done about the babies? We 're not all capable of your prodigious feats. A couple of olive branches usually suffices to absorb all the strength of an average woman, no matter how keen her wits may be. Ought we all to swear virginity or adopt Malthusianism? All the shops today are full of Easter Eggs. As I looked at them I reflected how much better it would be if we laid eggs like the happy and decent hens. I know I would take care not to hatch mine!

In the following anecdote Florence told of Anna's impact on men:

> A man who was taking the Botany Course for a Medical degree at the Regent's Park Botanic Gardens at the same time as she was told me that Mrs Kingsford habitually sat at the very back of the class, as if to avoid attracting attention. But one day, the Professor happening to observe about some plant that it had no utility to man as medicine or food, 'but its great beauty and the pleasure we derive from that entitle it to our admiring notice ' – with one accord, all the men on the front benches turned round and fixed their gaze for a moment on their beautiful fellow-student.

Florence mentioned Anna's unusual number of names in her life:

> ...corresponding I suppose, to her varying, almost Protean personality! 'Mrs Algernon Kingsford' on her visiting cards, she signed her letters 'Ninon Kingsford.' Her husband and her friends (myself included, when we reached that stage of intimacy) always called her 'Nina.' Her home name, by which her mother and brothers called her to the last, and which they inscribed upon her tomb, was 'Annie.' She took her medical degree as 'Anna,' and her biographer, Mr Edward Maitland, entitled his book 'Life of Anna Kingsford;' but he refers to her in it always as 'Mary,' on the ground that he believed her to be a reincarnation of Saint Mary Magdalen. One of her early letters to me concludes thus: – 'Annie Mary Magdalen Maria Johanna Kingsford – for that is really the elaborate length of my too tremendous name. I concisely shorten it into Ninon.'

Notes

1. Florence Miller's father was a ship captain employed by Anna's father from 1857 to 1864. Florence practised midwifery until 1876 when she was elected to the London School Board for three consecutive terms. She married Frederick Alfred Ford in 1877 but retained her maiden name. She had two daughters, Irene Florence (b.1880) who became a suffragette and Helen Caroline (b.1881). Florence concentrated on journalism from 1883, and operated her own paper, *The Woman's Signal,* from 1895 to 1899. Family legend holds that Frederick left her for a music hall actress, probably around 1894. Florence obliterated all traces of what happened, leaving only these poignant words, 'I paid a terribly heavy price for my poisonous draft of love, but I had it.' (Van Arsdel, 215) In her seventies Florence wrote her autobiography covering the first twenty five years of her life. Chapter 10, 'A Unique Personality,' is a thirty three page memoir of Anna providing details of Anna's personal life not found elsewhere. Miller's autobiography, *An Uncommon Girlhood,* reference GC/228, is held in the Wellcome Library, London.
2. Dr Charles Drysdale (1827-1907) qualified as an engineer, then under the influence of his brother George 's ideas, completed his medical training in 1862. In 1867 he joined the staff of the London Medical College, which was founded in 1864 to give women training in midwifery equal to that of men. He became an authority on venereal disease and in 1872 published a major work, *Syphilis, its Nature and Treatment.* In 1877 he founded the Malthusian League to promote birth control as the answer to overpopulation and poverty. Alice Vickery (1844-1929) became his partner, giving birth in 1874 to their first son, Charles Vickery Drysdale. After defying convention for many years they married in 1895. Alice Vickery spent time between 1873 and 1877 studying medicine in Paris, so she and Anna may have known each other. She finally obtained her medical degree from the London School of Medicine in 1880.

Chapter - 6

Medical Studies

In the Autumn of 1873 Anna discussed with Florence her preliminary steps for medical studies. They exchanged letters using male names as a comment on the fact women were barred from the medical profession in Britain. After mentioning to Anna the story of Agnodice, the ancient Greek woman who disguised herself as a man in order to practise medicine, Florence continued:

> I, half jestingly, talking over the slammed and barred doors facing Englishwomen, suggested that she and I should do the same. But so far as she was concerned, at any rate, I was not serious; for her beauty and her extreme femininity would have invariably betrayed her. Personally I might have carried it through, for I could 'be friends' with men; but she was not the type. However she was enchanted with the idea of the adventure, and tells me in one letter:
>
> 'I feel that life is not to be played with. You and I, and such as we, are the women on whom the Future depends. Others can afford to make game of their youth – we cannot, we dare not. I have resolved to do the course at St George 's if my certificates at Apothecaries Hall will admit me next session in male attire. Among all the scores of students who went up in September, are the examiners likely to remember that Ninon Kingsford was a woman?...Look here – in my Apothecaries' Certificate they have taken "Ninon" to be a male name and have reported themselves satisfied with *"his"* proficiency. Now, *Ninion* is a male name. Can't I go to St George 's as Mr Kingsford on the strength of that certificate?...If we went together I might be of service to you in assisting you with your money difficulty, since we might chum together.

A toi, mon cher Francis Fenwick,

Johann-Maria Kingsford'

In another letter to Florence, Anna told her of her experiment to look like a man:

> Last night I attired myself in my husband's garments, screwed my hair up tight and came into the boudoir, where I lit a cigarette, sat down and awaited results. My husband, coming in with the lamp, failed at first to recognise me. In his boots I was exactly his height: a little padding about the shoulder and waist would make everything complete. Positively, I think I shall try St George 's; are you still ready to undertake the enterprise?

Florence Miller wrote that Edward Maitland met Anna in the same year she met her, namely1873. There is no reliable information as to where Anna met Maitland, but a likely venue was a Dialectical Society lecture, as they were both interested in progressive thought. Writing to Anna in 1876 Maitland referred to 'the speakers and speeches at the Dialectical Society on the night of my paper, at the reading of which you were present.' Maitland was very impressed on first seeing Anna, describing her as follows:

> Tall, slender and graceful in form, fair and exquisite in complexion, bright and sunny in expression, the hair long and golden, of the 'Mary Magdalen' hue, but the brows and lashes dark, and the eyes deep set and hazel, and by turns dreamy and penetrating; the mouth rich, full, and exquisitely formed; the brow broad, prominent, and sharply cut; the nose delicate, slightly curved, and just sufficiently prominent to give character to the face; and the dress somewhat fantastic, as became her looks.

Maitland thought she 'had it in her to equally to be artist, poet, orator, musician, singer, scholar, savant, preacher, apostle, reformer and prophet.' She told him, 'And now I am completing my education by studying medicine. Not that I believe it will be complete even when I have my diploma; for the subject is limitless, and really leads to other subjects. For all things are related.'

On paying his first visit to Anna's home in Shropshire in February 1874, Maitland saw her this way:

> Anna Kingsford seemed at first more fairy than human, and more child than woman – for though really twenty seven, she appeared scarcely seventeen – and made expressly to be caressed, petted, and indulged,

> and by no means to be taken seriously; and the last characters to be assigned her were those of wife and mother, sufferer and student, while the bare idea of her studying medicine, or even taking a journey by herself, as she was then doing, shocked one by its incongruity.
>
> These impressions, however, were considerably modified when she spoke, so musical, rich, sympathetic, and natural were the tones of her voice. And when, as presently was the case – for there was no barrier of strangeness to be overcome, so ready had been the mutual recognition – she warmed to her favourite themes, her whole being radiant with a spiritual light which seemed to flow as from a luminious fountain within, her utterances were in turn those of a savant, a sage, and a child, each part suiting her as well as if it were her one and only character. Never had I seen anyone so completely and intensely alive, or comprising so many diverse and incompatible personalities.

Maitland stated, 'there was a connection between [Anna's] husband's family and my own,' though he did not produce any details. Isabelle de Steiger, who later befriended Anna, wrote in her memoirs that Maitland was Anna's step-uncle by marriage. However, this could not be possible, as Maitland only married once, and this was to Esther Bradley in Australia. No evidence showing a connection between Maitland and Algernon's family has been found.

Edward Maitland (27 October 1824-2 October 1897) was born at Ipswich, Suffolk, and attended a private school at Brighton, Sussex. His father, The Rev. Charles David Maitland, was perpetual curate of St James Chapel, Brighton. Edward entered Caius College, Cambridge on 19 April 1843 as a pensioner (fee paying student), gaining his BA in 1847. From an early age he was conscious of having a mission in life. He was repelled by the teachings of 'the strictest of evangelical sects' in which he was brought up, and resolved to do all in his power to abolish such teachings. Maitland felt his life had been 'one of much isolation and meditation. I had felt myself a stranger even with my closest intimates. For I was always conscious of a difference which separated me from them, and of a side to which they could not have access.'

Belonging to a family with clergymen, Maitland was expected to join the Church on his graduation from Cambridge. But he saw his inherited religious beliefs were 'a veritable strait-waistcoat, stifling life and restraining development.' He 'longed to get away from all my surroundings in order to think myself out of all that I had been taught, and so to make my mind as a clean sheet whereon to receive true impressions and at first hand.' Seeking adventure, freedom, and, hopefully, gold, Maitland set his sights on California.

Maitland left England in 1849, and after an eventful trip via the Caribbean, Panama and Mexico, he arrived in California. Although he found little gold, Maitland had many new experiences, and pondered much on philosophy and religion. He particularly liked to linger among the giant redwoods of California, and the outdoor life fostered in him a pantheistic philosophy. On hearing of gold discoveries in Australia Maitland set sail, arriving in Sydney around 1852. He told of his travels in his semi-autobiographical first novel *The Pilgrim and the Shrine* (1867).

In 1855 Maitland married Esther Bradley (1834-1856) in Sydney. Her father, William Bradley MP, was the wealthy owner of extensive grazing lands in Goulburn and the Monaro district of southern New South Wales, and the notable explorer Captain William Hovell was her grandfather. They had one son, Charles, who was born in January 1856 (d.1901), and in the following May Esther tragically died from consumption. In January 1858 Maitland returned to England and settled into a writing career. His other novels were *Higher Law: a Romance* (1870) and *By and By: an Historical Romance of the Future* (1873), and he also wrote many book reviews and pamphlets, mainly on religious subjects.

After having poems, pamphlets, stories and a novel published, and owning a paper, Anna now embarked upon a medical career. Florence Miller wrote in her autobiography about Anna's efforts to persuade her to study medicine in Paris with her early in 1874:

> However, at the end of March, she obtained permission to study in Paris. She was then very anxious that I should go with her there. I have a long letter telling me that she had learned about the fees and general expenses, and it goes on:
>
> 'Algy has promised to take me with him to Paris and wait there until I am settled. Will you join us? We might be very happy together, for I am sure we are not likely to disagree being so much at one on most subjects. Will you be frank with me and tell me how much you could afford to lay out per month? I should then be better able to calculate *our* resources.'
>
> There is also in my archives a copy of a letter from her to Dr C.R. Drysdale, (in his handwriting) asking him to try to influence me to go with her and let her pay part of my expenses.

> 'Miss Miller says very frankly and nobly that she could not stoop to being indebted to me for anything. But in any small help I might give her, you understand, she would *far more* than repay me by giving me her company. I am not the unselfish saint she seems to fancy, judging by her letter, for I am a terrible baby and can't get on without love. I am a spoilt child. Don't you think you, who have great influence with Miss Miller, could by dexterity and persuasion incline her to come with me? Tell her that you know she will be doing me a *downright kindness* in bearing me company, for she is a girl of much greater pluck than I. Oh dear, *do* persuade her, I shall be so lonely in Paris else!'

Florence wrote that 'for many reasons' she could not accompany Anna to Paris. Unlike Anna, Florence did not have independent means. She could not afford to study medicine for five or six years, only to find she could be prevented from practising in Great Britain. In her obituary of Anna Florence wrote that certain leaders of the medical women's movement tried hard to deter Anna form taking her degree. Florence did not provide any details, but indicated Anna's independent personality was frowned upon in conventional quarters. In April 1874 Anna enrolled at the Paris Medical School, having passed an exam in London which was accepted in lieu of the Paris entry exam.

A woman who very likely inspired Anna by her example was Elizabeth Garrett Anderson (1836-1917), the first woman to gain her medical licence in Britain. Elizabeth, the daughter of a successful businessman, Newson Garrett, was brought up in the seaside town of Aldeburgh, Suffolk. She was the second eldest of ten surviving children, and in her young womanhood she was expected to stay at home waiting to be married. By reading about then meeting Elizabeth Blackwell in London in 1859, Elizabeth was inspired to become a doctor. Miss Blackwell (1821-1910) was born in Bristol and as a child her family migrated to New York State, where, in 1849, she became the first Englishwoman to qualify as a doctor. In 1860 Elizabeth Garrett commenced nurse training at Middlesex Hospital. Her attempts to enter medical schools in England and Scotland were thwarted, largely by the male medical students, causing her to study under private tutors. The Society of Apothecaries examined and passed Elizabeth in 1865 because the sex of candidates was not specified. The Society then promptly closed this loophole to prevent any more women from qualifying. To command more respect, Elizabeth Garrett presented herself for examination, and gained her MD from the Paris Medical School in 1870. In 1873 she had a long letter in *The Times* (5 August) about women and medicine in Britain. Because women at this time were prevented from becoming doctors in Britain, she advocated that aspiring women should study at the Paris Medical School. Anna may well have read this letter and been influenced by its advice.

Anna joined a growing band of trailblazing women determined to become doctors despite considerable diffculties. In 1867 the Russian Nadezhda Suslova (b.1843) gained at Zurich 'the first medical degree awarded to a modern woman in a recognised university of high academic standing.'1 News of her success spread quickly across Europe and America. Women went to Zurich and Paris from countries which were slow to give them equal medical education: Russia, Germany, Austria, Britain and America. In the early 1870s only the Paris and Zurich medical schools were regularly open to women. When the Johns Hopkins University School of Medicine opened its doors to women in 1893, it compared its training with that of 'the great foreign schools of...Paris and Switzerland.'[2]

In Paris, Adolphe Wurtz (1817-1884), a renowned chemist and Dean of the Faculty of Medicine from 1866 to 1875, and Victor Duray, Minister of Public Instruction, were sympathetic to the admission of women into medicine. The liberal reformer Paul Broca (1824-1880), a surgeon and pioneer anthropologist on the medical faculty, was a strong supporter of women. He encouraged the career of Madeleine Brès, who enrolled in 1868, gained her MD and was allowed to practice in 1875. Despite this high level support, there was still widespread opposition to women in medicine, and few French women had the qualifications necessary to enter medicine. In 1870 only four women were enrolled in medicine in France. In the academic year of 1873-74, the year before Anna commenced, there were eighteen women enrolled in medicine in Paris. Many were Russian, because their government had banned women from attending Zurich through fear that they would be influenced by the exiled revolutionaries living there. At the time of Anna's graduation in 1880 thirty seven women were studying medicine in Paris.

Anna's stories, *Rosamunda the Princess, an Historical Romance and Other Tales,* which has been previously mentioned, was published early in 1875. This was the first publication of the title story, which, having a pantheistic and pagan atmosphere, indicates it was written after the other stories. Anna based this story in part on the account given in the eighth century by the Lombard, Paul the Deacon, in his *History of the Lombards.* Rosamunda is usually depicted as a villain by (male) historians, but Anna presents her as a heroine:

> And of such a race came the Gepide virgin, Rosamunda, exemplar and model of the true strong-minded woman. Born and reared in the lap of a nation whose customs made but small distinction in the training of the sexes, and whose laws permitted any able-bodied person – man or maid – to carry arms, the daughter of Kunimond was from childhood an Amazon in heart and physique. Not the less a woman, because so unlike the feminine portraiture of emasculated times; but such a woman as suited most fitly that age of iron, a woman who would have deemed the reproach of cowardice and fear as a great disgrace to her womanhood as the charge of falsehood and wantonness. Such, as please God, the return of virile strength to the heart of our palsied world may again bring forth in the good days to come, but then with purer and higher aspirations than were possible to the pagan Rosamunda.

In Anna's story, Alboin, king of the Arian Christian Langobards (or Lombards) desired to marry the beautiful Rosamunda, daughter of Kunimond, king of the Gepidae. Rosamunda, however, wanted none of Alboin. As the arrogant Alboin stooped to kiss the lips of the 'fiery' Rosamunda, she 'spat her hatred into his smiling face.' Shortly after she was captured and taken away by Alboin. The Gepidae then attacked the Langobards and freed Rosamunda.

After Alboin's wife Chlotswinda died, he sent an envoy to the Langobards demanding Rosamunda be delivered to him or war would follow. Rosamunda boldly told the envoy:

> ...that if he triumph over my people and carry me again to captivity within his palace, I and his death-warrant will enter its doors together! Let him force his love upon me if he dare, and the hand of a woman and not of a warrior shall compass shamefully the overthrow of your heroking!
>
> Standing erect and defiant before the Langobard she waved her queenly hand in sign of dismissal with such an air as a goddess might have fitly assumed toward some ignoble suppliant after pronouncing an adverse and irrevocable oracle.

Alboin went ahead and attacked the Gepidae, killing King Kunimond. Alboin married Rosamunda against her will. On the night of her marriage Rosamunda prayed to her gods:

> ...Give me power to redeem the honour of the Goths, give me might to avenge the shame that lies upon the glory of my father's race! We must die, we must perish – I and my people, yea we must perish; but like the

sun, let us go down in blood! Ye also, gods of the Norse, are passing away from our world; already your mighty shapes grow dim and shadowy in the upper air – obscured by the incense smoke of Christian altars. Weaker deities with beardless faces, mild and childlike, usurp the thrones your giant forms so long have filled! Where once the majestic form of the war-god Odin towered in huge divinity, stand the feeble and lacerated feet of the pale Christ! Where once we beheld a stately and fertile goddess – Hertha, the live-giving mother and queen – there kneels a slender and timorous maiden with downcast eyes and wounded heart, a vestal, unmated and sorrow-stricken! These are the new divinities, these – the rejected, the mean, the suffering; and to give these place, O grand and sturdy gods of the ancient faith, are ye and yours dethroned! Stoop from your eternal seats, steel my hungry spirit, strengthen my eager hands...

These defiant words are in sharp contrast to the meekness and martyrdom of Beatrice, Anna's former heroine.

In 568AD Alboin conquered northern Italy and at a 'triumphant banquet' he made Rosamunda drink from a goblet made out of her father's skull. Burning with indignation, she vowed Alboin must die. Rosamunda and Helmichis, the Gepide armour bearer who has fallen in love with her, hide in Alboin's room and attacked him. Rosamunda, true to her word, delivered the fatal blow with a spear thrust into the chest of Alboin. This is Anna's addition to the story which does not appear in Paul's account.

As a Lombard himself, Paul the Deacon had cause to paint Rosamunda in the blackest of colours, not only because she was an enemy of his tribe, but also a woman. Anna's portrayal of Rosamunda raised the ire of Walter Macleane, a complete unknown, who reviewed the book in *The Academy*.3 As she was a strong woman, he called Rosamunda 'one of the most detestable characters in history.' When he overstepped the mark and implied Anna advocated adultery, she complained to the editor, who grudgingly apologised in *The Academy*,4 but hypocritically added that no harm was intended.

The reviewer of *Rosamunda the Princess* in *The Athenaeum*5 saw merit in Anna's book:

Mrs Kingsford's volume will be read with interest by all Anglican or Roman Catholic devotees whose bent is to a fanciful and sensuous type of religion. The general reader will find her didactic strain occasionally wearisome, and her eloquence sometimes verbose and

> over-strained. The tales which please us best are the floral allegories, in which a good deal of poetic fancy is exhibited, while the moral deduced from each is unobjectionable. The story of 'Rosamunda,' which gives its name to the book, seems to us in questionable taste, being a revival in bold character of the circumstances of Alboin's death, and of horrors which, except for historical purposes, are better forgotten. The story of the Puritan weaver's daughter and that ardent controversialist Lord Maxwell is a glaring anachronism. The purely religious stories are even less to our taste, but on that point we would speak with reserve. Rapturous descriptions of the personal beauty of choristers, and exaggerated praises of the moral efficacy of music, are apt to become a little cloying if much insisted on. But Mrs Kingsford has power of a sort, and at any rate deserves more respect than novelists of the ordinary type. With a little concentration and more tolerance, she might do better things.

According to Maitland, at the request of Algernon he accompanied Anna to Paris in April 1874 for her enrolment. On returning to England Anna resumed her studies under private tuition in preparation for the Autumn term in Paris, dividing her time between her home in Atcham and London. In the Summer of 1874 Maitland's mother died and he left Brighton to take up chambers in London where he assisted Anna as required. Anna passed her exams 'with the highest credit' and was granted permission to continue her studies in England until the following Autumn. After spending the Christmas of 1874 at the parsonage she returned to London 'where she studied physiology at the school recently opened in Henrietta Street for women students of medicine, attended classes in Botany at the Regent's Park School, and took private lessons in the other subjects required.' The records of the London School of Medicine show that Anna was number 17 on the register of students.[6]

In the Autumn of 1875 Anna returned to Paris, this time with Algernon and Eadith, and moved in with a family of Irish ladies named Dawson in the Rue Vaugirard. The following letter from Anna to Maitland recounts one of her experiences as a hospital student:

> 24 November, 1875
>
> Here is a pretty story for you. There is in one of our wards a little deaf and dumb boy about ten years old, suffering— poor child—for the sins of his parents, with abcess in the scapulo-humeral articulation. He is an intelligent child, and talks to the students on his fingers. Yesterday

he complained in this manner of the bad smell arising from the wound in his shoulder, which is dressed with an ointment not too fragrant. I therefore conceived the idea of buying him a large bouquet of violets, and got him one last night at a flower-shop. This morning I arrived at the hospital very early, before G. (the professor) appeared, and gave my violets to the boy. He was greatly pleased, and hugged them close up to his breast. Then I went back to the salle to wait with the other students for G. After the 'call' was over we went our usual rounds with him. When we came to the bed where the deaf and dumb child was, there he sat up on his pillow with the violets in his hand, smiling. G. looked round, and asked rather sharply, 'Who gave him these violets?' I was dreadfully frightened, for I thought he was going to be angry about it. One of the students answered, 'C'est Madame Kingsford, monsieur.' 'So!' said G. 'She is a woman after all. Only a woman would have thought of doing such a thing as that. Not one of you, messieurs, would have brought flowers to a sick child in the wards.' Think of that! I have actually won him over by that simple little affair of a nosegay!

Anna continued her studies in Paris while Maitland dwelt in London. In discussion of vivisection in their correspondence, Maitland advised Anna to stand up to a professor who wanted to undertake vivisection at her lessons. He cautioned her not to let it be known that it was her intention to gain a diploma without witnessing any vivisection, 'for they might pass a rule making it obligatory.'

Maitland wrote to Anna on developments in the campaign for women's suffrage:

I send you to-day's *Times*, with a report of the debate on the Women's Suffrage Bill, which will show you how much you are needed in that movement. For the debate shows why it does not advance. They are all on the wrong tack, supporters and opponents alike. The franchise is claimed in hostility, not sought in love. The women are demanding it as a means of defence and offence against men, instead of as a means of aiding and perfecting men's work. They want a level platform with man expressly in order to fight him on equal terms. And, of course, the instinct of the majority – both of men and women – revolts against such a view.

The debate Maitland referred to took place in the House of Commons on 26 April 1876. Voting was 240 against the bill and 154 in favour. The campaign for women's suffrage was long and arduous. The bill went before the House twenty eight times from 1867 until 1928 when all adult women achieved the vote.

The medical school laboratories were near the lecture-rooms, and the cries of the animals so distressed Anna that she was forced to take up private tuition. Some years later Anna wrote of her experience in an article for *The Heretic*:

> Very shortly after my entry as a student at the Paris *Faculté*,and when as yet I was new to the horrors of the vivisectional method, I was one morning, while studying alone in the Natural History Museum, suddenly disturbed by a frightful burst of screams, of a character more distressing than words can convey, proceeding from some chamber on another side of the building. I called the porter in charge of the museum, and asked him what it meant. He replied with a grin, 'It is only the dogs being vivisected in M.Béclard's laboratory.' I expressed my horror; and he retorted, scrutinising me with surprise and amusement – for he could never before have heard a student speak of vivisection in such terms – 'Que voulez-vous? C'est pour la science.' Therewith he left me, and I sat down alone and listened.
>
> 'Much as I had heard and said, and even written, before that day about vivisection, I found myself then for the first time in its actual presence, and there swept over me a wave of such extreme mental anguish that my heart stood still under it. It was not sorrow, nor was it indignation merely, that I felt; it was nearer despair than these. It seemed as if suddenly all the laboratories of torture throughout Christendom stood open before me, with their manifold unutterable agonies exposed, and the awful future an atheistic science was everywhere making for the world rose up and stared me in the face. And then and there, burying my face in my hands, with tears of agony I prayed for strength and courage to labour effectually for the abolition of so vile a wrong, and to do at least what one heart and one voice might to root this curse of torture from the land…[7]

After considerable public debate, the Cruelty to Animals Act received Royal assent on 15 August 1876. However, far from protecting animals as the pro-vivisectionists claimed, the Act protected 'the freedom to use living animals as tools of research...The Act only dealt with experiments calculated to inflict pain.' Robert Sharpe has observed, 'There has never been a conviction for cruelty. The Act was designed to protect the scientist and not the animal.'[8] Three inspectors, from the medical profession, were appointed under the Act of 1876 to monitor experiments. In 1879, 270 licensed experiments took place.

In his history of the antivisection movement Richard French remarked, 'Anti-vivisectionists foresaw the cold, barren, alienation of a future dominated by the imperatives of technique and expertise. It was not only experiments on animals they were protesting, it was the shape of the century to come.'[9] Anna and other campaigners, such as Frances P. Cobbe and W.S. Lilly, were concerned about the loss of spiritual values in society caused by burgeoning materialism.

After passing her examination with distinction, Anna wrote an article on vivisection for the *Spectator*. She then divided her time between the vicarage and her mother's place in St Leonards. Anna obtained permission to continue her studies in England, so she stayed with a relative at Chelsea and attended the Children's Hospital in Great Ormond Street, Bloomsbury. Founded in 1852 by Dr Charles West, it was the first children's hospital in the English speaking world. It is still operating today, under the name of Great Ormond Street Hospital (GOSH). The hospital's Annual Reports list Mrs Algernon Kingsford as donating two guineas each year from 1877 to 1880.[10]

The relative Anna stayed with, whom Maitland does not name, was her aunt by marriage, Mary Ellen Kingsford (1833-1916), of 59 Oakley Street, Chelsea. She was born Mary Ellen Tennant in Lincoln and was the second wife of Henry Baldock Kingsford (1821-1872) whom she married in 1864. He spent seven years in India as a tea plantation manager, then returned to England and worked as a chartered accountant. Aunt Mary had one daughter and three sons. Maitland did not state his address for this time, only that he was living alone in his chambers two miles away from Anna.

Notes

1. Bonner, 37.
2. Ibid., 75.
3. The Academy (20 March 1875): 291.
4. Ibid., (8 May 1875): 475-6.
5. The Athenaeum (20 February 1875): 258.
6. Communication from Victoria North, Archivist, Royal Free Hospital Archives Centre, London.

7. *Anna Kingsford: Her Life, Letters, Diary and Work,* I. 75-6. (I refer subsequently in these notes to Maitland's biography of Anna as 'Life.') In Great Britain in 1968 not even a member of parliament had the right to visit a vivisection laboratory. In the same year, at the University of California laboratories at La Jolla, a witness saw over one hundred large dogs, such as collies, German Shepherds and huskies, all in utter silence. Their vocal cords had been severed to prepare them for torture. (Vyvyan, 133.)
8. Sharpe, 13.
9. French, 412.
10. Communication from John Clarke, Librarian at the Great Ormond Street Hospital.

Chapter - 7

Anna's Mystical Illuminations

Beginning in late 1876 and persisting for some ten years, Anna received a series of mystical illuminations in which spiritual truths concerning life and cosmic reality were revealed to her from her past memory. She wrote down her illuminations and later published them, offering spiritual nourishment to a famished humanity.

In November 1876, when Anna was living in Chelsea, she had a vivid dream of travelling on a runaway train. The other passengers were oblivious of their impending doom. Anna managed to reach the engine, and with Maitland's help unhooked it. The engine sped off into the darkness, and the passengers were saved. This dream was published as 'The Doomed Train' in *Dreams and Dream Stories* (1888). Maitland explained the dream in terms of the materialism which was 'fast sapping the very life of humanity by the rejection of the ideal and the spiritual.' Humanity was unconsciously hurrying to extinction 'under the impulsion of blind force, which materialism alone recognises.' In Anna's dream there was no one in the engine, indicating the forces of materialism lack any intelligent control. Nothing can save the engine from crashing over the precipice, which is why the train and its passengers had to be detached from it. Maitland noted the current age of materialism was 'the winter solstice of the human soul, and spiritual perception was at its lowest ebb.' He observed they 'were living in Bible times, which in reality had never ceased, nor ever do cease, except for those who are devoid of the spiritual consciousness, and for these those times never begin and have no existence.' Anna's vision of the doomed train is a graphic metaphor for a civilisation that is self-destructing.

Also in November Anna had this illumination about Mary and the Christ:

> If his be the glory of the full noontide, his day has been ushered in by a goddess. Aurora has preceded Phoibos Apollo; Mary has been before Christ. For, mark that he shall do his greatest work at her suggestion. To her shall ever belong the glory of the inauguration; of her shall the gospel be born; from her lips shall the Christ take the bidding for his first miracle; from her shall his earliest inspiration be drawn. The people are athirst for the living wine, which shall be better, sweeter, purer, stronger, for need of it. The Christ is in their midst, but he opens not his lips; his heart is sealed, his hour is not yet come. Mark that the first inspiration falls on the woman by his side, on Mary the Mother of God; she saith unto him, 'They have no wine.' She has spoken; the impulse is given to Divinity.
>
> His soul awakens; his pulse quickens; he utters the word that works the miracle. Hail, Mary, full of grace: Christ is thy gift to the world! Without her he could not have been; but for thine impulse he could have worked no mighty work. This shall be the history of all time; it shall be the sign of the Christ. Mary shall feel; Christ shall speak. Hers the glory of setting his heart in action; hers the thrill of emotion to which his power shall respond. But for her He shall be powerless; but for her He shall be dumb; but for her He will have no strength to smite, no hand to help. It is the seed of the woman shall bruise the serpent's head. The Christ, the true Prophet, is her Child, her gift to the world. 'Woman, behold thy Son!'

Anna was to later explain in *The Perfect Way* that symbolically the soul is Mary, and when purified can unite with the Holy Spirit to produce the Christ within.

Meanwhile, Maitland was experimenting with a meditation technique whereby he would trace his ideas back to their source and try to reach the very centre of his consciousness. On one occasion he saw 'the Great White Throne of the seer of the Apocalypse.' He found that his experiences were generally in accord with those of other mystic writers, in particular the Neoplatonist, Plotinus. He took issue with 'that view of Nirvana which identifies it with the mergence of the individual in the universal to the loss of his individuality.' Rather, Maitland learnt from his mystical experiences that 'the one becomes many, the end of evolution being not the absorption of the individual in God, but the individuation of God.'

In mid-January 1877 Anna returned to London and her studies. She moved into the house of Letitia Going, in Jermyn Street, London. Isabelle de Steiger, who became Anna's friend, wrote of Anna's new companion in her memoirs:

> Mrs Going was a young [Irish] widow lady of ample means, an advanced Mystic, and quite a new sort of character to me. In after life I had good reason to believe that she was one of those rare beings, inwardly a saint, though not an adept, for no miracles happened to her of which I knew, and I had a thorough reverence for her. She was not intellectual. Her retiring, shy, nature, indeed, shrank from ordinary conversation. She was a vegetarian and took very little food. Her exquisite little late dinner was the first purely vegetarian meal that I ever had, although common abstention from meat eating was not new to me.

In 1877 Maitland finished his book, *England and Islam,* a long, rambling affair which was an appeal to William Gladstone to oppose Russian expansion in the Middle East more vigorously. Maitland's brother, the Reverend Brownlow Maitland, opposed the book's publication, and raised questions about his brother's sanity. The brothers argued over religious matters, resulting in their estrangement. Despite the controversy, the book was published by William Tinsley (1831-1902), who also published works by Thomas Hardy, Anthony Trollope, Florence Marryat, Ouida, Mrs Oliphant and Wilkie Collins.

Anna returned to Paris with Algernon, Eadith and her governess in April 1877. She took an apartment in a small street in the Chaillot quarter, No. 26 Rue Boissiere, about halfway between the Arc de Triomphe and the palace of the Trocadero, not far from the Dawson ladies. Algernon went home after Anna had settled in, taking with him the manuscript of a story by Anna to post to an American magazine. She wrote to Maitland that she had received a letter from Florence Marryat, enclosing a cheque and a copy of the February number of *London Society* containing her story.

Maitland's next book, *The Soul and How It Found Me,* was published in the Autumn of 1877. This work contains his religious ideas and experiences, and also includes a selection of Anna's visions and dreams. Throughout the book he called Anna 'the Seeress' or 'Mary' to preserve her anonymity. Maitland stated the function of religion is the culture of the soul by means of pure living and thinking, and 'the encouragement of aspiration towards the highest perfection conceivable.' Accounts Maitland gave in the book of various séances he attended caused the press to disparage the book. The reviewer in the *University of Dublin Review1* found that Maitland had published his visions prematurely and suggested he should 'digest his revelations before pouring them out on the world in an unrestrained flood.' The review said Maitland's 'wild metaphysical enthusiasm [would] very likely be mistaken by homely people for insanity.' It continued, 'Mr Maitland's book is mainly an account of his spiritualistic experiences; he gives in full many visions, most of which had better been omitted, for though possessed of much beauty and colour they have evidently projected upon a mental tissue so preternaturally sensitive and excitable as to present the details in portentously enlarged, and, as it were, gaseous forms, too much like the weird imaginings of a Wilkie Collins.'

This review also stated, 'In deplorably ludicrous juxtaposition to what profess to be world-revelations, are details of changes that are taking place in the author's personal habits, which it would have been well for him to reserve for a separate work on the Diet and Dress of Prophets.' Here the reviewer referred to advice Maitland received from spirits that he eschew woolen underwear in favour of silk or linen. Spirits also told him to take a purge after eating lobster.

A scathing review in *The Academy*[2] also made fun of these personal injunctions, and called Maitland's assistant 'an hysterical female friend.' The review concluded, 'If the general public can be persuaded to look inside the mysterious binding, they will wisely content themselves with reading no further than the first page of the book, on which the author has inscribed the tell-tale text, "And there was given unto him a mouth speaking great things and blasphemies." '

The Soul and How It Found Me contains the only personal observation Maitland put into print about Algernon:

> Even the Seeress's husband, though one of the least imaginative of Englishmen, was not exempt from the operation of the same influences. For a vision was given to him in which the church in which he was ministering had become a tavern, while the prayer-book in his hands became refuse, to be flung away in disgust as containing doctrines derogatory to the divine character.[3]

Maitland admitted that *England and Islam* and *The Soul and How It Found Me* damaged his reputation as an author, and when Anna opposed the latter book he withdrew it from circulation.

One night in November, after thinking about Eadith, Anna had a dream which she called 'The Difficult Path.' In the dream she and Eadith were walking along a narrow path up a high cliff above the sea. Eadith kept stumbling and thereby hindering Anna's progress. Far below Anna could see a fishing village with a large crucifix at its centre. Suddenly a fisherman appeared on the path before them and asked to take Eadith to live in the village. Anna only relented when Eadith showed her willingness to go with him. Anna continued her ascent, seeing mountain peak upon peak rising before her through breaks in drifting masses of cloud. We can see in this dream that Anna's unconscious mind was prompting her to go forward on her mission. Also, perhaps, that she perceived Eadith as holding her back.

In Paris less than a fortnight later Anna had a short dream which she called 'A Lion in the Way.' This dream offers a clue to her state of mind at the time:

> Owing to the many and great difficulties thrown in my way, I had been seriously considering the advisability of withdrawing, if only for a time, from my course of medical study, when I received the following dream, which determined me to persevere:
>
> I found myself on the same narrow, rugged, and precipitous path described in my last dream ['The Difficult Path'], and confronted by a lion. Afraid to pass him I turned and fled. On this the beast gave chase, when, finding escape by flight hopeless, I turned and boldly faced him. Whereupon the lion at once stopped and slunk to the side of the path, and suffered me to pass unmolested, though I was so close to him that I could not avoid touching him with my garments in passing.

As well as her studies, Anna found time to write short stories. 'The Turquoise Ring' and 'Meg Myrtle ' were published in *Tinsley's Magazine* in 1877,4 while 'A Cast for Fortune, the Holiday Adventures of a Lady Doctor,' was published in *Temple Bar: a London Magazine for Town and Country Readers,* December 1877. Although it is a work of fiction, Anna put some of herself and her ideas into the story. For example, she must have been thinking of herself when she penned the story's opening words:

> I am one of those women who, being endowed with a love of knowledge, a disposition to gratify it, and means, mental, pecuniary and otherwise, of accomplishing that object, have devoted to serious study the years which most persons of my sex give to croquet, kettledrums, and other matrimonial machinations.

The story takes place in Germany where Dr Mary Thornton is on holiday after completing her medical studies at a 'continental university.' Staying at her hotel is Lady Pomeroy, a rich widow in very poor health. She consults Dr Mary about her condition and explains she is being cared for by her brother-in-law Dr George Pomeroy. Dr Mary speedily ascertains that Dr Pomeroy is slowly poisoning Lady Pomeroy with the view of acquiring her fortune, upon which she whisks Lady Pomeroy away to another town to escape his dastardly clutches. He gives pursuit, and when cornered by the police he kills himself. The story moves at a fast pace and grips the reader from beginning to end. Although it is a lightweight story which Anna must have enjoyed writing, she had a serious intent in presenting in print a woman doctor as the heroine.

In June 1878 Maitland claimed evil spirits began to try and sow discord between Anna and himself. He said 'the enemy took advantage of this period, by artfully causing discussion to generate into controversy, and controversy into altercation, when any subject arose between us respecting which we saw differently.' This was not the only time Maitland blamed 'evil spirits' for disagreements with other people.

For example, Maitland related an incident which occurred in May 1880 showing discord with Anna. When a lady of Anna's acquaintance invited her to a reception, Anna replied that she could not afford the time due to her studies. According to Maitland the lady pressed Anna to Maitland said that he wrote privately to the lady explaining Anna's situation. The friend then communicated his letter to Anna 'in terms of bitter resentment.' On Anna reproaching him, Maitland wrote:

> On my remarking that I had acted only as I should desire to be acted by in the matter, and judged her friend by my own best, she replied that it was a great mistake to judge others by onself. She knew that the person in question would act as she had done, because she read her as she actually is, and did not read herself into her.

One month later, Maitland reported he and Anna were working under 'strained conditions':

So great was the tension that no mutual discussion of the situation was possible. Speech and silence were alike dangerous; rather than run the risk of it, I devoted my evenings to long solitary walks, pleading the need of such exercise to my deranged circulation, though aware that the real motive was no secret to her.

As Anna's life is filtered through Maitland, we do not know her side of the story, although it is clear relations between her and Maitland were strained for some time.Unfortunately, Maitland did not choose to be more forthcoming on the matter.

Notes

1. *University of Dublin Review* (November 1877).
2. *The Academy* (13 October 1877).
3. Maitland, *The Soul and How It Found Me*, 175.
4. 'The Turquoise Ring,' *Tinsley's Magazine* 5 (20 January 1877): 1-31 and 'Meg Myrtle ' *Tinsley's Magazine* 5 (20 Jan.-June 1877): 293-324, 389-420. The former includes a long speech in favour of vegetarianism, and in the latter the heroine becomes secretary to a British MP, showing some of Anna's social concerns.

Chapter - 8

New Friends and Medical Graduation

In the late 1870s Anna met Lady Caithness and Isabelle de Steiger, two women who became close friends and were in complete sympathy with her spiritual beliefs and endeavours. After the death of her first husband, the Count de Medina Pomar, Lady Caithness (1830-1895) married James Sinclair, the 14th Earl of Caithness, Scotland, in 1872.

Though nominally a Roman Catholic, Lady Marie Caithness embraced spiritualism and Theosophy, and wrote books on religious subjects. Maitland first met her in 1875 at a reception in her London home in Portland Place. When Anna and Maitland visited her in Paris in 1878, she introduced them to works by the German mystic Jacob Boehme (1575-1624) and the French occulist Eliphas Levi (1810-1875). That year Anna and Maitland also wrote and published numerous articles, letters and pamphlets against vivisection. In addition to these activities Anna passed her exams with distinction.

Anna returned to England and spent Christmas at the vicarage. To safeguard her written revelations, Maitland carried them in a 'wallet' strapped to his shoulders for the journey, and he was much relieved he did not lose any of this valuable material. Anna had read in a newspaper that a woman was refused entry at Dover because she was carrying her pet lamb. This news caused her some apprehension, but she was extra careful and managed to smuggle Rufus into England without detection.

On returning to Paris Anna and Maitland visited Cardinal Guibert, Archbishop of Paris, to talk about vivisection. Though expressing his love for animals, the Cardinal suggested that scientists should attend confession and then they would find that the Church disapproved of their practices. Anna left him a short paper she had written on vivisection which he put to one side to read later. She came away 'dumb with amazement and disappointment, her high hopes utterly evaporated.' Maitland said nothing, and waited for Anna to speak. Only after they had walked a considerable distance did she exclaim:

> How the mighty are fallen! I could not have believed it had I not seen it myself. There is but one word to express the condition of the Catholic Church in France – it is abject. And I believe all through its own fault. The Gods haven't come to the rescue a moment too soon. Oh, what a work we have to do! The Church wants as much saving as the world, and will probably be our greatest hindrance to saving the world. Oh, those priests! those priests! Priests of religion and priests of science, I do not believe there is a pin to choose between them.

In June 1879 Anna gained another friend, Isabelle de Steiger, whom she met through their mutual acquaintance Mrs Letitia Going. Isabelle related in her memoirs that at a meeting of the British National Association of Spiritualists Mrs Going invited her 'to go to her house in park Street to meet a very dear and interesting friend of her.' Isabella continued:

> Mrs Going and I were sitting in earnest conversation when Mrs Kingsford was announced, and I was struck on her entrance by her remarkable appearance. She was a tall, pale, fair and really beautiful woman, much draped with black silk and lace. [Writing her memoirs in the 1920s, Isabelle added a footnote saying she found '…it impossible to imagine that tall graceful figure dressed in a short narrow dress, like a theatrical nightgown, with seemingly bare legs only covered by thin pink or flesh-coloured silk stockings, and all the other barebackness as we see in most women today.']
>
> …[Anna] soon became deeply interested in the earnest conversation which she speedily began with Mrs Going. It was concerning a subject of which I then knew little, for it was the transmutation of the human body, one of the last Miracles of the 'Master.' I did not know then who the Master was or to whom they referred…
>
> When Mr Kingsford came to fetch his wife, as we parted, I said to Mrs Kingsford: 'I do hope I shall see you again some time,' for we certainly were in a worldly sense utter strangers. She stooped and said, looking at me – I well remember her concentrated manner – 'There is no question of hope, we assuredly shall; you and I were bound to meet, we have met in other lives and we have the same work to do.' I felt impressed and deeply interested, and remained silent.

Anna studied hard and passed her chemistry exam with flying colours. To escape the Summer heat of Paris she and Maitland went to the seaside at Cabourg, near Trouville. They had intellectual arguments which Maitland attributed to the influence of evil spirits trying to thwart them. He began to have health problems; his pulse rate accelerated to 110-120 beats per minute and he suffered disturbing head noises. Nor did the sea air give him the recovery for which he had hoped, although he enjoyed swimming in the surf. Anna and Maitland returned to Paris in the welcome knowledge that Lady Caithness was going establish her principal residence in the capital.

From November 1879 to April 1880 Paris experienced freezing conditions. Apart from the bad weather, Anna was too busy with her studies to return to England. She and Maitland went daily to the Bois where the lakes had frozen over, and Maitland resumed his favourite pastime of skating, while propelling Anna over the ice in a chair. Maitland reported his circulation and ears gave him much trouble, and the treatment he received did not relieve his sufferings.

Anna persistently refused to allow her professors to vivisect at her lessons, which resulted in many altercations and 'a constant change ' of teachers. Maitland asked her to put the question of vivisection directly to the *chef* of her hospital. 'She rather shrank from the task, saying it would be an unheard of presumption for a student to interrogate a *chef* of the wards,' but, Maitland continued, 'She was English, and had a prescriptive right to be eccentric; and above all she was a woman – not to say a good-looking one – and by that fact was accorded privileges denied to men, so that her very weakness was her strength.' Anna subsequently challenged the *chef* and he admitted that vivisection had no practical utility; scientists only used it to assert their independence from 'interference by clerics and moralists.'

On 7 February Anna had the following illumination in which woman symbolises the soul:

A Prophecy of the Kingdom of the Soul, mystically called the Day of the Woman

And now I show you a mystery and a new thing, which is part of the mystery of the fourth day of creation.

The word which shall come to save the world shall be uttered by a woman.

A woman shall conceive, and shall bring forth the tidings of salvation.

For the reign of Adam is at its last hour; and God shall crown all things by the creation of Eve.

Hitherto the man hath been alone, and hath dominion over the earth.

But when the woman shall be created, God shall give unto her the kingdom; and she shall be the first in rule and highest in dignity.

Yea, the last shall be first; and the elder shall serve the younger.

So that women shall no more lament for their womanhood; but men shall rather say, 'O that we had been born women!'

For the strong shall be put down from their seat; and the meek shall be exalted in their place.

The days of the covenant of manifestation are passing away; the gospel of interpretation cometh.

There shall nothing new be told; but that which is ancient shall be interpreted.

So that man the manifestor shall resign his office; and that women the interpreter shall give light to the world.

Hers is the fourth office; she revealeth that which the Lord hath manifested.

Hers is the light of the heavens, and the brightness of the planets of the holy seven.

She is the fourth dimension; the eyes which enlighten; the power which draweth inward to God.

And her kingdom cometh; the day of the exaltation of woman.

And her reign shall be greater than the reign of man; for Adam shall be put down from his place; and she shall have dominion for ever.

And she who is alone shall bring forth more children to God than she who hath a husband.

There shall no more be a reproach against women; but against men shall be the reproach.

For the woman is the crown of man, and the final manifestation of humanity.

She is the nearest to the throne of God, when she shall be revealed.

> But the creation of woman is not yet complete; but it shall be complete in the time which is at hand.
>
> All things are mine, O Mother of God; all things are thine, O Thou who risest from the sea; and Thou shalt have dominion over all the worlds.[2]

Anna passed her exams that year and all that remained was to complete her thesis. She chose vegetarianism as her topic and entitled her thesis *De l'Alimentation Végétale chez l'Homme.* Students had to discuss and defend their theses in open disputation before an audience of professors and students. Anna was full of confidence and looked forward to this experience which many students faced with dread. However, at the last moment, Professor Le Fort, the *chef* of her hospital, informed her that her thesis could not be accepted as it stood. The examiners had no quarrel with its scientific integrity, he said, but it was 'moral.' Le Fort said he himself would make the necessary changes to render it acceptable. Anna and Maitland discovered the chief objector to the thesis was a man 'most violently opposed to the admission of women to degrees.' Anna's presentation, on 22 July, was a friendly and informal occasion, and Anna 'was perfectly at her ease, doing full justice to her faculty of eloquent and lucid exposition.' Her professor warmly shook hands with Maitland and congratulated him on her success, saying,' "Madame is now one of us;" 'to which I mentally replied,' "Yes, but with a very considerable difference." According to information given by Sophia Jex-Blake in her book on medical women, Anna was the seventh British woman to graduate from the Paris Medical School, and overall the eighteenth British woman to qualify as a doctor. Thus, Anna was joining the ranks of a select group of pioneering British women doctors.

As Anna and Maitland had not anticipated a delay, they had allowed the lease of their apartment to expire, and could not renew it for the short period before they left Paris. Lady Caithness came to the rescue with a most welcome offer of residence in her home. Anna and Maitland had been studying the works of the Neoplatonists, Hermeticists, Rosicrucians and various 'seers, mystics and occultists' in Lady Caithness's 'excellent library.' They now studied the literature of modern spiritualism and confirmed the assurance they had received that they had 'nothing to do with spiritualism, our work lay far above that.'

Anna and Maitland then spent a few weeks by the seaside at Boulagne. They bathed and walked, but only partially revived their flagging energies after the 'wear and tear' of Paris. Rufus 'died of sheer old age, after nine years of pettage as never before fell to rodent.' He was sealed in a tin box and taken home to the parsonage for burial under a rose bush. Anna's 'grief was great,' as the furry fellow was so attached to her and used to pine dreadfully when she was absent. His death occurred on 15 August, the Feast of the Assumption of the Blessed Virgin Mary, a day Anna would always remember. While at Boulagne Maitland received a hurried visit of farewell from his son Charles, who had received his appointment as an army doctor in India. Father and son were not close, and they did not meet again for nearly ten years.

Notes

1. Isabelle de Steiger (1836-1927) was the daughter of Joshua Lace, a solicitor in iverpool. At twenty five she married Rudolf von Steiger, a Swiss cotton merchant. He died ten years later, and she became a painter and spiritualist. Isabelle was an inveterate joiner of occult groups. She joined the British Theosophical Society in 1878, attended 'The Perfect Way' lectures in 1881, and later joined Anna's Hermetic Society. She was in the Society for Psychical Research, and joined the Hermetic Order of the Golden Dawn in October 1888. When the Golden Dawn fragmented in 1903 Isabelle joined the 'Independent and Rectified Order' of the Christian mystic Arthur Edward Waite. After becoming disenchanted with the Theosophical Society she followed the teachings of Rudolf Steiner. She translated Karl von Eckartshausen's mystical work *Cloud Upon the Sanctuary* (1896) into English, and wrote *On a Gold Basis: a Treatise on Mysticism* (1907), *Superhumanity* (1916), and *Memorabilia* (1927)
2. Kingsford, Clothed With the Sun, 6-7.

Chapter - 9

Back in England

In the Autumn of 1880 Anna returned to England with the Swiss maid who had been with her for the latter part of her stay in Paris. Anna leased 11 Chapel Street, Park Lane for a period of twenty one months.[1] Here she conducted her medical practice, though Maitland gave no details of the practice. In her obituary of Anna, Florence Miller wrote she understood Anna had 'peculiar success with hysterical girls.' Although Anna did not register as a doctor, being qualified she was allowed to conduct a private practice. Registration was required for doctors to work in the armed services and other government positions. In 1874 the British Medical Association inadvertently elected Dr Garrett Anderson as a member, and banned membership to all other women until 1892.

Anna continued to receive illuminations explaining various aspects of esoteric philosophy. The following illumination relates to thoughts she had about seeking solitude in nature:

> If you would become a Man of Power, you must be master of the Fire. The man who seeks to be a Hierophant must not dwell in cities. He may begin his initiation in a city; but he cannot complete it there. For he must not breathe the dead and burnt air. In a city you respire air upon which the flame has passed; you breathe fire and it consumes your blood. The man who seeks all power must be a wanderer, a dweller in the plain and the garden and in the mountains. He must seek the sun and the breath of night. He must commune with the moon, and maintain direct contact with the great electric currents of the unburnt air, and with the unpaved grass and earth of the planet. It is in unfrequented places – in lands such as that of the East, where the abominations of

Babylon are unknown, and where the magnetic chain between earth and heaven is strong – that the man who seeks power, and would achieve the great work, must accomplish his initiation.[2]

The year 1881 opened with an extremely cold Winter and 'the Serpentine was frozen well nigh to the bottom.' Maitland continued, 'My colleague was far too precious and fragile an article to be exposed to the perils of a crowded London ice-rink, and so we made the reading room of the British Museum our recreation ground.' Anna and Maitland again saw two friends, the artist John Varley and his wife Isabella, whom they had first met in Paris. John Varley (1850-1933), like his painter grandfather, was an astrologer, and he aroused Anna's interest in the subject. Varley was an active member of the Theosophical Society, being a vice-president of the London Lodge in 1885.[3] Isabella Pollexfen Varley (1849-1938) was an aunt of the poet William Butler Yeats.

Maitland read in the newspapers in Easter that vines and fruit trees had been grafted onto cactus plants in western Mexico, a place he had once visited. It was hoped that crops could be raised and then 'the desert shall rejoice and blossom as the rose ' (Isaiah 35:1). Maitland saw this as a good omen for their proposed lectures and Anna's aim of bringing new life to the spiritual desert that was materialistic civilisation. Maitland also made the comment that Anna's 'spiritual emblem' was the red flowering cactus.

Anna and Maitland were members of The International Association for the Total Suppression of Vivisection, founded on 21 June 1876. Maitland's first mention of the Association referred to late 1878 when he and Anna wrote articles for it. Early in 1881 they were appointed to its committee. In Easter 1881 Maitland produced a twenty one page pamphlet called *'The Woman" and the Age: a Letter Addressed to the Right Hon. W.E. Gladstone, M.P.'* by Sundry Members, Clerical, Medical, and Lay, of The International Association for the Total Suppression of Vivisection. (At this time a bill to abolish vivisection was before parliament.) The committee was upset because Maitland falsely claimed authorship to the Association, when the pamphlet was entirely his own work. Throughout the pamphlet Maitland used the term 'we,' and his name is absent from it. W.H. Llewelyn, the Association's secretary, wrote to *The Zoophilist* disclaiming Maitland's false attribution of authorship.[4] In his letter of reply Maitland claimed the committee approved the original draft, and offered to pay for its publication. This, he thought, gave him the liberty to attribute authorship to the Association. Maitland and Anna later left the Association, but still vigorously campaigned against vivisection. On 6 June 1883 the Association merged with Miss Cobbe's Victoria Street Society For the Protection of Animals from Vivisection.

The British census, held on the evening of Wednesday, 3 April 1881, showed Anna's address was 11 Chapel Street, London, Middlesex. Anna had one servant, the unmarried Emma Bulloz, 28 years old and born in Switzerland. Anna was listed as the head of the household and Maitland as a 'visitor.' This contradicts what Maitland wrote in his biography of Anna, where he claimed he also lived at 11 Chapel Street with Anna.[5] For example, he wrote, 'I reached home after my last sitting only just in time to join her at the dinner table.' If Maitland had been moving in and out of Anna's place, he gives no explanation of the circumstances. Isabelle de Steiger referred to it in her memoirs as 'a house rented by Mrs Kingsford's husband, in a fashionable street adjoining Park Lane.'

On this census day Algernon was at Hinton Hall, Pontesbury. Also present was his housekeeper Margaret Willner aged forty years, and the twenty two year old George Waring, the footman and domestic servant. Eadith was with her grandmother Mrs Bonus in St Leonards on Sea where she attended a school of nineteen girls at 1 & 2 Markwick Terrace, a few streets to the north west of Warrior Square. Anna's brothers Albert and Henry lived in the parish of Hollington, to the north of St Leonards, within easy reach when Anna visited her mother. In 1881 Anna's sister Emily Louisa was living with her husband the Reverend Edward Gilliat and their four daughters in High Street, Harrow on the Hill, Middlesex. Although Maitland does not mention these siblings of Anna, she more than likely kept in touch with them.

Anna planned a series of lectures to be held in the Summer of 1881 in London, based on her insights into the higher aspects of religion, received through her illuminations and her study of esoteric writings. Because the subject matter was esoteric and not accessible to everyone, the audience had to be carefully chosen. As Maitland wrote, 'there are spiritualists and spiritualists—those who seek to *spirits,* and those who seek the Spirit itself.' Anna and Maitland therefore sought their audience from among the latter group. Maitland anticipated that members of the British Theosophical Society would attend the lectures because of their common religious beliefs. The Theosophical Society was founded in New York in 1875 by Madame Helena Blavatsky[6] and Colonel Henry Steel Olcott, and the British branch was established in London three years later. Maitland had read Blavatsky's *Isis Unveiled* (1877), which he found somewhat 'ill-digested and ill-arranged,' but thought it 'showed both power and knowledge of an unusual kind.' He was struck by the fact a man and a woman were working to restore the esoteric philosophy of the West—himself and Anna—while at the same time a man and a woman were doing the same for the esoteric philosophy of the East—Olcott and Blavatsky.

Maitland's chief intermediary with the British Theosophical Society was its president Charles Carleton Massey, who attended Anna's lectures. According to Maitland, other attendees included Dr George Wyld, the Hon. Roden Noel, Sir Francis Hastings Doyle, J.W. Farquhar, Dr Inglis, Rev. John Manners, Hensleigh Wedgwood, Rev. Stainton Moses, Herbert Stack, Gerard B. Finch, Frank Podmore, Elizabeth V. Ingram, Francescsa Arundale, Isabelle de Steiger, and members of the Kenealy family.[7] Maitland wrote of these people, 'it will be seen that we had an audience of more than average intelligence and culture of the kind required for the appreciation of our results.' The 'Perfect Way' lectures, as they were called, were held in the drawing room of Anna's residence in Chapel Street. Sir Francis Doyle said of them, 'they were something quite new in the world; there was nothing in literature to compare with them. And to hear them was like listening to the utterances of a god or an archangel.'[8] Mme de Steiger noted in her memoirs, 'I have only since (at the time I don't think I much noticed matters of money) become aware how generous Mrs Kingsford and Mr Maitland were in unobtrusively paying all expenses in connection with their meetings.'

On 15 August 1881 Anna wrote sadly in her diary of the passing of her pet Rufus, followed by some thoughts on astrological symbolism:

> …today is one of sorrowful memory to me – the first anniversary of the death of my dear little friend Rufus. And it is also the Feast of the Assumption of the Virgin. There is an association between these two ideas, for is not Maria the same as Venus, and is not Venus our Lady of Love? And is it not from her Golden Book that I got my assurance of the continuance of the life of all creatures and the uses of love towards them? Love 's rising heralds the rising of Justice, our Lady the Enlightener. Sure it is that Love and Justice are one, and the equal rights of all creatures before the Lord God of Spirits are revealed and assured to us by Her who is Mistress of the fourth Day. For what are these words – Justice and Rights? How should we know the meaning of either but for Love? And Love is the Woman of Heaven, Maria, Astraea, Venus, Aphrodite, by whatever name she is known and is dear to us.
>
> Yes, dear Goddess, that sign of Thee in Heaven is my comfort, for I know no sign could be there if the Reality did not invisible exist. How

> idle it is to refer us to all this wonderful text-book of the Zodiac, and to expect us to believe that the mere Letter is all there is of it! 'Thy word, O Lord, for ever is written in Heaven.' Yea, but the writing is not the Word, This holy Lamb, this Lion, this Virgin, this Cup-Bearer – they are but so many hieroglyphs of True Persons, whose signatures they are. Can Astronomy satisfy Love? Can the soul be content with symbols? That I love, that I have a soul – nay, that I *am* a Soul, these are evidences to me that Heaven too loves, that the Universe is spiritual.
>
> History is the Body, Science is the Mind, the Soul is that inner and central Cause which answers to Religion. No one but a fool or a lunatic could suppose that all the wise and illuminated men of all ages and lands combined and agreed to represent these various figures in the Starry Sphere according to one universal chart out of pure fantasy! And if such an assumption is difficult on the face of it, how much more is it difficult to the man who has experience of life, and who knows how perfectly these figures correspond to the intuition of the heart and mind! I need no history, for my part, to convince me of the truth of the Parables of the Zodiac, and of their eternal application to the experience of humanity.

While in London, Anna continued with her more earthly pursuit of opposing vivisection, resulting in the only known contact between Anna and Annie Besant, which occurred when Mrs Besant wrote an article for *The National Reformer9* in support of vivisection. She was the editor of this paper, which was owned by Charles Bradlaugh, her coworker for secular causes. Besant argued the pain caused to a few animals justified the 'benefits' ensuing to mankind. She thought vivisection contributed to the advancement of science, and wrote, 'It is sometimes pretended that those who advocate vivisection are indifferent to animals. That is certainly not so in my own case.' To prove her love for animals, she said that as she wrote she had three dogs with her, birds were flying in a large cage, there was an aquarium, and a squirrel was playing in the greenhouse outside.

Anna's strong reply to Mrs Besant appeared in the paper on 6 November 1881. She quoted esteemed medical authorities who said vivisection had not resulted in medical progress. Anna pointed out that Mrs Besant used the same argument as the Inquisition: it was justified to torture and burn 'a few to save thousands.' Anna also expressed her views on the promotion of health in society:

> As I am against the orthodox priest, I am against the orthodox 'doctor.' In my view, the best means for obtaining health and preserving it are,

whether for men or beasts, natural, clean, hygienic means. True prophylactics consist, not in the inoculation of disease, but in living so as to make disease impossible. Sanitary measures, properly carried into practice, in home, in city, in meadow, in pasture, in diet and in life, social, physical and moral, are, with time, sufficient to rid us of all the devils to which dirt, poverty, barbarity, ignorance and vice have given birth in the past. But of these devils we shall never be rid as long as 'prophylactic' science goes on collecting, preserving, bottling, inoculating, disseminating, and perpetuating their 'germs,' from generation to generation, and thus undoing on one hand what hygiene is doing on the other.

Mrs Besant later wrote in her *Autobiography* (1889) that Anna's article was instrumental in causing her to change her attitude and oppose vivisection. She stated her own article was 'the one thing that I ever wrote for which I feel deep regret and shame, as against the whole trend and efforts of my life.' Anna's article had 'touched that question of the moral sense to which my nature at once responded.'

When the 'Perfect Way' lectures were over Anna and Maitland separated for a holiday, Anna going to her mother at St Leonards and Maitland to Warwickshire to his niece, the married daughter of his deceased brother Charles. After their rest they were busily occupied revising and proofreading *The Perfect Way,* the book of the lectures.

In the following letter to Lady Caithness Anna discussed the progress of the book:

4 November 1881

My Dear Lady Caithness – Thank you very much for your welcome and sympathetic letter. I doubt not that Mr M – keeps you posted up in the progress of the Book, which we are doing our utmost to get out as a Christmas present to the world. You can have no idea what a labour it has been, and still is. For not only has it been exceedingly difficult to compress into moderate dimensions, and to express clearly in popular language, the enormous mass of truth we have to put forth, but we have also found it necessary to elucidate the text by means of woodcuts, the designing, the copying and perfecting of which, having been exclusively assigned to me, have occupied a considerable amount of time.

The little woodcut which I have had stamped on this paper has been kindly lent me by Mrs Kenealy. It was cut for use by the Doctor, but he died before the book in which it was to have appeared could be produced. The design is from a reproduction from an old picture; hence the conventional stiffness of the limbs and drapery. Apart from this, I find everything in the symbolism of the picture, and for that reason have adopted it. The divine Mother is of course the heavenly Arche, or Wisdom, the primary substance of things manifest, holding in her arms the Life or Spirit, that is God, the vital Principle, who is to the Soul what the sun is to the system. And the seven doves are the seven spirits of God, or the seven messengers, the dove or pigeon being selected as the type of the carrier messenger. For the dove it was which went out of Noah's ark and brought him back tidings of the cessation of the flood, bearing in her mouth an olive branch, symbol of peace and of wisdom; and the throat of the dove, encircled by a ring resembling the rainbow, indicates it as the special emblem of the sevenfold spirit, whose hues are figured as those of the seven rays which make the One Invisible Light.[10]

As regards the Book, I am anxious that it should become known. Once known, I am confident of its success on every plane. But it is no easy thing to reach the public eye and hand...The interpretation which you suggest of the celebrated 666 is an admirable one, and commends itself more to my mind than any I have yet heard. The three sixes would thus be the number of the beast, in that the date 1881 would indicate the year which should limit and end his power; the beast being Denial, the spirit of Unbelief and Materialism...I regard the prophecy regarding this year as already fulfilled in the production of our Book, which will, for the first time in the world's history, 'make straight the way of the Lord' – the Perfect Way.

For a long time I have had no visions or direct illuminations, but I look on these as suspended merely in order to permit occupation in the active work needed for the production of our Book. And I hope when it is safely launched that I may have time for rest and thought, assisted by the Light which has already taught us all to discern so much. You must remember also that, unlike the ordinary medium, I have no power to attract or influence my 'Voices.' If it should seem good to the Gods to show or to tell me anything concerning your special guardian, of course you shall know at once; but as a rule, the affairs of Souls and their Angels are as strictly concealed from other Souls as are the secrets of penitents by their directors in the Church. Nor are the communications made to me often of a particular nature. They concern rather principles and interior interpretations, doctrine, and so forth. For these only, or chiefly, hitherto have I found myself clairvoyante or clairaudient.

I am glad to know you feel interested in my little treatise to which I ventured to give the *family name* of the 'Perfect Way' (*The Perfect Way in Diet*) – and I regard it as a forerunner of the Book, a sort of John the Baptist heralding the fuller Gospel. And it sets forth the physical foundation on which the spiritual structure must be raised; it clears away the blood from the steps of the Christ. And unless a man can make up his mind to *live the life of Eden* he will never have right to the Tree of the Garden, 'whose leaves are for the healing of nations.

I send you herewith a copy of the last number of the *Food Reform Magazine*, thinking you may be interested in my last letter on Pure Diet therein. Also the *Réforme Alimentaire* of the Paris Society.

Always most affectionately yours, Anna K.

When Anna's thesis was published as *The Perfect Way in Diet* in 1881, it attracted attention and was translated into a number of foreign languages. An unsigned review in the reactionary *Saturday Review* attacked the book and Anna in a most unseemly manner.[11] After stating, 'The vegetarian very frequently kills himself,' the author lambasted Anna's arguments and the very concept of vegetarianism. The reviewer launched a personal attack on her, writing that he did not know how she gained her degree, and judging by her thesis it must not be very difficult to become an MD in Paris. In response to Anna's threat of legal action, the editor published an apology, of sorts. He claimed the comments were meant to be light-hearted, and he and the readers knew the high standing of the Paris medical degree. The incident was yet another example of opposition to women's progress by conservative forces in society.

In 1882 Algernon was appointed vicar of Atcham. His patron was John Lingen Burton (d.1896), the eldest son of the widow Catherine Sophia Burton of Longner Hall, one and a half miles to the north west of Atcham. In 1893 the parish of Atcham had a population of 370, and the church could accommodate 250 souls. The vicarage had thirty acres of glebe, and net income was £247 p.a. *Crockford's Clerical Dictionary* informs us that the incomes of beneficed clergy had been steadily falling, and in 1893 were 38% lower than in 1875.

Notes

1. An earlier famous inhabitant of Chapel Street was Beau Brummel who lived at No. 13 in 1816. Percy B. Shelley eloped with Harriet Westbrook from her home

at No. 23 Chapel Street in 1811. Anna admired Shelley's poetry and his advocacy of vegetarianism.

2. *Life*, I. 409.
3. John Varley (1778-1842), grandfather of John Varley the Theosophist, was an important watercolour painter and art teacher. He was a friend of William Blake, and an avid astrologer.
4. *The Zoophilist* 5 (1 July 1881): 58.
5. *Life*, I. 374.
6. Helena Petrovna Blavatsky (1831-1891) led an extremely colourful life. She was born at Ekaterinoslav in the Ukraine, and after her mother died went to live with her grandparents when she was eight. On impulse, when nearly seventeen, she married the forty year old General Nikifor Blavatsky, Vice-Governor of the province of Erivan in Armenia. After three months she left her husband and embarked on a life of travel, intrigue and adventure. There is no reliable information on her complete travels, but she spent time in Egypt, the Caucasus and Europe. There is scant evidence for her claim that she went to Tibet. During her travels she learnt and practised mediumship. In 1873 in New York she met Colonel Olcott (1832-1907) through a common interest in spiritualism. In 1875 they formed the Theosophical Society, but because it was making little headway in America, they set sail for India and arrived in Bombay early in 1879.
7. Charles Carleton Massey (1838-1905) was a writer and barrister. His father was an MP and Under Secretary of the Home Office, and later Minister of Finance for India. Charles Massey BACK IN ENGLAND 89 gave up a flourishing law practice to devote himself to the study of philosophy, psychology and psychic phenomena. He was the first president of the British Theosophical Society and was a foundation member of the Society for Psychical Research in 1882. At Anna's suggestion he translated Carl du Prel's *Philosophy of Mysticism* (1889) and dedicated his translation to her. Dr George Wyld (1821-1906) was a Scottish homeopathic physician and a Christian who took an early interest in spiritualism and mesmerism. In 1854 he met the famous medium Daniel D. Home. For many years he was a director of the District Railways, and in 1886 he instigated the founding of the Liberal Unionist Party. He was an associate of the Society for Psychical Research and a member of its first Council. He met Mme Blavatsky and Henry Olcott when on their way to India Roden Noel (1834-1894) was the son of the Earl and Countess of Gainsborough. He obtained his MA from Cambridge in 1858. He was a poet and writer, and from 1869 to 1873 he was a groom of the Privy Chamber. He had a long term interest in spiritualism and was an associate of the Society for Psychical Research. Sir Francis Hastings Doyle (1810-1888) was a barrister, receiver-general of customs (1846-1869) and commissioner of customs (1869-1883). He was also a poet and held the chair of poetry at Oxford from 1867 to 1877. He took an abiding interest in spiritualistic phenomena. The Rev. John Manners (1806-1893) was born in Ruddington, Nottingham. He gained his BA in 1833 and MA in 1837 at Cambridge. In 1841 he was appointed deacon at Lichfield. From 1861 to 1986 he was curate of St James-the-Less, Bethnal Green. Hensleigh Wedgwood (1803-1891), philologist, was the grandson of Josiah Wedgwood the famous potter. He graduated from

Cambridge with an MA in 1828. His major work was the *Dictionary of Etymology* (1857). In his later years he became a confirmed spiritualist and contributed to the spiritualist journal *Light*. William Stainton Moses (1839-1892) was a curate, then English master at University College School. He had mediumistic powers and was prominent in Spiritualist circles. He wrote various articles and books on spiritualism under the pseudonym 'M.A. (Oxon)' John Herbert Stack (1828-1892), born in Ireland, was a journalist, author, and council member of the Society for Psychical Research. Gerard Brown Finch (1835-1913) gained his MA from Cambridge in 1860. He was called to the Bar in 1864 and later taught law at Cambridge. He was ordained in Canterbury in 1888 but did not proceed to priest's orders. Frank Podmore (1855-1910) was the son of Rev. Thompson Podmore, headmaster of Eastbourne College. Frank graduated from Oxford with a first in natural science in 1877. He began to study psychic phenomena and write papers on the subject while at Oxford, and was an early member of the Society for Psychical Research, though he later became skeptical about psychic matters. He was a founding member of the Fabian Society in 1884 and wrote a biography of the socialist and spiritualist Robert Owen. He wrote a number of books on psychic and spiritualistic phenomena. He took a higher division clerkship in the Post Office, retiring in 1907. Francesca Arundale (1848- died c. 1924) was a wealthy spinster who joined the British Theosophical Society in its early days. She became treasurer of the Society and later Olcott appointed her assistant treasurer of the Theosophical Society as a whole, with responsibility for Europe.

8. *Life*, II.16.
9. *The National Reformer* (4 and 11 September 1881).
10. This drawing appears in Adolphe Didron's *Christian Iconography,* first published in English in 1851. See 1886 edition, vol.1, 476.
11. *Saturday Review* (5 November 1881): 569-70.

Chapter - 10

A Public Figure

Anna was very busy early in 1882 disseminating her ideas. She spoke on 'Vivisection' before the Zetetical Society in the Winter Term Session 1881-1882, with Bernard Shaw also speaking at this session on capital punishment. There is no evidence of a meeting between Anna and Shaw, but there is little doubt that he would have been impressed by Anna's intelligence and womanly presence. The Zetetical Society ('truth-seeking') was formed in 1878 as a 'junior copy' of the Dialectical Society. Shaw and Sidney Webb, the Fabian socialist, were prominent members of its committee. Anna's speech brought forth an attack in print by a 'Miss P.,' which prompted the following reply by Anna:

> It is morally permissible to use the lower animals for the benefit of man, but not to abuse them. Miss P. confounds use and abuse. In using an animal humanely and intelligently, both the user and the used benefit...Miss P. assumes that I would ride a horse to death to save a friend. No, I would not, *because my horse is my friend also.* I would urge him as far as reason and humanity permit, and for the rest I would have faith in God. The hypothesis of the vivisector is that of the atheist. By it all possibility of God's help is omitted from the system of things. The scalpel, the saw and the pincers are to do everything for man. Prayer and love and will, and all that is divine in him, are to do nothing. Under the doctrine of modern vivisectional science the nations are fast becoming atheistic. 'If,' say the people, 'it be necessary in order to *know,* and in order to obtain health and healing, that deeds abhorrent to moral feeling should be performed, then, obviously, Justice is not the essential principle of the universe, and religion has no substantial basis.'I am doing my best to show both that knowledge is the supremely good

> thing, and that it is to be got only by divine methods. 'The scientists,' says Dr Garth Wilkinson, 'are in a hurry to be scientific, but God opens no gates to hurry.'

Anna wrote two important papers against vivisection early in 1882. One was called 'The Uselessness of Vivisection,' which appeared in the February issue of the journal *The Nineteenth Century*. The other was an address entitled 'Violationism or the Sorcery of Science,' delivered before the British National Association of Spiritualists on 23 January. Anna noted that in ancient times the true physician was a priest: he healed the body and the soul. He knew the way to the divine was through sacrifice of the lower nature. There grew up, 'like a poisonous weed,' the sorcerer or black magician, who sacrificed others for his own benefit. The vivisector, 'like the sorcerer, finds it easier to propagate disease than to discover the secret of health. Seeking for the germs of life he invents only new methods of death, and pays with his soul the price of these poor gains.' She continued, 'It is impossible to serve humanity by the sacrifice of that which alone constitutes humanity— justice and its eternals principles.' Anna's lecture attracted much attention both at home and abroad, and was reproduced in various languages.

Anna's attacks on vivisection stung the physician Sir William Gull (1816-1890) into action with an article entitled 'The Ethics of Vivisection' in *The Nineteenth Century*.[1] As a wealthy man with influential positions, Gull shows the powerful forces Anna was up against in her fight against vivisection. Gull defended vivisection with the usual arguments, namely, the practice contributed to scientific 'progress,' and it was justifiable to inflict some pain on animals in order to relieve 'human misery.' He referred to Anna as follows:

> As if this controversy on the rights of vivisection had not already had enough of feeling imported into it, Mrs [not Dr] Kingsford would raise the cry of Atheism. She sees in the pursuit of physiological science a concealed attack upon all religious and sympathetic sentiment, and a repudiation on man's moral responsibility...
>
> This accusation needs little reply. We need not here, in the cause of science, discuss the grounds of religious belief, nor the relation of scientific knowledge to religious conviction. We have it on the highest authority that 'the kingdom of God is within' us, and from the earliest time it stands recorded that we cannot 'by searching find out God.' Science has to do with that which is external to us, with our material nature, its forces and their relations; with what is ponderable and

measurable...There cannot be anything atheistic in knowledge, and science is nothing but exact knowledge.

Gull adhered to the tradition of materialistic science formulated by the likes of Francis Bacon (1561-1626) and Rene Descartes (1596-1650) and advanced by Isaac Newton (1642-1727). This tradition postulated a mechanical universe which has no place for the human or divine soul. In this system man's reason is given god-like status, and the organic unity of existence is fragmented. The poet and mystic William Blake (1757-1827) wrote that materialism can only be atheistic, for it postulates matter as the primary cause in the universe. No doubt Anna would have been in agreement with Blake 's words on this lifeless mechanical view of the world:

May God us keep
From Single vision & Newton's sleep![2]

Anna continued her busy schedule of activities, including public speaking. In her autobiography Florence Fenwick Miller described the occasion when Anna spoke for the Sunday Lecture Society. This Society was formed in 1869 by William Henry Domville, a London solicitor in London. Its objective was to present lectures on the arts, history, literature and science on Sunday, a day when wholesome recreation was scarce. Anna's lecture took place at 4 p.m. on Sunday 5 February 1882 in the Society's usual venue, St George 's Hall at Langham Place. Anna's lecture was entitled 'Foods: Their Chemical Constituents, Comparative Values, and Relation to National & Domestic Economy.' Florence Miller gave amusing background material on the lecture, showing an impish side to Anna's character:

As the leading scientific advocate of vegetarianism she was invited to lecture before the Sunday Lecture Society; and the Hon. Secretary, Mr Domville, came up to me at a Meeting one evening, and said:

'You are a great friend of Mrs Kingsford's, I know. Could you ask her to dress more plainly to appear upon our platform. You know we are a scientific Society, and we avoid anything of the Stage order, so I feel that she is not suitably dressed now for our platform.'

I looked across the room at Nina, and the request fixed in my mind her aspect as she stood there. She was clad elegantly but simply in a Lincoln green face-cloth gown, sparingly relieved with touches of golden braiding, and fitting her exquisite figure perfectly; on her golden hair was a rather wide-brimmed hat in the same tone in velvet, wreathed around with a long ostrich feather to match.

'Why, really, she is quite simply dressed,' I said to Mr Domville. 'But you would like her, perhaps, all in black? I can tell her that.'

'Nina,' I said to her presently, 'have you got an all-black platform gown? Mr Domville says his committee like their lady lecturers to be all in black.'

She understood, and made a *moue* [face] at me, but she did appear in black – and looked more beautiful!

In the Autumn of 1885 Anna gave an address to the Vegetarian Society. In her opening remarks she explained her attitude to public speaking:

I always speak with the greatest delight and satisfaction in the presence of my friends the members of the Vegetarian society. With them I am quite at my ease, I have no reservation, I have no dissatisfaction. This is not the case when I speak for my friends the Anti-Vivisectionists, the Anti-Vaccinationists, the Spiritualists, or the advocates for the freedom of women. I always feel that such of these as are not abstainers from flesh-food have unstable ground under their feet, and it is my great regret that, when helping them in their good works, I cannot openly and publicly maintain what I so ardently believe – that the Vegetarian movement is the bottom and basis of all other movements towards Purity, Freedom, Justice, and Happiness.

We can imagine there were times when Anna had feelings about lecturing similar to those of Annie Besant, who wrote these words in her Autobiography:

And, indeed, none can know, save they who have felt it, what joy there is in the full rush of language that moves and sways; to feel a crowd 94 A PUBLIC FIGURE respond to the lightest touch; to see the faces brighten or darken at your bidding; to know that the sources of human emotion and human passion gush forth at the word of the speaker as the stream from the riven rock; to feel that the thought which thrills through a thousand hearers has its impulse from you, and throbs back to you the fuller from a thousand heart-beats. Is there any emotional joy in life more brilliant than this, fuller of passionate triumph, and of the very essence of intellectual delight?[3]

Opposition to women speaking from the platform was deeply entrenched in the nineteenth century. When Harriet Beecher Stowe, the author of *Uncle Tom's Cabin,* toured England and Scotland in 1853, her husband spoke for her, because convention dictated that women did not speak in public halls. Harriet had to sit with other women in the 'ladies' gallery,' an area partitioned off by a lattice. In 1867 Millicent Fawcett gave her first speech advocating votes for women in the company of Clementia Taylor. A then well-known member of parliament, 'Mr C. R.,' referred in the House to 'two ladies, wives of members of this House, who had disgraced themselves,' and he 'would not further disgrace them by mentioning their names.'

One Margaret Lonsdale, in her article 'Platform Women' in *The Nineteenth Century,*[4] set forth common arguments used against public speaking by women. Women, she said, because of their physical constitution, when they feel strongly on any subject, 'become mentally warped in that direction.' Lonsdale supported the continued subjection of women. In her view,

> ...a man may be narrow- minded and warped as well as a woman, but I believe that we women have this one-sided tendency to such a marked degree that we are usually unable to control it. Education only increases our unfitness as public teachers and speakers, since with education our power of using influence fairly or unfairly also increases...
>
> In self-assertion we lose respect. By insisting upon our own opinions on subjects of which, owing to our condition as well as our education, we cannot see or understand all the bearings, we let go the justly and righteously high honour in which on certain points the instincts of a woman have always been held.

According to Lonsdale, a woman should use her influence only within her private circle. 'Women who are exhibiting themselves' upon A PUBLIC FIGURE 95 the platform 'are unconsciously helping to lower the standard of womanhood in the eyes of the world at large.' Platform women lose their 'gentleness, softness, and quiet dignity,' and in Lonsdale 's view, self-assertion in a woman 'gradually thickens and becomes a brazen front.

Anna was the living contradiction of Lonsdale's arguments against platform women. She was highly educated and intelligent, and she knew the subjects on which she spoke. As Florence Miller showed, by mounting the platform Anna did not lose her femininity one iota. After all, William Domville was concerned that she would look too feminine on the platform!

In February 1882 *The Perfect Way, or the Finding of Christ* was published anonymously to allow it to be assessed on its own merits, not on the reputation of the authors. A revised edition naming the authors was published in January 1887. Of the nine lectures, Anna wrote numbers four and six, with Maitland writing the rest based on Anna's illuminations. There is a contrast between Anna's lucid prose and Maitland's toilsome style. In *The Perfect Way* Anna was the first person in the modern era to show that the ancient Mysteries are at the core of Christianity. Maitland related that he and Anna were not unduly surprised when the press either ignored or misunderstood it. However, its intended audience, students of the Hermetic philosophy, saw the merits of the book, with Lady Caithness writing to Maitland as follows:

> Nice, 13 February 1882
>
> Dear Mr Maitland,
>
> Yours of the 10th has just arrived. One [copy of the] Book came yesterday morning, and I gave up going out, although I had some engagements, in order to devote the whole day to reading it, *here, there* and *everywhere,* which is my vagabond way, for I could never read anything straight through on end.
>
> I can now write to you at once, and give you my first impressions. And I do not think that it will surprise you to hear that my soul has everywhere so far responded, Amen, Amen, Amen…
>
> You tell me not to be in haste to judge, much of it being very profound and needing long pondering before it can be comprehended. Such is not at all my appreciation of it. All that I have read so far I have not had even to read twice over; for it has been like a magnet to my soul, which has flown to it page after page, and jumping about all over the Book! I have freely used my red and blue pencil to mark those passages I know I shall often turn to with real pleasure and delight. So I may at once say for your satisfaction that I have got another Bible.
>
> Thank you for sending me the number of *Light* containing the splendid address by Mrs Kingsford. You may well be proud of her wonderful powers. She is decidedly *The Woman* of the present age, and has no doubt been The Woman of many previous ages! She makes one feel very small and insignificant. Please give her my most hearty congratulations on all she has done and is doing. May god bless her, and He will.
>
> I earnestly congratulate you also on the very able manner which you have performed your very arduous and difficult part of the grand work. May God also bless you with a full measure of His Love, prays your sincere friend, M. C.

Less than one month later, Lady Caithness wrote to Maitland, again expressing her admiration for Anna:

> Many thanks for yours of the 22nd to which I now reply. And first let me thank you for sending that splendid letter [against vivisection] written by our dear and much venerated Seeress, A.K., to the Kensington News. Like all she writes, it is very able and very remarkable. She has a wonderful talent for expressing a very great deal in few words. She certainly is a very remarkable woman.

Alfred Sinnett gave *The Perfect Way* a mixed review in *The Theosophist,*[5] which began thus:

> The curious book, which bears this title, may be welcomed with the heartiest cordiality by all true theosophists. It bears evidence of being an upheaval of true Spirituality, breaking through the leaden crust of artificial religious formulas. There are certain tendencies, on the authors' part, which we deplore, and a good many straightforward mistakes in reference to occult matters, which we shall endeavour to meet by appropriate explanation of the point dealt with; but, on the whole, *The Perfect Way* is a grand book, by noble-minded writers, and the foremost regret it creates, is that the educated Western mind is, for A PUBLIC FIGURE 97 the most part, too deeply corrupted by false interpretations of religious doctrine to take such a book into consideration.

It is clear from his review that Sinnett had trouble understanding religious symbolism. He took issue with the Hermetic practice of symbolising the soul and intuition as 'woman.' He wrote, 'to call these faculties "the Divine Woman" is to give rein to an arbitrary fancy, and they might as well be called the divine humming-bird.' Sinnett also failed to grasp the symbolism inherent in Christianity, which Anna had explained in *The Perfect Way.* He wrote that Christianity was 'a scheme of thought which throws reason and logic altogether overboard and tests its claims entirely on sentimentality – it is a religion in fact for women and not for men...we must examine the curious theory which, as another prolonged flaw running through the whole of the volume under notice, has to do with the notion about woman and man being the spiritual complement of each other.'

Anna especially resented 'what she regarded as an affront to her sex' by Sinnett in his review, and she and Maitland had a 'controversy' with Sinnett in the September and October issues of *The Theosophist.* Mme Blavatsky weighed in and called for peace, stating her belief in the concurrence of religious symbolism from the West and the East. She wrote that *The Perfect Way* was a 'remarkable work' and she valued 'the sympathies of that highly advanced school of modern English thought of which our esteemed correspondents [Anna and Maitland] are such intellectual and fitting representatives.'[6]

Samuel L. MacGregor Mathers, the noted occultist and co-founder of the Hermetic Order of the Golden Dawn in 1888, was also impressed by *The Perfect Way*, as he showed in the preface of his translation of *The Kabbalah Unveiled* (1887):

> I have much pleasure in dedicating this work to the authors of the 'Perfect Way,' as they have in that excellent and wonderful book touched so much on the doctrine of the Kabbalah, and laid such value on its teachings. The 'Perfect Way' is one of the most deeply occult works that has been written for centuries.

The Perfect Way found its way around the world. The American Elizabeth Cady Stanton (1815-1902), editor of the *The Woman's Bible* (1895), read *The Perfect Way* in 1883. By the 1890s it was in the library of the Queensland Lodge of the Australian Theosophy Society. A spiritual group in Melbourne, Australia, also had it in its library at this time. Dion Fortune (1890-1946), arguably the leading occultist of the twentieth century and one time member of the Golden Dawn, recommended Anna's Hermetic writings, and in his *Access to Western Esotericism* (1994) the noted scholar Antoine Faivre called *The Perfect Way* a 'wonderful book.' A fifth edition appeared in 1923 and was favourably reviewed in *The Times Literary Supplement:*

> The influence of Mrs Kingsford and Edward Maitland was a wellknown phenomenon some forty years ago. They set out to interpret the mysteries of religion, revive 'Esoteric' doctrines, and break down Sacerdotalism, which they thought perverted the truth of Christianity. They might be described, in fact, as nineteenth-Century Gnostics. And they were, of course, vegetarians. They published a good many books – the present one in its first edition contained nine lectures delivered before a private audience. The fifth edition will be welcomed by those who follow them for the long new preface of sixty-seven pages contributed by Mr S. H. Hart.[7]

As a well known figure, Anna attracted a variety of responses. In the following letter to Lady Caithness Anna revealed the attitudes of various women toward her:

> London, 17 April 1882

My Dear Lady Caithness –

Your letter proved a great support to me; and not to me only, but to others who – more feeble-hearted than I – were more half disposed to press on me the necessity of obeying Mrs Grundy's behests. One of these friends of mine was here yesterday, and seeing that she wished to renew the subject of a former conversation on this point, I read her your letter by way of preface. The effect was singular. 'Does Lady Caithness say that?' she asked with emphasis. 'Then I think that letter is a great support to you,' and – after a little hesitation – 'I quite agree with her.' She then rehearsed to me some recent conversations she had had with several friends (heavens! how women gossip!) – and the burden of the strain seems to have been:

– Mrs Kingsford is a brilliant and gifted person.

– She will never be like other women, nor do anything like anyone else.

– If we force her to be conventional, she will only be a failure, and the work she might do to help us (most of these folks are antivivisectionists) will fall through.

– If we leave her alone, she will be a great success, and will do our work as no one else can do it.

– She may be 'improper,' but she will never compromise the cause in any really serious way.

– She is certainly eccentric, but then that is only all the more remarkable; and the more she is known, the less evil people will see in her.

– To change, or to attempt to change, her way of life now would be only to admit the justice of the charges made against her, and to brand herself as a 'penitent' who has seen the error of her ways.

– She will never change her way of thinking and speaking; therefore the reform would be but partial and Mrs Grundy would certainly remain unappeased.

– Therefore we will support Mrs Kingsford, and let her do the work for us in her own way.

But whether I should have heard all this if I had not opened the campaign by reading your letter I cannot guess. The fact appears to be that people cannot 'make me out.' The lady who recounted all the above to me yesterday confessed that I seemed to her a 'resuscitation of a Bible character' belonging to an age either long past or far into the future, and quiet unnameable to present conventionalities and by-laws, 'Nothing in our world seems to fit you', she said. 'When I hear you talk I seem to be living in a Bible-age, and the application of society rules and proprieties to you seems as incongruous as it would be to Isaiah. It is the people that don't know you that talk scandal. Let the world in general only know and hear you, and those who now treat you as they would other women will change their minds and think as I do.'

So far my visitor. But before we can really determine on any settled course, we must see what becomes of the Book and what its course is, under any circumstances, I do not think of remaining in this house. It is both too small and too expensive. I should like to live in some place where I should be free from the trouble of servants and of housekeeping generally. It is impossible to leave one's house for any time without anxiety; but if one lived in an hotel or club chambers, the servants and officials of the house would make it their business to see to the safety of everything.

To-morrow evening a few of the friends whose advice we think most worth having are coming to talk over the project of enlarging the scope or our work, and of appealing, as you suggest, to a larger audience...

I think that you would do a good and helpful thing by writing to Madame Blavatsky on the subject of the Book, which by this time must be in her hands. You would thus encourage and strengthen any commendation she may have it in her mind to give the New Gospel. For the rest, it seems to me best to trust the Gods and go on doing the right thing, confident that though the heathen may rage, the issues will be triumphant.—Yours very affectionately, Anna K.

Shortly later, Anna was on the move again, giving 'A Lecture on Food' to the students of Girton College, Cambridge, on 24 April 1882.[8] In her lecture she made strong points in favour of a vegetarian diet, observing that the meat people eat contains blood, and 'the blood is the vehicle of the sewage of the body.' She summed up her arguments against meat: 'As regards the consumption of flesh, it has been shown that being unsuited to the structure and organs of man, comparatively innutritious, largely impure and unsafe, and extremely costly, it certainly cannot be recommended on utilitarian grounds.' She spoke of education in her forthright manner, 'Education, if it is to be really humanising, refining, and elevating in it results, must be moral and spiritual as well as intellectual. And such an education as this will never be given by men who inculcate on human beings the diet of the tiger, and who teach science by the method of the Spanish Inquisition.'

She concluded her speech with a pro-vegetarian quotation from 'The Revolt of Islam' (Canto V) by Percy B. Shelley, whom she acclaimed as 'the king of poets.' The lecture shows Anna's abilities as a public speaker, for it is well constructed and the arguments are put forth with logic and force. The lecture was twenty three pages long, and printed as a pamphlet by the Vegetarian Society, Manchester.

On 9 June 1882 Maitland received a letter from Dr Ernest Grysanowski, the 'most formidable opponent in Germany' of vivisection. He was also a vegetarian and a student of Hermetic philosophy, and henceforth Anna and Maitland corresponded with him on a regular basis. Dr Grysanowski (1824-1888) conducted his medical practice in Tuscany, Italy,9 and in 1878 he published the first booklength discussion of vivisection by a medical doctor.

Anna went to her mother in St Leonards where Eadith had been living for some time, and Maitland joined them for a promised visit to Lady Caithness in Paris on 15 July. Anna wrote to Lady Caithness explaining some of Sinnett's criticisms of *The Perfect Way:*

> St Leonards, 3 July1882
>
> My Dear Lady Caithness,
>
> I hope you will not be misled by the misinterpretations of *The Perfect Way* given in the June *Theosophist.* The most serious and most incomprehensible of the reviewer's mistakes is that in which he finds fault with the fourfold division of Human Nature, and actually pretends that he can find in that division no place allotted to the Soul! – when the whole book is nothing else than the history of the Soul and her apotheosis! The blunder is so gross and palpable that I find it hard to believe it has been committed innocently…The very reviewer – Mr Sinnett – writes with much pseudo-authority in the Theosophist and has, within a year's time, completely altered his views on at least one important subject – I mean Reincarnation…
>
> I have no fear that the Immortals will deceive me; nor I am in the least disconcerted by adverse criticism. That others do not see, and cannot understand, proves only how greatly our work is needed in the world, and how far it surpasses all minor labours and teaching...

After a two week rest with Lady Caithness in Paris, Anna and Maitland went on to Lucerne, Switzerland, then on to the higher and drier airs of Berne. They spent most of August at the Pension du Cèdre, Lausanne, attracted by its 'charming position in the open country and the vegetarian regimen.' Anna possessed letters of introduction to some of the leading residents which were used to facilitate her lecture tour. Initially, Anna and Maitland found women to be the most responsive to the cause, but men were soon won over by 'the charm of her personality' and her eloquence. The enormous amount of energy Anna expended caused a local magnate to remark 'that it was fortunate for them that she was a vegetarian, for as a flesh-eater her fierceness would have made her dangerous.' Anna and Maitland then went to the Pension Vautier in the village of Les Planches, an ideal base for their climbing and walking expeditions. At these higher altitudes Anna found her health was greatly improved and she was able to take 'ecstatic delight' in the magnificent scenery.

On 19 October 1882 Anna and Maitland departed for Paris, breaking their journey on Anna's account at Marseilles, Lyons and Dijon, and reaching their destination on the 23rd. Maitland stayed with Lady Caithness who was preparing to depart Paris for her Winter residence at Nice, and Anna joined Eadith at the Misses Dawson's place.

Anna had been discussing with Mrs Kenealy and her daughter Arabella the possibility that she and Arabella could set up a medical practice together. Arabella Madonna Kenealy (1859-1938) was the fifth of twelve children. Her father, Edward Vaughan Kenealy MP (1819-1880) was a barrister, poet, journalist, and the author of long forgotten mystical works. His outspokenness, including his vigorous defence of the claimant in the famous Tichborne case in 1873, gained him widespread notoriety. Arabella trained at the London School of Medicine for women where she was an outstanding student. She then graduated from the Royal College of Surgeons at Dublin in 1883.[10]

On 1 November Anna wrote to her friend Mrs Elizabeth Kenealy about her health and her plans.[11] Although Anna had been in Paris 'nearly ten days,' she was 'far from being in my usual health…Country air is poison to me, and it is quite clear to me that my unfortunate malady will not permit me to travel, unless indeed my visits are confined to large cities.' Anna had been thinking of going to Birmingham, but saw drawbacks to this plan. A certain Miss Barker had a practice there already, with many women patients.[12]

Anna abandoned Birmingham in favour of London; she wished to pursue her research at the British Museum, and also had 'a circle of friends in London whom I should be sorry to leave.' Besides, she desired to 'superintend' the education of her 'little girl' in London because it had facilities not found in Birmingham. To avoid 'the bother of keeping servants,' Anna proposed to Arabella they live in a private hotel in the West End, 'with an entrance of our own.' Under such an arrangement 'there would be no necessity for Arabella to adopt Vegetarianism, as she could have her *repasts à la carte* in the hotel, and Edith [*sic*] and I could have our own table.' Anna added that under the new Married Women's Property Act she could make a contract jointly with Arabella. Anna intended to stay in Paris for about three weeks more visiting the hospitals, and had heard the 'religious' in the hospitals and been replaced by lay nurses 'of the stamp common in England.' She thought this a pity, because 'the presence of nuns served to keep the students in order.'

Ultimately, Arabella's studies, together with Anna's travels and various commitments, precluded a joint practice. Throughout 1883 Anna was to lecture on the Continent, in Scotland and around England. She was based at Atcham, though she spent time in London and St Leonards.

Notes

1. *The Nineteenth Century* (March 1882): 456-467. William Gull was the son of a barge owner and wharfinger from Thorpe-le-Soken, Esex. In 1871 he attended the Prince of Wales, and the following year was created a baronet and appointed physician extraordinary to the queen. His personal wealth at death was £344,023.00 besides landed estates.
2. Blake, 818.
3. Annie Besant also told in her *Autobiography* how, when still married to a vicar, she practiced delivering lectures in the empty church. It is possible Anna took advantage of her situation to practice in her husband's church.
4. *The Nineteenth Century* (March 1884): 409-15.
5. *The Theosophist* (May and June) 1882.
6. Blavatsky, *The Theosophist* (January 1883): 88.
7. *The Times Literary Supplement* (19 April 1923): 275.
8. The *Girton College Register* 1869-1946 shows that many women of attainment passed through the College doors. In 1882 when Anna gave her lecture, Harriet Isabella Cooper (1854-1914) was a student at Girton. In 1884 she married Alfred Oakley, a Cambridge man, then they joined the Theosophical Society and went to India with Mme Blavatsky. Harriet became a prominent organiser for Theosophy at an international level and published collections of her articles in book form. Edith Mary brown (later Dame) and Emily Louisa Dove were also

students at Girton in 1882, and both went on to study at the School of Medicine for women. Edith Brown founded the first medical school for women in India.

9. Dr Grysanowski was born in Konisberg where he gained his Ph.D. after his study of mathematics, astronomy and Oriental languages. He was an attache to the Prussian embassy in Rome when he decided to commence medical studies. He received his MD in Heidelberg in 1855, and then practised among the foreign residents in Pisa and Florence. He was friendly with the Brownings, the Trollopes, and other celebrities residing in Florence. In 1862 he married the daughter of a British parson. He was in contact with Frances Power Cobbe, herself a frequent visitor to Italy. He had long opposed vivisection, but only after meeting the wealthy antivivisectionist Marie-Esperance von Schwartz (1818-1899) in 1877 did he become active for the cause. The German anti-vivisection movement held Anna in high regard, calling her 'our' Anna Kingsford.
10. Arabella's practice was first in London, then she moved to Watford. She was forced to give up her practice in 1894 due to a severe attack of diphtheria. She then took to writing novels and various works on social issues. She became most reactionary in her views on the place of women in society. Despite being unmarried and independent herself, in her writings she argued that woman's place was in the home.
11. Anna Kingsford to Mrs Kenealy, 1 November, 1882. Edward Kenealy, Autograph book, Harvard Law School Library, MS 527. Anna gave her address as 'Chez Miss Dawson, 21 Avenue Carnot, Champs Elysses, Paris.' Anna's writing was neat, upright and very legible. She added large swirls from right to left under her signature. Stamped on the top left hand corner of Anna's notepaper is the Virgin and Dove icon she borrowed from Lady Caithness. This is the only original letter by Anna that has been located.
12. Annie Reay Barker took her MD at Paris in 1877. Anna must have known her in her student days in Paris, but Maitland makes no mention of her.

Chapter - 11

President of the British Theosophical Society

The British Theosophical Society was in disarray. Dr George Wyld, the president, had resigned, and was replaced by his predecessor Charles Massey. Massey kept in touch with Anna by letter, and sent her a circular distributed to Theosophical Society members wherein he proposed Anna be elected president. Anna and Maitland gave their consent 'on condition that we retain absolute freedom of opinion, speech, and action, acknowledging no superiors, nor any allegiance save to our own illuminators, and reserving the right to use as we might deem fit any knowledge we might acquire.' On 7 January 1883, when they were still in Paris, Anna was elected president and Maitland co-vice-president of the British Theosophical Society. Dr Wyld was elected as the other vicepresident. On 11 January Anna wrote to Mme de Steiger explaining she would not be able to take up her duties for some time. She concluded her letter, 'Remember me to all our friends, especially to Miss Arundale and her mother, and accept my love and best wishes for the new year. Mr Maitland, who is spending the afternoon with me, sends his kindest regards.' We do not know where Anna was staying at the time, but her words indicate it was not with Maitland.

Anna helped organise the Paris Anti-Vivisection Society, of which Victor Hugo became president. In the middle of March Anna and Mailtand returned to Switzerland to resume their 'crusade.' Anna lectured in Berne, Lausanne, Montreux and Geneva. At a meeting with the notorious vivisector M. Schiff she accused him of unscrupulous practices and statements. In Geneva a vociferous pro-vivisection faction claimed Anna did not have a genuine medical diploma, 'affirming it was of American manufacture.' These and other false allegations were swept away with the contempt they deserved, wrote Maitland. The pair made the acquaintance of the 'native poet,' Jules Charles Scholl, who wrote a 'touching appeal on behalf of the animals.'

They arrived back in England on 22 May and two days later Anna gave a lecture on vegetarianism in Norwich. Then she returned to London and commenced duties as president of the British Theosophical Society. Anna changed its name to the London Lodge of the Theosophical Society, for reasons explained in a letter to Lady Caithness:

> Atcham Vicarage, 8 June [1883]
>
> I did this because there are in London a vast number of 'Societies,' good, bad, and indifferent, and I wish the character of our fraternity to be entirely distinct from that of the ordinary run. We are a secret society, too, and our members are, or should be, brothers and sisters. But chiefly our aim is to establish branch societies throughout the world, and as the members of all these will be in constant intercommunication, and will be virtually be brothers of one fraternity, I think it best to designate the different groups by the name of the Lodge, the meaning of which is now classical and explains itself. There is really but one T.S., as there is but one Society of Freemasons, and all its various sects are really its lodges. Mr Sinnett adopted this idea with great zest, and it was carried immediately and unanimously. Pray do not let yourself be drawn away from the original idea by giving your Society such a name as 'Oriental.' It will mean nothing, and will put you into communication with no one either in India or in England. As a Theosophical Lodge you will have everything we of England or India can give you, and I have by me some very interesting papers to send, which you shall have. But you know you must not communicate their contents to any uninitiated person.
>
> I am going to do my utmost to make our London lodge a really influential and scientific body...Besides, we do not want to pledge ourselves to Orientalism only, but to the study of all religions esoterically, and especially to that of our Western Catholic Church. Theosophy is equally applicable to such study; but Orientalism can relate to Brahmanism and Buddhism...as you see, I have left London...

Anna wrote to Lady Caithness on 25 June mentioning she was in correspondence with the French esotericist Madam Adam. Anna would return to London to preside at a Theosophical Society meeting, 'and also give a lecture at a garden party upon vivisection.' After her constant activity

Anna was glad to slow down, for her letter concluded, 'It is very pleasant to me to have this quite little country retreat to resort to, to think and write. But for it I could never have done the article for Madam Adam; for in London I was constantly interrupted.'

Anna and Maitland assumed the helm of the London Lodge, but there was to be no plain sailing, for storm clouds appeared on the horizon in the form of Percy Alfred Sinnett (1840-1921). He was returning to England after losing his editorship of the Pioneer of India because of his Theosophical views.His main books were *The Occult World* (1881) and *Esoteric Buddhism* (1883).[1] Maitland wrote:

> The arrival of Mr Sinnett, and the publication of his *Esoteric Buddhism*, had completely revolutionised the status of the Theosophical Society. No longer now was it a private group of students engaged for their own satisfaction in mastering the philosophy of the Orient, and pledged to secrecy respecting its nature. It was a propaganda eager for notoriety, and claiming to be in possession of a doctrine resting on the infallible authority of an order of men divinised and hid away in the inaccessible fastnesses of the Thibetan uplands. This made it all the more necessary for us to see that we were committing ourselves to nothing that could impair the authority of the teaching received by us.

On Thursday, 17 July 1883, the London Theosophists held a conversazione at Prince 's Hall, Piccadilly to welcome Sinnett on his return from India. Some 270 people were present to hear speeches by Anna and Sinnett. Anna spoke first, then Sinnett took the platform for upwards of an hour and a-half and it was nearly midnight when the meeting closed.

Anna outlined her understanding of Theosophy and the object of the Theosophical Society: 'Theosophy is the science of the Divine...Our relations to the divine we hold to be relations, not to the exterior, but to the within; not to that which is afar off, but that which is at the heart of all being, the very core and vital point of our own true self.' The objective of the Theosophical Society, she continued, was 'to unveil Isis; to restore the Mysteries.' Theosophy embraced all seekers of truth, whether they followed the Greek, Hermetic, Buddhist, Vedantist, or Christian paths. In the view of Theosophy 'these Lodges of the Mysteries are fundamentally one and identical in doctrine.' Through study of religious symbolism, the language of the Divine, Theosophists could penetrate the Mysteries. Because of their common origin, each particular religion could be enhanced by the study of other religions.

Anna concluded her speech with a statement of her high expectations for the Society:

> Some of us have dreamed that our English Branch of the Theosophical Society is destined to become the ford across the stream which so long has separated the East from the West, religion from science, heart from mind, and love from learning. We have dreamed that this little Lodge of the Mysteries, set here in the core of matter-of-fact, agnostic London, may become an oasis in the wilderness for thirsty souls – a ladder between earth and heaven, on which, as once long since in earlier and purer days, the Gods again may 'come and go 'twixt mortal men and high Olympus.'
>
> Such a dream as this has been mine. May Pallas Athena grant me, the humblest of her votaries, length of days enough to see it, in some measure at least fulfilled.
>
> Mme de Steiger recollected the meeting in her memoirs:
>
> It was unanimously decided to join in a great 'At Home' in the large rooms of the Royal Institute in Piccadilly, where important Picture Exhibitions were held…There was a large crowd and the meeting was a decided success. No entertainment was offered, and it was merely a conversazione.
>
> At the same gathering, however, Mrs Kingsford spoke. She went on the platform simply and quietly, 'making no compliments' – sans phrases as the French phrase has it. She had no affected movements or mannerisms. She was dressed in a long, rather trailing, white silk dress – how odd a long dress would look in these days – with much white lace, and gold chain ornaments. Her hair was dressed in the fashion of that time, which poetically inclined authors describe as an 'aureole of gold' – not so far wrong as far as looks went, though it required hairpins to keep up the aureole form. Even Pallas Athene probably had at least an ivory comb. Nevertheless, as she stood there, tall, graceful, beautiful and pale, she had a goddess-like effect, and as she had also a real gift for oratory both in style, choice, and a flow of words, she seemed to me like the living type of what a goddess should and does look like! I felt that Olympus was a real abode.
>
> Nevertheless, when *Truth* appeared with its next issue, Labouchere had an elaborate and ethereal editorial account of the evening, headed 'Tealess and Tiresome Theosophy'. Quite true! The stewards or the male friends, whose business it was to arrange the whole affair, utterly

forgot the inner man and woman. There was neither tea nor refreshments! But everyone went away having keenly enjoyed the 'food' so freely given.

Sinnett must have written to Mme Blavatsky about the meeting, for on 23 August 1883 Mme Blavatsky wrote querulously to Sinnett about Anna:

> Say – why was she dressed in a dress that looked like 'the black and yellow coat of the *zebras* in the menagerie if the Rajah of Kashmir?' And is it true she had roses on her hair 'which is like a flaming sunset, yellow gold'? And why mercy on us! Why did she have her hands and arms painted black, *jet black* – up to the elbows' for? or was it gloves? and then, is it true she had that night a brilliant metal pocket in front of her, with clasps and bells and something else; and 'crescentmoon, tinkling earrings' – symbolical of the growing brilliancy of the 'London Lodge.' This moon has borrowed light from the Satellite…But why – why had *she*, 'the mystic of the century' so much jewellery on her! How can she confabulate with the unseen Gods when she looks 'like a Delhi English Jeweller's front window.' Well, I too think I saw her and would like to have her portrait to compare. For *she* was *shown* to me.[2]

At the conclusion of the above mentioned meeting, Dr Christian Ginsburg approached Mme de Steiger asking to be introduced to Anna. Ginsburg (1831-1914), a Hebrew scholar born in Warsaw, became a Christian at the age of sixteen, then settled in England. Among his various works was a book entitled *The Kabbalah*. It was arranged Mme de Steiger would bring Anna some evening to dine with Ginsburg and his wife at their house at Virginia Water, west of London. The evening, however, as related by Mme de Steiger, 'was a doleful fiasco':

> Dr Ginsburg, on our arrival, greeted us with his usual warmth, and also with the cordiality of the Jewish host. He forthwith began to imitate the manners, rather prevalent at the time, of treating all his guests as famous people coming to visit a famous host. So he said: 'Mrs Kingsford, I have heard much about you. I am told you have read my book and that you are a prophet.' 'Yes, Dr Ginsburg,' she answered, 'I have read your book. It interests me very much, and it is true that I am a prophet.' Dr Ginsburg gasped. He did not like his visitors to agree to their own greatness; but he said, 'You mean, you may be a sort of prophet; but I mean a real prophet, a great one, let us say, Isaiah.'3 She answered: 'I am a prophet, and a greater one than Isaiah.' She said this

very quietly, but I could see from her face that she would have liked to have returned mockery for mockery. She instantly felt his intention of exploiting her for the amusement of himself and the rest of his visitors, so she desisted, and merely replied with those few words.

Dr Ginsburg seemed staggered at the failure of his joke, and also became silent, but Mrs Ginsburg, who was a Christian of the Evangelical School, and greatly rejoiced in having married a famous converted Jew, at once started a chaffingly surprised argument at the impossibility of there being any truth in such an audacious statement. But Mrs Kingsford, who had no capacity for repartee when she meant honestly what she had just said, also became silent.

Of course, what Mrs Kingsford meant was that she was of the race or school of the prophets, and being a Christian aspired as to rank with Elizabeth or Anna in the New Testament as prophesying the coming of the Christ.

It was to me no rhapsodical remark but one made in good faith to Dr Ginsburg, who was supposed to be learned in the profundity of the Kabbalah, and to whom she perhaps over-hastily, announced her rank.

Needless to say, the evening was a dull one. Dr and Mrs Ginsburg continued somewhat to tackle their guest. The two male strangers also seemed puzzled as to what sort of people we were, so, after some strenuous and over-powerful musical efforts by the daughters of the house (whose interests were prominently sporting), poor Mrs Kingsford, myself, and the two bachelors – who seemed unmistakably disappointed at having wasted their Saturday – all managed to find our way safely on foot through the thick dark fog to the Virginia Water station.

I was the only one who had any knowledge of the way through the narrow lanes which required very decided intimacy in the thick fog at night. No masculine energy could suffice to help utter strangers in such a thick mist. But I knew the ditches and several awkward turns. I had been often on foot, on account of the portrait business. Poor Mrs Kingsford silently clung to me, not exactly with physical fear. She seemed hardly alive, and the men were rather alarmed about her, and they, too, were silent. I was thankful to hand her safely to the friend sent by her husband who came to meet her at the station.

Mme de Steiger's observations indicate that Algernon was supporting Anna in London at the time. Maitland gave no details of Anna's meeting with Dr Ginsburg, and did not mention this or other times Algernon was in London with Anna.

In his *Occultists and Mystics of All Ages* Ralph Shirley remarked on Anna's unfortunate encounter with Dr Ginsburg:

> Endowed with courage far greater than falls to the lot of most women, with great independence and an utter fearlessness of conventionality, she had no hesitation in avowing her own profound belief in her divine mission…Such mockery, however boldly she faced it, caused her the most acute pain. There was, indeed, nothing undignified about her avowal of her claims, nothing that jarred, nothing of the charlatan in her composition. If she deceived herself, she never dreamed of deceiving others. She never posed or attempted to gain a hearing by acting a part which was not natural to her. She was too genuine, too intense in her convictions, and withal too natural and too unaffected to be otherwise than always and everywhere true to herself. She was essentially a child of nature, and in some of the traits of her character she retained to the end the simplicity and wayward playfulness which most people say good-bye to when they reach years of discretion.

In the beginning of August Anna paid a visit to her mother at St Leonards, while Maitland remained in London. On the 11th Anna went to Atcham to prepare for a lecture tour on behalf of the Vegetarian Society, which ran from 11 September to mid October, taking in Chester, Carlisle, Longtown, Silloth, Ambleside, Stirling, Dundee, Dunfermline, Glasgow, Edinburgh and Dumfries. At Edinburgh they 'had the the high privilege of spending an evening with that ripest and tenderest of souls, Dr John Pulsford, and of hearing him preach one of his profoundly mystical discourses.' Pulsford (1815-1897), a Christian mystic, was the author of *Quiet Hours* and other religious works which enjoyed considerable popularity.

Notes

1. Alfred Percy Sinnett (1840-1921) was born in London and educated at London Univesrity School. In 1870 he married Patience Edensor (1843-1908). He was a journalist then became editor of the *Pioneer* of India in 1872.He returned to London on 25 April 1883 and met up with Mrs and Miss Arundale at 77 Elgin Crescent, Notting Hill, where he first met Anna Kingsford. Koot Hoomi told him among his past lives he was a priest in ancient Egypt and a high ranking Roman in the first century A.D. Sinnett also claimed to have been Sir John Spencer in Elizabethan times. (Sinnett 1986: 2-3.)
2. Blavatsky 1925, Letter to Sinnett No. 25.

3. We only have Mme de Steiger's word for this incident. Isaiah is a problematic figure. According to George Knight, of the 66 chapters of the book of *Isaiah*, only 'Chs.1-23 and 28-34 are substantially from the hand of the prophet whose name we know as Isaiah, and who lived in Jerusalem in the second half of the eighth century BC.' See George Knight, *Prophets of Israel: Isaiah* (London: Lutterworth Press, 1961). There is nothing particularly enlightening in the book of *Isaiah*. Its theme is Yaweh's wrath against the Jews for their sin and threats of punishment if they don't change their wicked ways.

Above left: Anna aged 11 with her mother
(Courtesy of R.H. Bonus, Canada)
Above right: Anna, aged 23
Below: Anna in her early 30s

Above: Ethelind Bonus, daughter of Anna's brother John.
Below: Anna's brother John Bonus
(Courtesy of R.H. Bonus, Canada)

Obituary.

Dr. John Bonus.

Many Vegetarian friends have pleasant recollections of the late Dr. John Bonus, who passed away on Thursday, December 16th, aged 81. Born in 1828, the eldest son of John Bonus, of Maryland Point, Stratford, Essex, he was one of a brilliant family. His beautiful and charming sister, the late Dr. Anna Kingsford, the well-known Vegetarian lady doctor, was one of the pioneer lady medical graduates of Paris, where she received her M.D. in 1880. Dr. John Bonus was also a Vegetarian, although not, in his later years, one of the strictest school. He was a pioneer, in fact, in many movements for reform. Intellectual freedom was the watchword of his life, and in the cause of intellectual freedom he fought fearlessly and well. At Oxford, where he was educated, at Wadham College, his principles brought him into conflict with the authorities; the formalities then necessary in taking a degree were against his conscience, and he therefore went down without taking a degree, and pursued his studies elsewhere. He visited both Paris and Germany, and eventually took his degree (Ph.D.) at Louvain. His fight for freedom of conscience brought him into sympathy with all who had experience of that struggle, from whatever point of view. One of his life-long friends was Professor St. George Mivart, the biologist, whose text-books, "The Common Cat," "The Common Frog," are still well known to students. He was Professor of Biology at University College, London, in 1874; and Dr. Bonus at one time acted as his assistant in his work. Dr. Bonus had, in fact, that breadth of sympathy which is always characteristic of a truly great mind; and while he was thus in touch with Catholicism through Professor Mivart and many other friends, his personal friendships included also some of the well-known leaders of free thought, in the usual and restricted sense of the term.

Dr. Bonus resided at Lavender Cottage, Feewit Hill, near Walton, Suffolk, where he lived at once the simple life and the intellectual life; his interests included alike the great questions of the day and the pleasures of the home—his garden, his flowers, his books, and his pets. Dogs, cats, birds, and hares shared the hospitality of his home, and humanity to animals was with him not only a principle but a passion. His sympathies went out towards all oppressed creatures, whether men or quadrupeds, and he took a part in all the humanitarian questions of the day.

Dr. Bonus leaves one daughter, who has been the constant companion of her father's old age; and he is survived by one brother, Major-General Joseph Bonus, R.E., who served through the Indian mutiny and the Afghan war. Dr. Bonus was cremated at Golder's Green on Tuesday, December 21st. An address was given by the Rev. J. Page Hopps, followed by music; six pieces of music, favourites with Dr. Bonus, were rendered by the organist.

Dr. Bonus leaves to the world and to his many friends, the memory of an entirely unselfish man. His earnest desire was to help all who needed help; his chief ambition was faithfulness to Truth, at all and every cost.

Beatrice Lindsay.

On Sunday, March 6th, 1910, at 324 Central Park Road, East Ham, E., Mr. William Elliott Long died a painless and peaceful death of senile decay at the age of 85 years. He was formerly well known as pharmaceutical chemist and stamp distributor at 15 East Street, Chichester, but for the past eight years chose to live the life of a strict Vegetarian with his son, J. E. Long, Hon. Secretary of the West Ham Vegetarian Society, much to the alleviation of those minor ailments peculiar to declining years, and it may interest our readers to know that during the last three weeks of his life, when he lay more helpless than a child, he neither asked for or was given flesh meat foods or alcoholic stimulants.

John Bonus' obituary from 'The Vegetarian' April 1910 (Courtesy of R.H. Bonus, Canada)

Above: Anna, in her 30s
Below: Anna, aged 36

Above: Algernon Kingsford, aged about 55
Below: Anna's brother John Bonus

Above: Marie, Countess of Caithness, Duchesse de Pomar
Below: Madame Isabelle de Steiger; Florence Fenwick Miller

The Lady's Own Paper.

EDITED BY MRS. ALGERNON KINGSFORD.

No. 307.—Vol. X.] SATURDAY, OCTOBER 5, 1872. [Price Threepence.

ADDRESS.

In issuing this First Number of our New Series we do not profess so much to supply an already acknowledged want, as to inaugurate a new combination of ideas.

Advocates of progress and reform in politics, education, and social manners, are apt, in their zeal for the serious and useful, to ignore the æsthetic; and by the vehemence of their crusade against frivolity, have, in the minds of many among the conservative party, identified the ethics of the liberal school with Vandalism and insensibility. There has lately come into the world of women a vast and wide-spread reaction, which, like most revulsions of thought, whether national or individual, is disposed to be extreme and intolerant. Some years ago we were exclusively domestic; now we are inclined to be exclusively politic. Once we were all for the feminine monopolies of the Bona Dea; now we will have nothing but Minerva and her manlike paraphernalia. This is a state of affairs which is doing a good cause great harm outside the charmed circle of the Amazonian camp. Home-keeping wives and women of idealistic tendencies imagine us to be a hard unlovely crew, with no interests beyond polling-booths and school-boards, contemners of art and taste, barbarous, implacable Gorgons, in whose vicinity no fair or graceful thing can endure, but whose very aspect freezes into stone all living forms of that heaven-given beauty which ought to be "a joy for ever."

The Editor of this Journal feels, therefore, that time is ripe for the establishment of a new and æsthetic school among "political women,"—a school which shall aim at uniting the worship of the Graces with the pursuit of liberty, the members of which, while claiming and asserting their rightful dignity and individual freedom, shall, none the less, uphold and preserve the distinctive charm and gentleness of true womanhood.

And in this sense it is hoped that our retention of the title by which this Journal has been already known for six years, may not be unsuggestive. "Lady" is a term which has suffered more grossly in the way of misapplication than its masculine equivalent —"lord;" the false and degraded chivalry of modern days having made it a common term of address for all women above the rank of vassalage. Nevertheless, there exist some exquisitely lovely and thoughtful verses of Wordsworth's, which may furnish us with a fair excuse for our heading, and serve to remind us what sweetness and refinement of mind, what tenderness of heart, what purity of soul are expected of those among us who bear that honourable and significant Saxon title of "lady":—

"Three years she grew in sun and shower,
Then Nature said—'A lovelier flower
On earth was never sown;
This child I to myself will take;
She shall be mine, and I will make
A Lady of mine own.

"'Myself will to my darling be
Both law and impulse; and with me
The girl, in rock and plain,
In earth and heaven, in glade and bower,
Shall feel an overseeing power
To kindle or restrain.

"'She shall be sportive as the fawn
That, wild with glee across the lawn
Or up the mountain springs;
And her's shall be the breathing balm,
And her's the silence and the calm
Of mute insensate things.

"'The floating clouds their state shall lend
To her; for her the willow bend;
Nor shall she fail to see
Even in the motions of the storm
Grace that shall mould the maiden's form
By silent sympathy.

[New Series.—No. 1.]

The front page of Anna's paper

Above: Edward Maitland, aged 52.
From *The Soul and How It Found Me*
Below: Edward Maitland, aged 68

Above: Helena Petrovna Blavatsky
Below: Actham Vicarage and Church, 2006
(Courtesy of Sue and Brian Poulson)

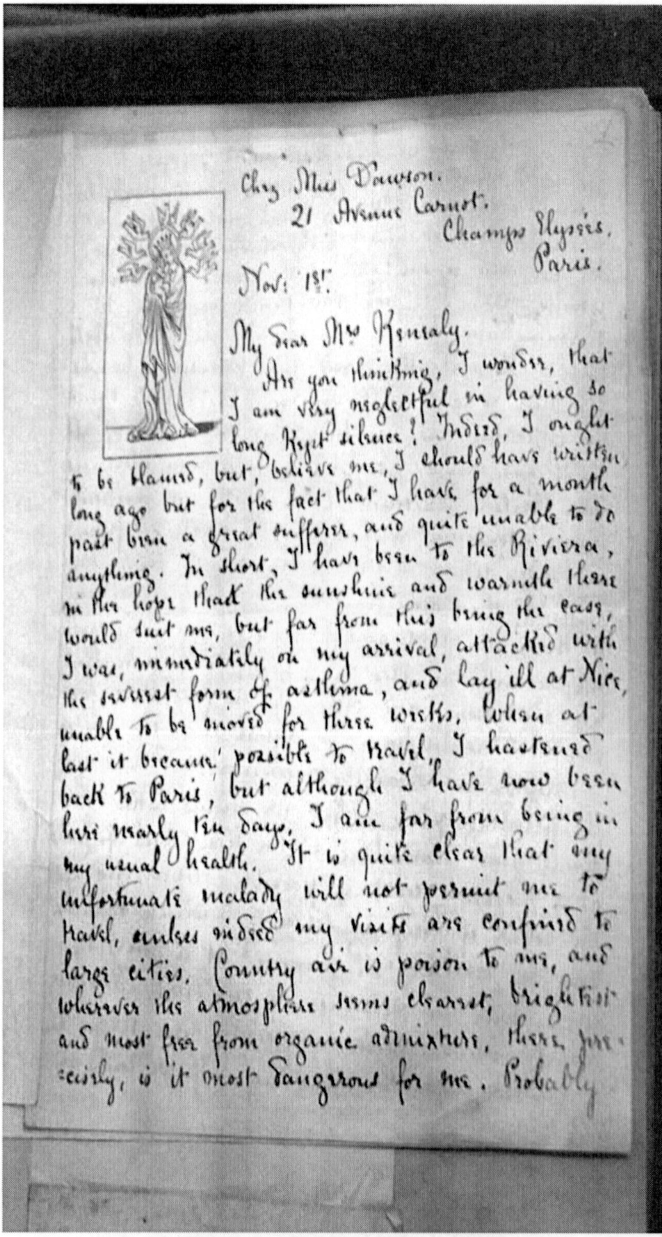

Chez Miss Dawson.
21 Avenue Carnot.
Champs Elysées.
Paris.

Nov: 18th.

My dear Mrs Kenealy.

Are you thinking, I wonder, that I am very neglectful in having so long kept silence? Indeed, I ought to be blamed, but, believe me, I should have written long ago but for the fact that I have for a month past been a great sufferer, and quite unable to do anything. In short, I have been to the Riviera, in the hope that the sunshine and warmth there would suit me, but far from this being the case, I was, immediately on my arrival, attacked with the severest form of asthma, and lay ill at Nice, unable to be moved for three weeks. When at last it became possible to travel, I hastened back to Paris, but although I have now been here nearly ten days, I am far from being in my usual health. It is quite clear that my unfortunate malady will not permit me to travel, unless indeed my visits are confined to large cities. Country air is poison to me, and wherever the atmosphere seems clearest, brightest and most free from organic admixtures, there, pre-cisely, is it most dangerous for me. Probably

Anna's Letter to Mrs Kenealy
(Courtesy of Special Collections Department, Harvard Law School Library)

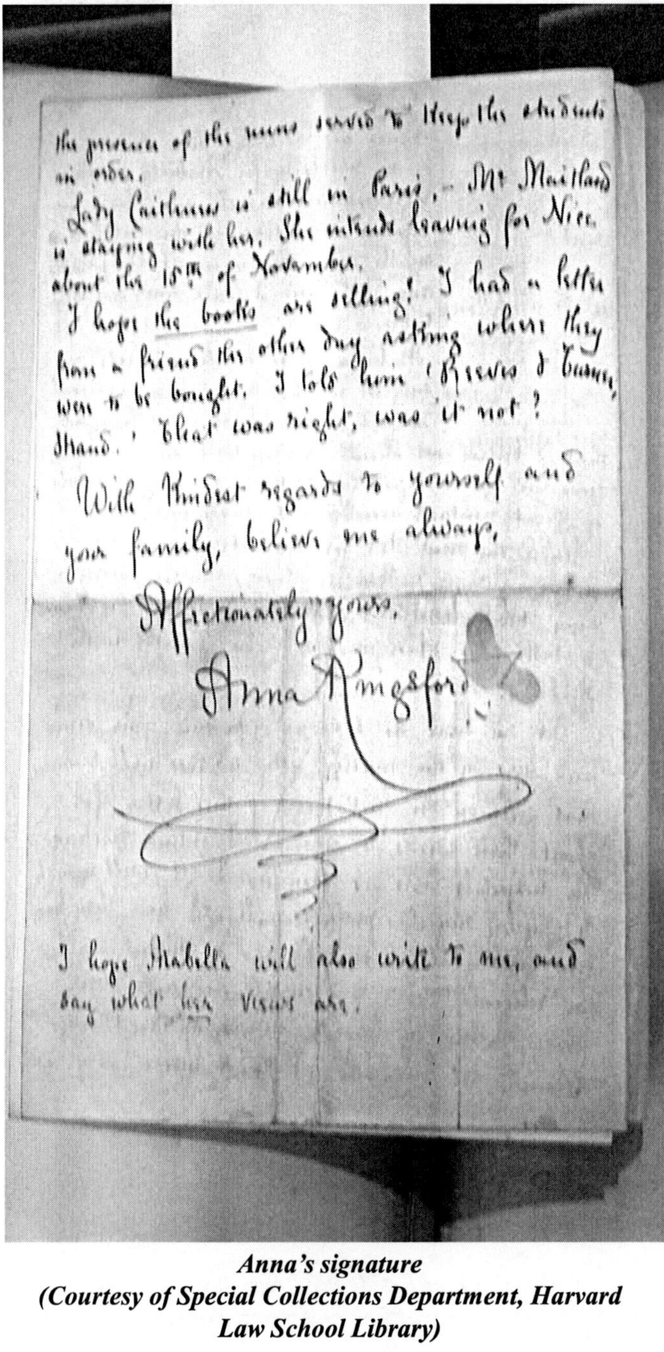

the presence of the men served to keep the students in order.

Lady Caithness is still in Paris, — Mr Maitland is staying with her. She intends leaving for Nice about the 15th of November.

I hope the books are selling! I had a letter from a friend the other day asking where they were to be bought. I told him 'Reeves & Turner, Strand.' That was right, was it not?

With kindest regards to yourself and your family, believe me always,

Affectionately yours,

Anna Kingsford

I hope Mabella will also write to me, and say what her views are.

Anna's signature
(Courtesy of Special Collections Department, Harvard Law School Library)

Anna's grave beside the River Severn, 2005
(Courtesy of Sue and Brian Poulson)

Chapter - 12

Controversy in Theosophy

Anna, although with the best motives, became embroiled in the machinations of Mme Blavatsky and Sinnett in the Theosophical Society. On 21 October 1883, Maitland read a letter[1] from Anna to the Society's members at a meeting of the London Lodge, for Anna was resting at Atcham. The letter dealt with advertisements from Charles Bradlaugh in *The Theosophist* and the 'Kiddle incident,' two matters currently causing concern to members. *The Theosophist,* published by the Theosophical headquarters in India, had been running advertisements for Freethought and anti-Christian literature by the likes of Bradlaugh and Tom Paine with the aim of countering the activities of Christian missionaries in India. In return, Bradlaugh advertised *The Theosophist* in his paper *The National Reformer.*

As an outspoken advocate of atheism and birth control, Bradlaugh was vilified by the establishment. The Council of the London Lodge of the British Theosophical Society passed a resolution concerning the inadvisability of advertising his Freethought literature in *The Theosophist.* Mme Blavatsky then wrote about the matter to the Secretary of the London Lodge from Madras on 16 August 1883. She was 'very much surprised that Mr Sinnett should have *seconded* the resolution,'[2] and would only drop the advertisement on an order from her guru, 'Morya,' who communicated to her through the mahatma or master, 'Koot Hoomi.'

Anna was concerned that 'the very unsavoury reputation attached to the name' of Bradlaugh would harm Theosophy. She was also upset because in advertising Bradlaugh's materialistic views 'an utterly false impression of the aims and teaching of our School' was being given. Her letter to the Theosophical Society said in part:

> Both Koot Hoomi and Madame Blavatsky ought to be informed that it is in a large measure owing to the presence of this unfortunate advertisement on the cover of our journal and to the terms in which it is couched, that many of us hesitate to introduce the 'Theosophist' to our friends or even to leave it lying on the tables of our drawing rooms. Personally I *know* of one case in which a friend, Mrs Molesworth, author of many charming books for children, declined to subscribe for the journal after becoming a theosophist, solely on account of the permanent Bradlaugh advertisement on its cover. She told me that before meeting me for the first time in Paris last winter, she had been warned against me by some of her lady friends on the ground that Dr Anna Kingsford was the new President of the British Theosophical Society, which was atheistic in its teachings and that she was moreover an ally and supporter of Mr Bradlaugh and Mrs Besant. The whole of this report was subsequently traced to the advertisement of those persons' writings on the cover of the 'Theosophist.'

Anna's letter also addressed the 'Kiddle Incident.' Henry Kiddle was an American spiritualist who noticed that in Sinnett's *The Occult World* Koot Hoomi had repeated verbatim some twenty four lines from a speech Kiddle himself had made in 1880. Kiddle wrote about this to *Light,* creating controversy in Theosophical and spiritualist circles. In a letter to Sinnett, Mme Blavatsky dismissed the charge of plagiarism by Koot Hoomi as 'absurd.'[3] Koot Hoomi later explained that a pupil, to whom he was transmitting a letter, inadvertently picked up Kiddle's ideas from the ether and wrote them down as if they came from Koot Hoomi.[4]

Anna gave her view on the dangers of relying on personalities instead of principles for truth, a tendency she saw evident in Sinnett and some sections of the Theosophical Society. Her comments are much to the point and show the acuteness of her religious understanding:

> I am not sorry to say that the Kiddle incident has arisen, since it gives me a good occasion of expressing my mistrust of all appeal to authority, and my conviction that no system having historical data and persons as its nuclei will ever successfully contend with time and criticism. I look with sorrow and concern on the growing tendency of the Theosophical Society to introduce into its method the superstitions; the exaggerated veneration for persons and for personal authority; an element which

has been the ruin of every other religious system in the past, and the inevitable outcome of which is a mere servile, hero-worship, degenerating into the substitution of events for processes; of personalities for principles; of authority for reason; of history for experience.

There is far too much talk among us about the adepts, our 'MASTERS,' and the like. Too much capital is made of their sayings and doings, doctrine is commended to us solely on the ground that they have affirmed it to be true, and reverence is expected for it to an excessive degree on that ground alone; insomuch that if one says 'I think Koot Hoomi is in error on such a point' or 'the Brothers appear to be insufficiently informed about so and so,' the statement is not unlikely to be regarded in the light of a sort of blasphemy, or at least as a disloyalty to Theosophy. But for the fate which befell Dr Wyld (and I do not defend his conduct, his method and manner being wrong throughout) I should myself perhaps have ventured to criticise some of Koot Hoomi's doctrines of *The Perfect Way.* It had not occurred to me then, that *Esoteric Buddhism* was expected to be viewed by Theosophists much in the same way as orthodox people view the Bible.

Let me, in very friendly and sincere feeling, assure Mr Sinnett and other members of our Society who have of late pressed upon us the personal and historic view of Theosophy, that they are making a fatal mistake, and one which, if persevered in, will inevitably bring contempt and difficulty upon us. The whole *raison d'etre* of the Theosophical Society is to rescue truth from superstition and to restore the 'Mysteries of the World.' Now the reason why Christianity has fallen into disrepute, and has failed to satisfy thinkers is because it has exalted persons in the place of principles, and has deified a Name in the stead of a Condition…Hence the need of a religious Reformation which shall demolish Atheism by unveiling the true nature of the Mysteries. Such a sublime function as this I hoped to have seen exercised by the Theosophical Society.

But if abandoning this *terra firma* is merely going to construct a new system of dogma on new authority, extraneous and arbitrary, it will speedily degenerate into a sect and become for the world no more than any other congregation of fanatics attached to some particular prophet. Koot Hoomi will be the oracle of the Theosophists, just as Joe Smith of the Latter Day Saints, Joanna Southcott of the Adventists, or Thomas Lake Harris of the community which acknowledges him as its

> King!...Our wise and truly theosophical course is not to set up new Popes nor proclaim new Masters, but to seek each for himself interiorly the realisation of the Process which is the Christ, which is Buddha, which is God with us. And this is the system we ought to proclaim to the world, on the authority of reason, of common sense, and of science.
>
> In the writings which from time to time I have published, whether alone or in conjunction with my co-worker, I have never appealed to authority nor even named those who appear to me to be my teachers. And this because I earnestly wish none to think I accept the teachings on authority, or that I would have others accept them on such ground. For how shall I convince anyone that I am not under an hallucination in such matters, or how even shall I persuade myself of the identity of the Gods? I know not – it may be the method of a poetic mind, it may be the phantasma of Thought, or of Psychic Memory. Therefore I judge and would have others judge by reasonableness only of that which is advanced for only this is capable of demonstration and endurance.
>
> 'Little children, keep yourselves from idols.' [1 John 5:21]
>
> I would have that text graven on the heart of every Theosophist.
>
> And so with fraternal salutations to you all, I trust you will take in good part the boldness with which I have spoken, and believe in my earnest zeal for the prosperity of our Brotherhood, which may under guidance become the Lever wherewith to purify the Church and destroy the canker of Infidelity.

It is not difficult to imagine that such a letter did not endear Anna to Sinnett and Mme Blavatsky. The controversy with Sinnett over his *Esoteric Buddhism* and the direction of Theosophy continued. On 31 October Anna wrote a long letter to Henry Olcott in Madras explaining her concerns. She thought Theosophy in England was too overladen with Eastern concepts which were 'meaningless and unintelligible, save to a few' in 'this quarter of the world.' She believed the esoteric study of Christianity would be more suitable for English speaking people. Anna also wrote to Mme de Steiger from Atcham on 2 November explaining her position vis-a-vis Theosophy. She thought Sinnett was giving too much prominence to the masters, and that this resulted in ridicule by the press, who called them 'Indian jugglers.' Anna continued:

> Mr Sinnett dislikes my being President for reasons of his own, and if I were to retire would not be slow to accept the vacant Chair. A hint is enough on this matter. The fact is patent to all who have eyes to see.

Following his lead, you have, most of you, read into my address a meaning I had not the least wish to convey, and I am heartily sorry so many of my friends should so much have misunderstood me. Mr C. C. Massey, at whose lead, as you know, I first joined the T.S. and became your President, under what we all then thought such happy auspices, is coming up to town to be present at Sunday's meeting, the 4th, and to do his best to break down the cabal raised against me. I hope you will support him, and I hope also that others of my friends will do likewise.

Can you manage to get a little private conversation with Mr Massey before the meeting, and exchange ideas with him? You will then learn exactly what it is he proposes to do. I have written him a letter to read at the meeting. Mr Sinnett will doubtless propose to call on me to retire from the Chair and from the Society; because this is his policy. Do not be misled by him. Both Mme Blavatsky and 'Mahatma K. H.' himself are, I have reason to believe, anxious to retain me as President. I had a long and cordial letter from Madame B. herself yesterday, with a kindly message from 'K.H.' I feel sure they would all be grieved to hear I was displaced.

Anna again wrote to Mme de Steiger outlining her position regarding the Theosophical Society:

Atcham Vicarage, 5 November 1883

Dear Mme de Steiger

In thanking you for your letter, which is a fair exposition of the present views of the London Lodge T.S., it would not be honest in me to leave you without a clear statement of my position in the matter that has arisen between us.

1. When I was invited to join the Society, I was emphatically and distinctly told that no allegiance would be required of me to the 'mahatmas,' to Mme Blavatsky, or to any other person real or otherwise, but only to Principles and Objects.
2. Consequently, I am no traitor to the express conditions on which I entered the Society when I say that I neither owe nor do I acknowledge the allegiance which now appears to be required of me to persons of whose existence and claims I am utterly unable to affirm or deny anything positively.
3. If it is the deliberate opinion of the whole Lodge – which it certainly was not six months ago – that it must have a president

whose allegiance to the mahatmas is *sans peur et sans reproche,* then I am certainly not, from the nature of things, fitted to occupy your Chair. And I do not see how anyone can occupy it, on such terms, who is not, of his own personal experience, in a position to testify to the existence and claims of the 'Brothers.' This even Mr Sinnett cannot do, as he only knows them 'through a glass darkly,' and not face to face.'

The utmost I can say in the present matter is – and this I say cordially – that I am heartily willing and anxious to hear all that comes to us from the East, with serious attention, provided I am not called upon to connect it with subservience to any personal authority claiming my belief and confidence as a duty; and provided also that I may fairly and freely criticize what I hear, and test it by reason and experience.

4. Mme Blavatsky calls the 'mahatmas' masters. Her experience and evidence may justify this epithet for her, but they do not justify me in using it. I do not, and will not, apply that term to any earthly being soever.

I may add that it is not I who seek to separate Esoteric Buddhism from Esoteric Christianity. First, the system expounded by Mr Sinnett is not – so far as I can see – esoteric at all, being simply a scheme of transcendental physics; and secondly, he is deliberately seeking to silence every other voice but that of the 'mahatmas.' If there is to be unification and brotherhood, there must be equality. It now seems to me that I am the only representative of [esoteric] Christian doctrine left among you!

Always affectionately yours, Anna Kingsford.

In her letters to Sinnett from India, Mme Blavatsky made uncomplimentary remarks about Anna. She blamed C. C. Masey for inviting Anna to become president of the British Theosophical Society.

'Well now thank him and keep her to turn all of you into a jelly. Of course she will wag you as her tail more than ever. I know it will end with a scandal.' She concluded this letter, 'Yours – but not Mrs Kingsford's.'[5]

On 30 October 1883 Anna wrote a letter to Mme Blavatsky outlining her position in the controversy. It was along the lines of her letter of 6 November to Mme de Steiger. Mme Blavatsky wrote to Sinnett on 26 November telling him about Anna's letter. Mme Blavatsky wrote, 'Three days ago I received a letter from her: 8 pages of her beautiful clear writing, with the usual celestial young lady surrounded with the seven pigeons and pressing to her heart the illegitimate offspring of her faux pas—stamped on the paper. A letter reasonable and refined, concise and clear to desperation.'

On 17 November 1883 Mme Blavatsky wrote to Sinnett, informing him Koot Hoomi had instructed her to drop the offending advertisement. This action was bound to happen, as Bradlaugh had stopped advertising *The Theosophist* in his paper four months previously.

Anna wrote a twelve page letter entitled 'A Letter Addressed to the Fellows of the London Lodge of the Theosophical Society' in December 1883 while at Atcham. She believed 'it is urgent that I should say a few words both in apology and vindication of the attitude taken by myself personally, in the present crisis of our history as a Theosophical Lodge.' She reminded her readers that she had been asked to become president of the British Branch by C. C. Massey because of *The Perfect Way,* her scientific qualifications, and 'certain natural gifts of seership.' She and Maitland joined the Theosophical Society 'on the express understanding that we should both retain our independence of position in regard to our own esoteric views.' However, she found Sinnett wanted his *Esoteric Buddhism* and other messengers from the masters to be the sole authority for Theosophists. She was not happy with 'the attitude subsequently assumed by him as the apostle of this system, the positive prohibition laid upon any expression of dissent from or criticism of it, or of its supreme authority, and the tone taken respecting certain attempts of my own to stem the current of a tide that appeared to me likely to lead us into an undesirable channel.'

Anna stated 'Pure Buddhism is in no radical respect different from pure Christianity, because esoteric religion is identical throughout all time and conditions, being eternal in its truth and immanent in the human spirit.' She found Sinnett's Esoteric Buddhism had the tendency'to divide, to scatter and to repel,' because it was 'materialistic, exoteric and unscientific.' 'In a word,' she said, 'this book is neither "Buddhistic" nor "esoteric."'[6]

Anna proposed that on the election of officials for 1884 two Sections be created in the London Lodge. One, headed by Sinnett, would study the teachings of the Tibetan Masters. The other Section 'should be composed by Fellows desirous, like myself, to adopt a broader basis, and to extend research into other directions, more especially with the object of encouraging the study of Esoteric Christianity, and of the Occidental theosophy out of which it arose.' This, she suggested, 'might be known as the Catholic Section of the London Lodge.' Anna meant Catholic in the sense of being universal. She envisaged members might move freely between the sections.

On 18 March 1884 Anna and Maitland issued their *Reply to the "Observations" of Mr T. Subba Row, C.T.S.*"[7] The Reply put its finger on the crux of the disagreement between Anna and Sinnett :

> It thus becomes obvious that the London lodge was in a fair way to become a place for those only who were prepared to yield abject submission to the authorities propounded by Mr Sinnett. And it was no secret that the resignation of all who were not so prepared was deemed desirable in order that Mr Sinnett, who had recently determined to remain in England instead of returning to India, should have the undivided direction of the Lodge. Meanwhile the belief was sedulously inculcated that the independent attitude of the recalcitrant members would be so deeply offensive to the Mahatmas as to lead to the withdrawal of their promised teaching.

Throughout the controversy Mme Blavatsky sent mixed messages about Anna in her letters to Sinnett and the London Lodge. Mme Blavatsky loved to manipulate people, but she met her match in Anna, whose principles and intellectual integrity were steadfast. Though she was very critical of Anna in her letters to Sinnett, she informed the London Lodge the masters supported Anna. However, early in 1884 the masters dropped their support for Anna and said members should have a free vote for president. The authenticity of certain mahatma letters was a controversial issue in Theosophy, with both Massey and Sinnett eventually falling out with Mme Blavatsky when they discovered certain letters they received, allegedly by masters, were written by Mme Blavatsky.

By all accounts Anna never criticised Mme Blavatsky. St George Lane-Fox, a member of the Theosophical Society, once stated:

> I remember well a conversation I had with Mrs K. shortly before her death. I had been speaking somewhat harshly about Mme Blavatsky and her methods, whereupon Mrs K. said, 'We must not condemn her, she is engaged upon a great work, and already has been a great service to mankind; her life may be far from perfect, but she is honestly seeking the way, and the way must be found before the life can be lived.'[8]

Anna kept Lady Caithness up to date with events in a letter dated 28 January. She concluded, 'Mr Ward (Uncle Sam)[9] sent me his vote, accompanied by an affectionate letter.' In a letter to Lady Caithness on 11 March 1884 Anna explained the source of her illuminations:

> ...I have no occult powers whatever, and have never laid claim to them. Neither am I, in the ordinary sense of the word, a clairvoyant. I am simply a 'prophetess'—one who sees and knows intuitively, and not by any exercise or any trained faculty. All that I receive comes to me by illumination, as to Proclus, to Iamblichus, to all those who follow the Platonic method.[10] And this gift was born with me, and has been developed by a special course and rule of life. It is, I am told, the result of a former initiation in a past birth, and the reason that I am enabled to profit by it is, that I am an 'old spirit' having, by thirst of life, pushed myself on to a point of spiritual evolution somewhat in advance of the rest of my race, but to which all can attain in time who have really once been initiated. My initiation was Greco-Egyptian, and therefore I recall the truth primarily in the language and after the method of the Bacchic mysteries, which are, as you know, the immediate source and pattern of the mysteries of the Catholic Christian Church.[11]

Plato wrote on knowledge as recollection in *Meno*:

> The soul, then, as being immortal, and having been born again many times, and having seen all things that exist, whether in this world or in the world below, has knowledge of them all; and it is no wonder that she should be able to call to remembrance all that she ever knew about virtue , and about everything; for as all nature is akin, and the soul has learned all things, there is no difficulty in her eliciting or as men say learning, out of a single recollection all the rest, if a man is strenuous and does not faint; for all enquiry and learning is but recollection.[12]

Anna wrote about the significance of her dreams in her preface to *Dreams and Dream Stories*:

> The priceless insights and illuminations I have acquired by means of my dreams have gone far to elucidate for me many difficulties and enigmas of life which might have otherwise remained dark to me, and to through upon the events and vicissitudes of a career filled with bewildering situations, a light which, like sunshine, has penetrated to the very causes and springs of circumstance, and has given reality and meaning to much in my life that would have else appeared to me futile and insignificant.

The potential for illuminative dreams was well known in Orphic religion and Pythagorean philosophy, as explained by A. E. Taylor: 'The familiar

Orphic doctrines, that the body is the "grave" of the soul, and that it is only when free from the body that the soul awakes to its true life, led naturally to the view that in sleep the soul converses with eternal things and receives communications form Heaven to which it is not accessible by day.'[13] Plato wrote that if the temperate man, 'before going to sleep has awakened his rational powers, and fed them on noble thoughts and enquiries, collecting himself in meditation,' and has subdued the passionate nature, in sleep he is then 'free to contemplate and aspire to the knowledge of the unknown, whether in the past, present, or future.'[14] Anna received illuminations through dreams, a facility which was once acknowledged by humankind, but has been disparaged and almost lost due to the prevailing materialistic philosophy.

Recollection of knowledge by students of the esoteric such as Anna is aided by study. She herself stated in her letter to Mrs Kenealy that one of the attractions of London for her was access to the British Museum; here she found a wealth of esoteric material which she studied with relish. Her writings show she was familiar with many significant works of esoteric thought, including works of Plato and the classical era, the Alexandrian School, Neoplatonism, Gnosticism, the Christian fathers, mystics from Meister Eckhart to Emmanuel Swedenborg. She also read prominent Eastern texts, Sufi works, and was familiar with alchemy, astrology, Kabbalah and the tarot. During the rest of the Winter and in the Spring Anna wrote in her diary a number of profound meditations on the mysteries of ancient Egypt, Greece, and the Kabbalah.[15]

Notes

1. Anna's letter was published in *Theosophical History* (July 1987: 82-5.
2. Blavatsky, CW v.5, 123.
3. Blavatsky 1925, Letter no. 29.
4. *The Theosophist* (September 1884): 287-88.
5. Blavatsky 1925, Letter no. 12.
6. In *The Secret Doctrine* (1888) Mme Blavatsky used virtually the same words as Anna when referring to *Esoteric Buddhism*. She wrote, 'as an eminent Pali scholar very pointedly expressed it, there was in the volume "neither esotericism nor Buddhism."' (I. xvii.)
7. Subba Row (1856-1890) was a Brahmin, a lawyer, and one of the leading Indian members of the Theosophical Society. He left the Theosophical Society in 1886.
8. *Theosophical History* 1, no.4 (Octber 1985): 74-80.
9. Samuel Ward (1814-1884) was an American lobbyist, financier and author. In an adventurous life he lost and then remade his fortune. He was 'warm-hearted,

charming and generous to the point of prodigality.' Ward lost two sons at a young age, and when Margaret, his only daughter, died at the age of thirty-four in 1875, he turned to 'Oriental mysticism.'

10. Iamblichus (c.250-c.325), a Neoplatonic philosopher who wrote on Pythagorean philosophy, is best known for *On the Mysteries.* Proclus (c.410-485), the last great Neoplatonic philosopher, was head of the Platonic Academy in Athens which was closed in 529 by Justinian. Proclus was a vegetarian, and greatly esteemed by his students for his holiness.
11. *The Eleusinian and Bacchic Mysteries, a Dissertation* (1790) by Thomas Taylor (1758-1835) is mentioned by Anna in *The Credo of Christendom* (127). Taylor was called 'the Platonist' because of his translations of Plato and Neoplatonists such as Proclus.
12. Plato, Meno 81.
13. Taylor, A. E., 31.
14. *The Republic*, Book IX 571.
15. *Life*, II.172-184.

Chapter - 13

The Hermetic Society

The controversy between Anna and Sinnett was approaching its climax. Mme Blavatsky and Henry Olcott headed for London from India to try and settle the dispute in the London Lodge. Olcott arrived on 5 April 1884 and two days later chaired a momentous meeting of the Lodge, held in the chambers of Gerard Finch in Lincoln's Inn. Maitland, Olcott, Sinnett and Charles Leadbeater have all given differing accounts of this meeting. Olcott gave the most plausible account of the proceedings as they related to Anna's role. Anna and Maitland notified him before the meeting they would not be standing for re-election. At the meeting Olcott offered to give Anna a charter to form the Hermetic Lodge of the Theosophical Society, and before leaving she presented him with a formal application for the charter. In her letter to fellows of the Theosophical Society of December 1883 Anna had proposed that two sections within the London Lodge be formed, but Olcott's charter proposed creating another lodge. In Olcott's words, 'the election passed off harmoniously,' with Gerard Finch being chosen president, Sinnett vice-president and secretary, and Miss Arundale treasurer.[1]

In their versions of the meeting, both Sinnett and Leadbeater wrongly claimed Anna stood for re-election and was soundly defeated. They wrote she was much annoyed with the result, and Leadbeater said 'her continual interruptions were more exasperating than ever.'[2] It is hard to imagine the highly cultured Anna behaving in such an unladylike manner. These two men had every reason to disparage Anna; she stood between Sinnett and his desire to become head of the London Lodge, while Leadbeater, a recent and ambitious convert to Theosophy, sided with the Sinnett camp.

Mme Blavatsky made an unexpected and dramatic appearance at the meeting, most graphically described by Leadbeater. He saw her enter at the back of the room and sit down. Some wrangling on the platform made her impatient and she jumped up and in a stentorian voice called out 'Mohini,' then walked out into the passage.[3] Mohini rushed down to the passage and threw himself prostrate at her feet. Sinnett hurried to the passage, re-entered the room and announced Mme Blavatsky to the assembly. Leadbeater continued, 'The scene was indescribable; the members, wildly delighted and yet half-awed at the same time, clustered round our great Founder, some kissing her hand, several kneeling before her, and two or three weeping hysterically.'[4] From this account, it appears that as her first entry went unnoticed, Mme Blavatsky staged a grand re-entry in order to attract attention. After everyone had settled down the meeting continued.

Only Maitland has mentioned that Mme Blavatsky bade him and Anna to shake hands with Sinnett. When 'She fixed her great eyes on us, as if to compel us by their magnetism to obey her behest,' he told her repentance ought to precede forgiveness. 'At this unexpected opposition her eyes flashed yet more powerfully on us, especially on Mary, who, as presumably the weaker vessel, might be expected to yield the more readily. Of course neither of us was in the smallest degree affected by her sorcery.'[5] Olcott stepped forward and said to Mme Blavatsky 'he would not have her trying to magnetise Mrs Kingsford.'

Anna and Maitland secured a charter from Olcott to form the Hermetic Lodge of the Theosophical Society. The new lodge was inaugurated on 9 April 1884 in the chambers of Charles C. Massey in London. Amongst those present were Olcott and Mohini Chatterjee, Lady Wilde, and her sons Oscar and William. Oscar Wilde was just seven weeks away from his marriage to Constance Mary Lloyd, a young woman with views in sympathy with those of Anna.[6] Lady Wilde was an inveterate collector of notable people for her soirées, and the writer Robert H. Sherard has mentioned meeting Anna at Lady Wilde 's house in Park Street, Grosvenor Square in 1883. Lady Wilde once said of Anna, 'no matter who was in the room, when Mrs Kingsford entered there seemed to be no one else there.'[7] Also present were Anna's friends, Mrs Kenealy and her two eldest daughters, Henrietta and Arabella.[8]

Light reported on the aims of the Hermetic Lodge as follows:

> The new Hermetic Lodge propounds as its platform 'freedom of opinion, expression, and discussion impartially conceded; the comparative study of all Esoteric teaching from an independent standpoint; conclusions on doctrinal matters based on reason rather than authority, and the special cultivation of personal development.'

The following supporters were listed: Dr Anna Kingsford, Mr Edward Maitland, Mr C. C. Massey, Lady Caithness, Mr Leslie Stephen, and the Baron Spedalier.[9]

Behind the scenes feverish activity was taking place. We catch a glimpse of this from a letter written by Maitland to Sam Ward dated 15 April 1884.[10] The letter provides hitherto unpublished information on events surrounding the formation of the Hermetic Lodge of the Theosophical Society.

In his letter Maitland thanked Ward for the offer of his rooms for meetings of the Hermetic Lodge. We then learn Maitland used Ward's name on the prospectus of the Hermetic Lodge without seeking his permission. Maitland wrote that in view of Ward's support in the past, he was confident he had his backing for the new Lodge. Maitland pointed out the Hermetic Lodge was 'no rival or opposition movement,' but was 'intended to supplement and complement' the existing London Lodge 'by one in which subjects can be studied and a liberty of discussion allowed, which do not find a place there.'

Maitland warned Ward that other members of the Theosophical Society might make 'trouble ' over the use of his name, as there was 'so bitter feeling against him and Mrs Kingsford by Sinnett and his adherents,' who were 'so mortified' with the granting of a new lodge, they were 'clamouring for our own expulsion from the society.' The opposition would 'jump' at anything to aggravate matters.

Maitland was concerned his and Anna's views were not getting a fair hearing, for 'the whole party from India' had taken up residence in Notting Hill with 'our opponents,' making it impossible for Maitland to see them.[11] He continued that 'matters have been much aggravated by Mme Blavatsky herself ' with her impetuosity and abruptness, 'when she ought to have gone softly, if at all,' and that she 'read evil meanings into words and actions perfectly guileless.' Maitland warned Ward not to quote or show his letter to anyone, because 'the utmost caution is necessary to avoid giving, in that quarter, grounds for antagonism.'

In the last part of his letter Maitland wrote that he and Anna had seen Ward's rooms at 1 St Stephen's Rd 'since writing the above.' They found them unsuitable for 'want of access,' and the largest room could only seat between eight and a dozen persons with comfort. However, he thanked Ward for his 'kind and generous thought and offer.' Maitland concluded by stating the meeting for 'Tuesday next at 5 P.M. will probably be held here or at Massey's.' This meeting was held on 22 April 1884, but rather than being a meeting of the Hermetic Lodge, it inaugurated Anna's own Hermetic Society.

Henry Olcott explained this turn-around in events:

> My Diary shows that the making of the 'Hermetic' group did not quite settle the disturbance in the old Lodge. The members generally wanted to profit by both courses of instruction and to belong to both Lodges. The effect was to keep up the excitement, so I was obliged to issue a new rule, to the effect that multiple membership would not be allowed; no person to be an active member in more than one Branch simultaneously; and where double membership existed, choice should be made in which group the individual preferred to remain. The effect was to threaten the disruption of the 'Hermetic' Lodge. So after consultations with Mr Massey, I suggested that Mrs Kingsford should return her charter and form her friends into an independent society, and thus make it feasible for them to belong to both.[12]

However, Olcott did not explain why the 'excitement' kept up; namely, that Sinnett's aim had always been to become president of the London Lodge. Sinnett wrote in his autobiography that the election of Gerard Finch as president was simply a temporary measure until he became president (which he did in January 1885). Because Anna stood in his way, Sinnett claimed 'she never realised the true character of the Theosophical movement'[13] He did not want to see any other lodge in London. In the words of Basil Crump, Sinnett's 'abnormal egotism and personal ambition grasped eagerly at the chance of becoming the Avatar of a great religio-scientific revelation to the Western world.'[14] Anna no doubt was greatly relieved to take the helm of her new Society and move on, leaving all the controversy behind her.

The first series of meetings of the Hermetic Society were held on 9 May 1884 at the home of Francis Lloyd, 43 Rutland Gate, London. Francis Lloyd (1853-1926), a distinguished army officer, was knighted in 1911.His main residence was Aston Hall, Oswestry, Shropshire. William Forsell Kirby (1844-1912) was the Hermetic Society's honorary secretary.[15]

The Society was another platform from which Anna could fight against the materialist philosophy she saw was corrupting society, so she wasted no time in pressing on with her task. At the Society's first session on 9 May 1884 Anna spoke on the inner meaning of the legend of St George and the dragon. Briefly stated, the people of Silene in ancient Lybia had to appease a monstrous dragon by feeding it their children. Even the king's daughter had to face the dragon, to be rescued by St George from the jaws of certain death. Anna explained the dragon stood for materialism, the king's daughter represented the soul, and St George was the higher reason or Hermes. Her explanation of the legend was included in her *Dreams and Dream Stories.* Her interpretation is a lesson for today, where we witness society 'feeding' its children to the dragon of consumerism.

The objectives of the Hermetic Society were set out in its prospectus:

> Its chief aim is to promote the comparative study of the philosophical and religious systems of the East and of the West; especially of the Greek Mysteries and the Hermetic Gnosis, and its allied schools, the Kabalistic, Pythagorean, Platonic, and Alexandrian – these being inclusive of Christianity – with the view to the elucidation of their original esoteric and real doctrine, and the adaptation of its expression to modern requirements.[16]

Various esoteric topics were discussed at the meetings of the Hermetic Society:

9 May 1884: 'The History and Character of Hermetic Philosophy' by E. Maitland.

19 May : 'Revelation as the Supreme Common Sense' by E. Maitland.

12 and 19 June: 'The Apostle 's Creed' by Anna.

26 June : 'Mystics and Materialism' by E. Maitland.

July: 'Indian Yoga' by Arthur Lillie.

July: 'The Apostle 's Creed' by Anna (meetings seven to ten).

Anna and Maitland made abstracts of their own papers which were published in *Light.* Some abstracts of Anna's lectures are reprinted in her work *The Credo of Christendom.*

On 12 May Anna wrote to Lady Caithness from 21 Henrietta Street, Cavendish Square. In part her letter said:

> Sometimes I think that the truths and knowledges we hold are so high and so deep that the age is yet unable to receive them, and that all we shall be permitted to do is to formulate them in some book or books to leave as a legacy to the world when we pass away from it. The truth we have is far in advance of anything the disciples of Madame Blavatsky and her Gurus possess. They know only the Lower Triangle of the Seal of Solomon [the hexagram]; and this is all that the Masons or the Buddhists know. This Lower Triangle is Solomon's Temple, which the

Masons are always rebuilding. But that which has been expounded to us, and which we hold in trust for the age to come, is the secret of the Upper Triangle—'the city not made with hands, eternal in the Heavens.'

I like Mohini Chatterjee. I think he knows more intuitively than Mme B. is capable of knowing. I have had two hour's conversation with him, and found him instructed and intelligent. I think him honest and free from malice, so far as I can judge.

With this letter Anna laid aside her tumultuous dealings with the Theosophical Society. She was now in a position to devote herself to her campaigns without unnecessary distractions.

Notes

1. Olcott, 93-94.
2. Leadbeater, 35. Sinnett 1922, 55.
3. Mohini Chatterjee (1858-1936) was an attorney-at-law and a leading Hindu member of the early Theosophical Society who lectured extensively in Europe and America. He had a falling out with Mme Blavatsky and Henry Olcott and resigned from the Theosophical Society in 1887.
4. Leadbeater, 36-7.
5. *Life*, II.186.
6. Oscar Wilde (1854-1900) was not a student of Hermetic studies, though he dabbled in spiritualism with visits to seances. Constance Wilde 's (1858-1898) father, Horace Lloyd, was Lady Mount Temple's cousin by marriage. When Constance was in her late teens Lady Mount Temple took her under her wing and they maintained a close relationship. Constance took an interest in Theosophy and knew the Theosophist Mrs Laura Cooper Oakley. Constance was a member of the Golden Dawn in 1888-89. Like Anna, Constance was an advocate of rational dress, and from 1888 she was editor of *The Rational Dress Society Gazette*.
7. *Life*, II. 225.
8. Olcott, 94.
9. *Light* (19 April 1884): 1.
10. Maitland's letter to Sam Ward is held in the F. Marion Crawford papers, call number bMS Am 2206 (21), Houghton Library, Harvard University. Quoted by permission of the Houghton Library, Harvard University. Sam Ward died at the age of seventy on 19 May 1884 in Pegli, Italy.
11. Henry Olcott and Mohini Chatterjee were staying with Mrs and Miss Francesca Arundale at 77 Elgin Crescent, Notting Hill. Sinnett recorded that after the meeting of 7 April 1884 he took Mme Blavatsky home with him, where she stayed for about one week, then went to Paris.
12. Olcott, 96-7.

13. Sinnett 1922, 54.
14. Cleather, 46-7.
15. Howe, 40. William F. Kirby was an assistant in the Zoological Department of the British Museum. He was a respected entomologist and wrote distinguished books on the subject. He was also a member of the Theosophical Society, and joined the Hermetic Order of the Golden Dawn in July 1893. When the Golden Dawn split he joined Arthur Edward Waite 's Independent and Rectified Order in November 1903. Kirby's translation of the Finnish epic poem *The Kalevala* was published in 1907. His interests were summed up in his entry in *Who's Who* as entomology, north European folklore, and mysticism.
16. *Life*, II. 195.

Chapter - 14

Multifarious Activities

In Maitland's words, he and Anna did not neglect their 'crusade on behalf of our rudimentary brethren, the animals.' Anna was in Paris when she showed affection for the late Sam Ward in her diary on 3 June C1884:

> I have come here for the Anti-Vivisection Congress, or rather Conference, which begins tomorrow. Matters look very gloomy for the cause of justice since the Pasteur investigation began. It may be that discoveries partially beneficial really may be made by this horrible system of inoculating madness and death. All the severer the ordeal for those who keep a perfect heart and a clear eye. And now dear old Uncle Sam [Samuel Ward] is gone to the other side. I shall not see him any more, nor hear his genial, gracious voice. It is always through the affections that we suffer. Uncle Sam died on Monday the 19th May. I had barely known him one year, and yet he had become part of my life, and was bound up with all my thoughts about the future. It seems to me that he cannot be dead; that some day he must return to us, and bring me, as was his wont, a basket of fruit or a bunch of roses. What will he be—this dear old man—in another life? He is a relative of mine now, acquired by my Karma, and I feel sure in another birth we shall be of one kin.
>
> How keenly, as one grows older, the idea enforces itself on the heart that all the events and experiences of this life are but Maya! How clearly one sees that all the light of this world is but a false radiance, and that all its seeming realities are the tricks and shows of illusion! Nothing is; everything passes, flits by, and vanishes.

In July 1884 William T. Stead's *Pall Mall Gazette* published an article by Anna on the Hermetic Society. It was given the misleading heading 'The Newest Thing in Religions,' causing Anna to write to the Gazette explaining 'the Society aims the recovery of what is really the oldest thing in Religion—so old as to have become forgotten and lost— namely, its esoteric and spiritual, and therefore its true, signification.' At this time Maitland noted they were receiving 'numerous letters from strangers from various distant regions' who 'desired information respecting our work.'

With both the season and their work in London for the Summer over, Anna went to Atcham. Here she continued her studies, assisted by visits to the occult library of Walter Moseley,[1] who lived at The Park in Buildwas, a village situated a few miles south east of Atcham. Anna found these studies opened 'fresh veins of buried knowledge,' recollected from her remote past and yielding 'results far transcending those contained in the books themselves.'

In December 1884 Maitland and Anna embarked on a lecture tour to Leeds, Hull, Birmingham, and Cheltenham, speaking on vegetarianism and vivisection. Anna spoke to large, enthusiastic audiences, and the tour was declared a success. She and Maitland returned to Atcham where they wrote a letter of resignation from the London Lodge of the Theosophical Society, dated Christmas Eve, 1884. Before taking this step they consulted their friend Charles Massey, who had resigned in the previous Summer. Maitland wrote that their reason for resigning was 'a narrow sectarianism' and lack of 'freedom of expression' in the Lodge. He and Anna also opposed the Lodge 's 'rejection of the Mysticism of the West.' However, they still had articles and book reviews published in Theosophical magazines. After Anna died Maitland maintained contact with some Theosophists, including attending meetings at Sinnett's home.

Towards the end of 1884 Anna undertook to write a weekly letter to the *Lady's Pictorial* on women's health. Maitland noted this involved 'a heavy correspondence with individuals as well as a considerable private practice ' and took time away from her spiritual work. Anna's youthful appearance created the impression that she was in possession 'of some magical secret which could be imparted to others.' Some of the women who consulted her wanted to improve their complexions, and Anna was appalled that their own doctors ignored diet and just wrote out prescriptions which were detrimental to the complexion. Anna explained to her patients that 'the look of their skin depends on the state of their blood, and this chiefly on the diet with which they nourish it.' A selection of her letters was published in *Health, Beauty, and the Toilet: Letters from a Lady Doctor* in 1886.

Anna's campaign against vivisection was ongoing. On 11 December 1884 she gave a lecture entitled 'Vivisection' in the Assembly Room at Cheltenham. She said 'it was impossible to draw the line on vivisection,' for once in the laboratory with an animal men got carried away by 'scientific enthusiasm.' The English did not want to get left behind the Continent on vivisection, but English medical men, she said, were playing into the hands of the materialists and utilitarians by pursuing the practice. After the lecture the committee and deputation dined together, and in the evening a *conversazione* took place, when other speeches were made by anti-vivisectionists.[2]

In December 1884 and January 1885 Anna contributed to a debate in *The Times* on vivisection. In her letter of 25 December she pointed out that details of a particular cerebral disease were learnt from examination of humans and not through the vivisection of animals, as claimed in a letter by a certain 'F.R.S.' She also mentioned Broca's discovery of the centre for language in the brain did not involve any vivisection experiments. In a letter of approximately 1,000 words on 5 January 1885 Anna further expounded on the subject, which was still being discussed in the paper. She concluded this letter, 'An attempt has been made to establish a case for vivisection, and that attempt has, I think, signally failed. Any exhibition of gratulation on the part of the vivisectors is, under the circumstances, to say the least of it, singularly misplaced and inconsequent.'

A major event for London in 1884 was the International Health Exhibition held at South Kensington. It generated great interest, with over 80,000 visitors on some days, and the exhibition received considerable coverage in *The Times* and *Punch*. The exhibition was officially opened on 9 May by the Duke of Cambridge for the Prince of Wales, and ran for the rest of the year. A number of attractions were of particular interest to Anna, such as displays on rational dress, the purification of water, and sanitary dwellings. Edwin Godwin, the noted architect and theatrical designer, spoke on rational dress. The Vegetarian Society opened a dining-room, distributed their literature, and presented public lectures.

At the end of the International Health Exhibition, Anna and Maitland were among the prominent vegetarians who spoke at a 'great meeting' of the Vegetarian Society at Exeter Hall, London, on 12 January 1885. Anna's speech was issued by the Manchester branch of the Vegetarian Society in

1886 under the title *Physiology of Vegetarianism.* In the five page pamphlet reactions from the audience have been inserted, giving us an idea of the talk's atmosphere. Anna 'was received with loud and prolonged cheers,' showing her popularity among fellow vegetarians. She had a sense of humour and knew how to use it in her lecture, for she drew laughter eleven times in all, six times on the first page. Anna stated one page from the end, 'I am afraid I have over-talked my time now,' but the audience were of a different mind, responding with 'Loud cries of "Go on; go on."'

Anna revealed some information about her own health and diet in her speech:

> In the hospitals again and again we hear the words, 'You must take flesh-meat,' or, 'You must get some port wine,' and that sort of thing. Well, my own experience is this – I cured myself of tubercular consumption by living on vegetable food. A doctor told me I had not six months to live. What was I to do? I was to eat raw meat and drink port wine. Well, I went into the country and ate porridge and fruit, and appear to-day on this platform!'
>
> Then, again, there is the Leather question. I was determined that on this point I would not have my boots thrown at my head as a reproach; so I went about London to find a man who would make boots without leather, and I found him, and have the boots on this evening. The argument about leather then is answered, for soles, uppers, and everything else are made without it. Two years ago I climbed the hills of Switzerland in boots made without leather. I have pretty well solved this question, then. When there comes a demand for boots made without leather, you will be able to get them…
>
> There have been a great many very illustrious names connected with Vegetarianism: men of such calibre as Gautama Buddha, whose life has been given to the world in that beautiful poem, *The Light of Asia,* which is now issued as cheap as possible – at one shilling. You should read that work and the teaching of Edwin Arnold, and if that does not convert you to Vegetarianism, nothing will; it is full of the most beautiful language and most pathetic sentiment possible to imagine. You will find that a book to smile over, and a book to weep over. It is the sort of literature I should like to see widely disseminated in London.'

This meeting at Exeter Hall was reported extensively in *The Times* of 13 January 1885. Edwin Collier, treasurer of the Vegetarian Society was in the chair. The Society had £100 in the bank after expenses, and this would provide free dinners in some of the largest towns in England. The president of the Society was Professor the Reverend John Eyton Bickersteth Mayor (1825-1910), a noted classical scholar who had a long association with St John's College, Cambridge. He attributed his robust health and longevity to a vegetarian diet. Among his many writings were a number on vegetarianism. Another prominent vegetarian present at the meeting was Dr Thomas Richard Allinson (1857-1918). His medical practice in the West End of London was linked to a private hospital that treated patients in accordance with his views on naturopathy. In 1892 he set up The Natural Food Company which produced wholemeal flour using the slogan 'Health Without Medicine.' His wholemeal bread won a high reputation, and the company continues today under his name.

On 17 February 1885 Anna wrote to Lady Caithness with her news. She had translated *Astrology Theologised* by the German mystic Valentin Weigelius (1553-1588), and would now write a long preface for it on the Hermetic doctrine. Anna concluded her letter with these heartfelt words:

> The extent of the work which lies before us seems so great and overwhelming that I despair when I think of it; and, alas! mankind care so little about it. The idea of a miracle or of an Adept is far more attractive to them than all the knowledge in the world. Write to me as soon as you can. It gives me always the greatest of pleasure to hear from you, for you are the one friend with whom I can converse with entire confidence and affection.

Anna had sufficient prominence for *Punch* to take a pot shot at her. The issue of 14 March 1885 printed without comment this piece of doggerel which obviously refers to Anna:

> To Mrs Anna Longshore Potts, M.D.
> (By Our Own Old Nurse)
>
> WERE JANES AND ANNES
> ALL POTTS, not pans,
> There'd be no work
> For the Doctor's hands.

Punch at this time was no friend of women's rights. The issue of 2 May 1885, for example, printed an anti-women's suffrage drawing depicting women holding a public meeting. To make them look ridiculous the women were given grossly distorted features.

Anna, however, continued on undeterred, as shown by her letter to Lady Caithness, written from London on 15 May:

> If I had written to you as often lately as I have wished to write, you would have had by this time a score of letters. But I think Mr Maitland will have told you the best of the news. Our Hermetic meeting last Wednesday was attended by thirty five people. As you know, we have taken the rooms of the Royal Asiatic Society in Albemarle St. for our reunions. I fear we shall be unable to visit you in Paris this year, greatly as I should enjoy it. After leaving London I think I shall have to go home and remain there quietly till the ensuing spring, as I did last year, unless I undertake some lectures in the autumn. I enclose you a form of petition, sent me for signature by Mrs Burton,[3] wife of the British Consul at Trieste. I have already obtained nearly seventy names to it, and I send a form to you, begging you to sign it, and to get all the friends you can to sign it also. As you see, it is a petition to Pope Leo XIII, calling on him to instruct the Catholic Church on the subject of humanity to animals.

The programme for the 1885 Hermetic Society meetings shows a range of esoteric subjects was discussed:

27 April: 'The Hermetic Fragment, Koré Kosmou the Virgin of the World' by Anna.

6 May: 'The Kabala and Buddhism,' by Arthur Lillie.

13 May: 'The Method of the Mystics,' by Anna.

20 May: 'The Revival of Mysticism,' by E. Maitland.

27 May: 'Karma,' by C. C.Massey.

3 June: 'The Symbology of the Old Testament,' by E. Maitland.

10 June: 'The Value of the Historical Element in Christianity,' by Roden Noel.

17 June: 'The Intention and Method of the Gospels,' by E. Maitland

24 June: 'Individuality,' by C. C. Massey.

1 July: 'The Communion of Saints,' by Anna.

Maitland noted that an Hermetic Society was formed in Boston, U.S. for the purpose of studying *The Perfect Way,* and he quoted the comments of a Boston paper:

> *The Perfect Way* is the title of a book which has excited great attention in London, and in Boston circles of modern scientific and theosophic discussion, and the name of the author has been sought in vain. Mrs

> Waters (Clara Erskine Clement), who has just returned from Europe, solves the mystery. The author of these remarkable lectures is Dr Anna Kingsford of London, a woman described as having the face and figure of a Greek goddess, so perfect is her beauty. She is of the goldenblonde type, and her manner is one of exceptional dignity and grace. The Metaphysical Club of Boston was deeply interested in *The Perfect Way* last year. A remarkable book it is, whether one accepts its ideas or not. Dr Kingsford's theory of life, in brief outline, is that it is a series of reincarnations, by means of which the soul acquires its experiences; that the deeds and aspirations of one life predetermine entirely the quality of the next incarnation.

On 15 June 1885 Anna wrote to Lady Caithness with more news:

> By the way, have you got some signatures to the petition to the Pope – which I sent you – praying him to cause humanity to the animals be taught and preached to the people in Italy, Spain and elsewhere ? Mrs Burton, the promoter of the petition, is now in London. She came to see me yesterday, and I am to meet her again next week, Lady Mount Temple having asked me to bring her to lunch with her. Mrs Burton is most nice; you would like her greatly. She reminds me wonderfully of you in some things. She pounced immediately on the picture of the Virgin and Seven Doves on our paper, and asked if it was reserved for you and me only, or whether she might adopt it too. I said she might, and then she begged me for a copy to take to the engraver's, and she preferred yours on account of the double Triangle and the Anno Dominae which greatly struck her. So I tore off a corner of your last letter and gave it to her. She says that she shall adopt one alteration, that of putting the cross in the centre of the two triangles, as it is in my ringseal. She also sees visions and is a spiritualist. Her special guide is St Joseph, she says, and he has appeared to her several times.

Miss Cobbe's anti-vivisection journal *The Zoophilist* reported Anna's busy schedule of lectures for the cause. For example, in July Anna spoke at Oxford, and also delivered a lecture at Mile End. It was reported her meetings drew large and enthusiastic audiences. Anna then visited her mother at St Leonards, writing to Lady Caithness about her hectic pace:

> 2 August 1885
>
> Dearest Lady Caithness,
>
> All the time I remained in London, I was so hunted about with all manner of lectures, at homes, calls, and engagements of all sorts, as

well as literary and medical work, that I thought it best to wait until I got away to the sea-side before sitting down to write to you. I have now been here since 31 July, and I hope to remain for about ten days before going back to Shropshire. I have quite given up the idea of going abroad or elsewhere this year; in fact, I have no possible time for a holiday ramble, seeing that my daughter's schooling is over, and I must take her home until the end of September; after which I have several lecturing engagements to fulfil in various parts of England, which will occupy me until the beginning of November…

No doubt you have by this time read *The Virgin of the World,* and our two essays prefixed to it. I am longing to hear what you think of it and them. Our Hermetic Session was far more successful at its close than at its opening. No doubt you have read the reports in *Light* of our weekly meetings. Next session I hope to go on with my lectures on the Creed, which I suspended this time in order to permit other speakers to be heard. It is extremely difficult to impress a catholic and mystic view of these things on the British mind. The fogs and clouds which enwrap their isle seem to enshroud their spirits also. And yet how lucent, how splendid, how entrancing this wonderful Truth is, could they only receive it! Is it indeed the fact I sometimes wonder, that a few of us have senses developed which are unknown to the majority of our race; and do we really walk about among a blind and deaf generation for whom the light *we* see and the words *we* hear *are not?*

I have been trying hard to persuade Lady Archibald Campbell to produce next year, as a pastoral play, in Coombe Wood, the story of Buddha, founded on Edwin Arnold's magnificent poem, 'The Light of Asia.' You know this has long been a dream of mine to educate the people by means of the stage, by reproducing in tableaux or spectacular drama the lives and teaching of the world's holiest and noblest. 'The Light of Asia' lends itself peculiarly to such an idea. The verse is melodious and dramatic, the situations are excellent, and the scenery, being mostly forest and jungle, quite easy to manage. I propose to give four acts – the Departure, the Ministry, the Triumph, the Return, and to introduce into these the chief episodes in Buddha's career.

I drew out a tableau of the acts, with the chief situations fully described, and rehearsed the whole at Lady Tennant's, in Grosvenor Square, in the presence of Lady A. Campbell, Lady Ribblesdale, Hon. Mrs Lyttleton, Hon. Percy and Mrs Wyndham, Mr Tennyson (the poet's son), Miss Tennant, Mr Godwin (the manager of the Coombe Wood plays), and some others. All were delighted, but the *technic* of the matter appeared to them to involve great difficulties. Edwin Arnold, to whom I wrote on the subject, said he would do everything he could do to forward the idea, and to ensure its success if it were found workable.

As for my novel, that is quite at a standstill. I hope to take it up again as soon as I return to Shropshire. I have a story coming out at Christmas in the Catholic magazine, *The Month.* All this time I have been talking about myself, and have not said a word about you. That is very egotistic of me.

The above mentioned gathering was obviously impressed by Anna's capabilities.[4] Margot Asquith, a daughter of Lady Tennant, wrote of their London home in her autobiography: '...at our house in Grosvenor Square...everyone met – Randolph Churchill, Gladstone, Asquith, Morely, Chamberlain, Balfour, Rosbery, Salisbury, Hartington, Harcourt, and, I might add, jockeys, actors, the Prince of Wales and every ambassodor in London.'

Notes

1. William Moseley, the local magistrate, was born in Buildwas 1831 and Maria his wife was born in 1845 in Burneston, York. Moseley's name appears in *The Theosophist* of April 1880 among a list of new subscribers.
2. *The Zoophilist* (2 February 1885): 203.
3. Isabel Burton (1831-1896) was the wife of the famous explorer and writer Sir Richard Francis Burton (1821-1890). She first met him in 1851 but did not marry him until 1861, still without parental approval. She was always concerned about the welfare of animals, and when living inTrieste she managed a local society for the prevention of cruelty to animals.
4. Lady Emma Tennant (1821-1895) was the first wife of Sir Charles Tennant (1823-1906), an industrialist with global interests in chemicals, mining, oil, railways and banking. Emma gave birth to six sons and six daughters. Their London town house was at 40 Grosvenor Square, and the family castle was located outside Edinburgh, Scotland. Their daughter Charlotte (1858-1911) married Lord Ribblesdale (1854-1925) of Gisburne Park, near Skipton, Yorkshire. Octavia Laura (1862-1886), another daughter, married the Rt. Hon. Alfred Lyttelton in 1885, only to tragically die after the birth of her first child. Laura's vivacious personality won her many admirers, including Alfred, Lord Tennyson, whose poem about her included the line 'Half child, half woman.' Lady Archibald Campbell (1845-1923) was an amateur actress who originated the Pastoral Plays, in which she also acted. She lived at Coombe Hill Farm near Kingston, Surrey, where plays were held in the open air. She and her husband wrote prolifically on Celtic folklore. Percy Scawen Wyndham (1835-1911), born at Drove, near

Chichester, was the Conservative MP for Cumberland West from 1860 to 1885. He was intrigued by spiritualism and attended séances. Hallam Tennyson (1852-1928) was the son of the famous poet Alfred, Lord Tennyson. Edwin Arnold (1832-1904) was the editor of the *Daily Telegraph.* He achieved fame with *The Light of Asia* (1879), a long poem based on the life of the Buddha. Arnold used to visit the house of Anna's friend, Alice Meynell, and read poems to her daughters.

Chapter - 15

A Busy Life Takes Its Toll

Anna's busy schedule did not let up, for in the Autumn of 1885 she undertook with Maitland a lecture tour to Gloucester, Malvern, Bristol, Clifton, Weston-super Mare, Clevedon, and Tunbridge Wells in the Autumn of 1885. At most places they visited, they 'were hospitably entertained in private houses, and had opportunities both of making fresh friends and of imparting of our more recondite teachings.' At Weston Anna and Maitland stayed with Professor Francis W. Newman (1805-1897), brother of Cardinal John Henry Newman. Francis Newman had been professor of Latin at University College, London. He was a supporter of women's suffrage, opposed vivisection, and was a strong advocate of a vegetarian diet. He wrote some fifty seven books on various subjects, including linguistics, mathematics, religion, and social and political issues.

Anna's strenuous workload is exemplified by the week commencing on Monday, 5 October 1885, when she gave four lectures in as many days. In the afternoon of 5 October she spoke in the room of the Young Men's Christian Association in Hereford, and spoke the same evening at a meeting chaired by J.H. Morley, the Mayor of Hereford. Anna next appeared on the afternoon of Wednesday 7 October at the Imperial Hotel. There was such a large and enthusiastic attendance that a new anti-vivisection society was formed with the intention to affiliate with the Victoria Street and International Association as a branch. On Thursday 8 October 1885 Anna spoke at an anniversary meeting of the Anti-Vivisection Society in Bristol. She was warmly thanked for her address, and a petition to Parliament against vivisection was adopted. The chairman, Mr Henry Fedden, referred to the death of Lord Shaftesbury, and remarked that the rest of the nobility should take his lead in supporting humanitarian causes.

Anna's long and arduous campaign against vivisection must have taken its toll on her, both mentally and physically. At least as early as 1872 she was vitally interested in the subject, and must have thought about it constantly. Such immersion in a very distressing subject would have had a debilitating effect, as shown by the American feminist Andrea Dworkin (1946-2005) in her comments about her own research on pornography:

> My work on de Sade came to an end, but not before I nearly collapsed from fatigue; physical fatigue because I hated to sleep [because of nightmares]; physical fatigue as I was often physically sick from the material; mental fatigue because I took on the whole male intellectual tradition that has lionized de Sade; but also moral fatigue, the fatigue that comes from confronting the very worst sexual aspiration of men articulated by de Sade in graphic detail, the fatigue engendered by sexual cruelty.[1]

In her article addressing the question as to why the majority of antivivisectionists were women, Coral Lansbury has put forward cogent arguments linking vivisection and sadism. She pointed out that in gynaecological practices and pornography of the Victorian era, women were strapped down and sadistically abused in a manner similar to the treatment of animals undergoing vivisection. Lansbury remarked that anti-vivisection novels like *Heart and Science* by Wilkie Collins and *The Beth Book* by Sarah Grand made it 'disturbingly clear that when women wept for tortured animals they were weeping for themselves.'

Further, as an advanced mystic, Anna saw much more deeply into the human condition than most folk. She must have pondered long and hard on the sin and evil in the world. Anna dedicated her life to bringing light into this fallen world. This condition has been remarked upon by Mary Atwood in her arcane tome *A Suggestive Inquiry Into the Hermetic Mystery* (1850):

> It is an awful thing that when the Divine Life is being elicited in a man [or woman], the sins of this world press heavily upon him, through his sympathy with it, and his perception of the evil; it is as if the individual soul was responsible for all.[2]

Early in 1886 Anna was in St Leonards and on 24 February she wrote to Lady Caithness about her plans:

> I have been intending to write to you for ages, but work has quite overwhelmed me of late; and, besides, I have been terribly bad with neuralgia and almost laid up. Now that I am away from our damp vicarage I am better. Thanks, many, for your Nice newspapers. I have

read the accounts of your festivals with interest, and fancied myself present. On Saturday next I go up to London with my little daughter, who leaves for Paris on Sunday under the charge of Miss Dawson. The child is going to spend a year in Paris to learn French and music. The change will do her an immense deal of good in every way and she is looking forward to it greatly. After the dull life she has led here it will develop her character for the better, I hope. As for me, I have taken a charming little flat for the six spring and summer months in London, and enter into possession on 8 March. My address will be 34 Wynnstay Gardens, Kensington, until next September.

Our Hermetic Session will very soon begin again now. Is it not extraordinary that this year of all years the Sphinx is to be dug out of the Desert sands that have hidden it all these centuries? 1886 is, you know, the prophesied year of Nostrodamus, who foretold that when St George should roll away the stone from the door of the holy sepulchre, then the new era should dawn. This year St George 's Day and Easter Day coincide – a thing that has not happened before, since many hundred years, I think – and all the other Festivals also coincide in very strange ways, but I have not the prophecy here to refer to. I will try to get it and send it. But no doubt you read all about it in Light. And the Hermetic Society was founded on St George 's Day eve! He is our Patron Saint. The Sphinx is to be uncovered by Easter, so the whole thing is most strange.

I have a new book just coming out, published by Redway. It is the *Theology Astrologized* of Weigelius, with a long introductory essay by me. I hope you will like it. But how about your book? Do let me know how it gets on. I am so glad you liked my story in the *Month.* It has lately been reprinted in America. I am very hard at work now with literary and other matters, and only wish my health was sufficiently good to allow of my taking up all the offers of literary work I get.

Meetings of the Hermetic Society resumed, and ran from 13 April to 29 July 1886. This session saw the appearance of Samuel L. Mac Gregor Mathers, who lectured on 'The Kabala' on 3 June. Dr William Wynn Westcott lectured 'on the Kabalistic book, *Sepher Yetzirah.*'

Maitland wrote enthusiastically about these meetings:

At all the meetings the papers were followed by discussions of the highest interest, the attendance varying from thirty to fifty persons, many of whom were notable for their talent, their erudition and their piety. A special feature in Mary's lectures consisted in the highly artistic diagrams, made by herself, of the symbols explained, such as the double Triangle and the Seal of Solomon, on which were shown the stations of the soul in the course of its elaboration; also her drawings of man in his two states, degenerate and regenerate, as indicated by the direction of the magnetic currents of his system, according to the view shown in her vision. Another feature worthy of mention was the occasional presence of theatrical actors and professional reciters, who came, they said, not because they could understand what they heard – that, they frankly admitted was beyond them – but in order to listen to the president, whose gift of elocution they declared to be so perfect that to hear her speak was a lesson in their own art. This proved to be the closing session of the Hermetic Society.

Anna again wrote about her activities to Lady Caithness on 11 May 1886:

> You know that it is not because I do not often think of you that I do not write often. Both Mr Maitland and I have been, and still are, so incessantly occupied with literary work that we find it hard to get time for correspondence further than the sending off of short notes and post cards. We are now very busy getting ready the revised edition of *The Perfect Way,* which will contain a new lecture and many alterations and improvements. Then there is my own book, which Redway is bringing out, and the proofs of which I have to correct, besides my weekly newspaper work, which is heavy, and my lectures. One is coming off on Thursday evening at Hampstead. It is a mere feat for me to get to bed earlier than 1 or 2 am, and, as you know, my health is very far from strong.
>
> There is a general feeling among the members of the Hermetic Society that we hold some meetings in the evening. Many of our men cannot come in the afternoons. At the last the Hon. Roden Noel gave us a paper on Boehme, which was extremely interesting, and led to my reading up what Mrs Penny has to say on the subject. I think I begin to understand Boehme much better than I did, though I think that he was very irregular in his aspirations, and the levels to which he attained; not rising always to the same height...

The lecture at Hampstead which Anna mentioned in this letter was entitled 'Pasteur: His Method and Its Results.' It was held on 13 May 1886 on behalf of the North London Anti-Vivisection Society and published for sale at twopence. Anna pointed out there was much dispute among scientists and medical men over Pasteur's claims for his vaccination experiments. As usual, she expressed her concern that he caused much pain to animals for dubious benefit. Her concluding remarks not only showed her passion for the cause, they were also prophetic:

> The natural heart, as well as the educated instincts, of Englishmen, at least, rise up in arms against the official formulation and recognition of such a system. Religious teachers, if only they were not blinded and gagged by professional and social terrorisms, could not fail to see and to proclaim the dangerous rock ahead on which the whole ship of the faith must inevitably go to pieces, if it be suffered to drift before the storm which Pasteurism has raised. For what becomes of the trust and belief in a good and all-compassionate God, who built the universe for good, if men are to be taught that the God-appointed way to knowledge and healing involves deeds which hitherto have been supposed to characterise only the worst and wickedest of cowards? Will not the very distinction itself between justice and cruelty, virtue and vice, good and evil, rot and fall asunder under the blow which such a doctrine must deal? What folly, what fatuous imbecility, to invoke the Name of God as that of a Deity of Goodness and mercy, of Love and beneficence, if the conditions which alone He sanctions and blesses for the attainment of his best gifts are such as mark Him as a Fiend!
>
> Only the other day, a lady who is deservedly honoured and revered, a lady of high intellectual attainments and reputation as a writer, said in a letter to a friend, 'My faith in the being and goodness of God is *strained to the utmost* by the achievements and the success of Pasteur.'
>
> O pregnant words! bitter words! prophetic words! Born of unbelief and agent of the Pit, the demon of vivisection will work havoc with many a soul before the time of his rage is spent. Of all the workers on the side of atheism there is none so potent as this particular Beelzebub.
>
> Only, the tyranny cannot last. Cannot last, because not evil but good is the ultimate and origin of all things, and because only the divine can stand the test of time. The universe is not a house divided against itself, nor can it own two masters. And unless the devil has built the world, it will not be possible for devilish means to triumph in the end. That which is morally wrong cannot be scientifically right. It is the character of the man of the future that is at stake in this matter; and the issues of a far vaster problem than any that physical science can determine depend

on the verdict which the heart of our country passes on the method of Louis Pasteur.

More evidence of Anna's busy social life comes from the author Thomas Hardy. In notes on his life, Hardy recorded a brief encounter with Anna and Maitland on 17 May 1886:

> At a curious soiree in Bond Street. Met a Hindu Buddhist, a remarkably well-educated man who speaks English fluently. [Most probably Mohini Chatterjee.] He is the coach of the Theosophical Society. Also encountered a Mr E. Maitland, author of a book called the Pilgrim and the Shrine, which I remember. He mentioned also another, written, I think he said, by himself and Dr Anna Kingsford in collaboration. If he could not get on with the work on any particular night he would go to her next morning and she would supply him with the sentences, written down by her on waking, as sentences she had dreamt of without knowing why. Met also Dr Anna Kingsford herself, and others; all very strange people.[3]

Anna wrote to Mme de Steiger in June 1886 to thank her for her gift of a painting:

> Your charming gift is as much a surprise to me as it is a delight! But – ought I to accept it? – for I fear you offer it to me under the impression that this flat is mine. I have only taken it for six months, to see whether I succeed in London or not; so it is not mine, as you appear to think. But I do hope this will not cause you to recall your gift. I admire this picture of yours greatly. It is a little jewel, and words fail me to thank you enough for it. Pray come and see it next Monday, and tell me if you like the place I choose to hang it. I shall then be better able to thank you than on paper; written thanks are always meagre. I know that it costs an artist to part with a 'child' that has grown under the hand in moments of love and insight. One 's picture is a part of oneself, more so by far than a book, for that may be multiplied by the thousand, while the painting is only one—a beloved offspring.

This same month the painter Louise Jopling met Anna. Jopling gave a glimpse into Anna's life and her reputation in her memoirs:

> In June [1886] I met that clever woman, Dr Anna Kingsford at the house of the poet, Alice Meynell.4 She invited me to a lecture, which unfortunately she could not give herself, as she was suffering from her throat. The author [Alexander Kinglake] of 'Eothen' read it for her.

Yet June was a restless month for Anna, as shown in this diary entry:

> 22 June – It is I see, nine months since I wrote a line in my diary. Time enough in which to have conceived and borne a child. And yet I am always standing on the same spot, moving my feet, indeed, but never advancing – marking time – marking time! I know what I want. I want to be away in strange places – overseas, there in the prairies of the West; there – overland, in the gorgeous South, among the palm fronds, and the broken shrines of the dead gods. Or eastward again, in the old world, where faces are brown and garments white and the stars drop out of heaven on the clear luminous nights! Or northward, among the fjords and the firs, – in Norway, in Finland, or the ice fields. Why must I stay here – here, where the Salvationists howl and blaspheme the Lord; where there are policemen and mad dogs and Societies and Journalism? And the hideous nightmare of the Devil Pasteur, blackening all the horizon with his looming shadow!
>
> Somewhere in the world is there no friend who will take me away, that I may forget this fallen Christendom? No friend with whom I may visit the solitudes that yet remain on the planet, – the long salt shores, the deep forests, the silences of earth, where still the Genii and the Spirits linger? In my dream the spray blows on my face, the stars shine, the meadows are daisy-sweet. When I was a child they always looked like that. Is it Love that I want? No, not the common vulgar cry, the cry of all sickly women-folk, the sing-song of the drawing room misses. I want a *friend*.
>
> There are too many men and women; there is too little Humanity. I had almost said there is no Humanity. There is a dearth of understanding, of nakedness of spirit. All of us are over-dressed; no man knows what heart beats in his neighbour's bosom. Truth is dead – is dead – or has she never yet come to birth?

As is common with people approaching mid-life, Anna went through a period of soul searching. Being a mystic, her fulfilment was to be found on the spiritual plane, preferably far from the madding crowd. Her passionate commitment to her causes held her in thrall to the mundane world, and she could not devise a practical alternative. It is instructive that Anna did not express a desire to go to the wilderness with Maitland, indicating they were not as close as Maitland often stated. Further, her desire for a friend suggests that Maitland did not truly fulfil her requirements for companionship.

Two months later Anna wrote to Lady Caithness from her flat in London:

34 Wynnstay Gardens, W., 19 August, 1886

Thank you so much for your very kind invitation. Yes, if the Gods are favourable, I will try to visit you for a week or two somewhere about 1 October. Next week I am going to stay with the Mount Temples at Broadlands.

Miss Dawson came unexpectedly to see me the other day, when my husband was here, and told us how kind you had been to Eadith, and said she thought the child much improved...Now that you are at Vichy, I suppose you will get on with your book. We, too, are going to try to do some literary work while on our proposed holiday. If we go on to Germany after leaving you, we shall have to be away some time. Mr M. even talks of wintering abroad, but I do not see my way to that, though I should like it very much from some points of view.—Ever yours lovingly, Anna K.

Anna's respite from her busy schedule was short but pleasant, as she wrote to her friend Miss Ethel Walker on 27 August about her visit to Broadlands:[5]

I have long been seeking a quiet half hour to talk with you, and it has come at last.

I am here for a brief while in 'Retreat,' in the midst of the most lovely country, the most perfect calm, the most glorious weather. Tomorrow I return to London; meanwhile I am at rest. This is the country seat of Lord and Lady Mount Temple, and I never saw any lovelier place. We have had Canon Wilberforce and his wife, Mr Percy Wyndham (whom you have often met at the Hermetic Society), and one or two other kindred spirits with us. How I have wished you could have been of the number! All day long we have spoken together of spiritual things – nothing else – whether through the gardens, or sitting on the sunlit lawns, or pacing the terraces under the beautiful stars at night. In the morning we have services of song and prayer and reading of the Scriptures, with exposition; and after that we meditate alone for some time. Then meet again at lunch, and spend the rest of the day in discoursing about sacred things.

I am writing this to you in my own room, while the others, under the direction of a young clergyman, are singing hymns in the oratory.

> It is indeed a convent life, only with all the beautiful surroundings of wealthy circumstances and the refined and cultured accessories which wealth procures.

Lady Georgina Mount Temple (1822-1901), the daughter of Vice-Admiral John Richard Delap Tollemache, was 'the youngest and most beautiful of nine beautiful sisters.' In 1848 she married the recently widowed William Cowper Temple (1811-1888), but they had no children. Anna and Lady Mount Temple were well suited to be friends, for 'The dominant note of Lady Mount Temple's character was her passionate indignation against cruelty and injustice...Her husband shared to the full her zeal for social service; and, as this zeal was allied with an absorbing interest in religion, ethical, and psychological problems, the result was that Broadlands became the scene of strange gatherings' from 1874 onwards.[6] In 1883 Lord Mount Temple MP was a vice president of the Victoria Street Society against vivisection, and his wife was on the central executive committee. Lady Mount Temple embraced a range of what today are called New Age spiritual beliefs.

On 19 September 1886 Maitland received a letter from 'our highly esteemed correspondent, Mrs Mary Atwood of Bridlington. Mrs Atwood (1817-1910), born Mary Anne South, was a devout student of alchemy and allied esoteric subjects. Her father was Thomas South of Bury House, Gosport, Hampshire, a man of leisure and independent means. He had a fine library of classical, philosophical and metaphysical works, many of them old and rare. Mary studied with her father and in 1850 her *A Suggestive Inquiry into the Hermetic Mystery* was published, but she soon withdrew it because she thought she had revealed too much secret knowledge. Later she said the work was incomplete and she was dissatisfied with it. In 1859 She married the Rev. Alban Atwood, vicar of Leake, near Thirsk, Yorkshire. After his death in 1883 she led a secluded life in Thirsk, though she corresponded with like-minded people such as Mrs Penny, Walter Mosely and C. C. Massey. Mme de Steiger was her good friend and republished the *Suggestive Inquiry* in 1918. Mrs Atwood's letter reads:

> I have followed—picturing to myself with amazement—the amount of your London labours this season. I was vexed to find that paper on the evolution of the true Ego so abridged in *Light,* but conclude that it will be forthcoming complete in the new edition of *The Perfect Way.* We are sorry, though not surprised, that Mrs Kingsford can find no recruit of health without going further afield. Her constitution plainly calls for more supply of vitality than those midland counties yield.

> I trust that the project of wintering in Rome will be carried out after a trial of sea air for a while after leaving Paris. Has she ever stayed at Arachon?
>
> The beautiful old priory here is an object of interest. There is an aroma to me of sanctity about it still. I will send with this a copy of the little guide, which may amuse Mrs Kingsford if she has leisure to read the rigmarole concerning the famous alchemist, Canon Ripley, etc. You are right about the Inquiry. I sent it for you to keep, please.

Anna's book *Health, Beauty and the Toilet: Letters to Ladies From a Lady Doctor* was published in 1886. As Anna stated in her preface, these letters first appeared in the *Lady's Pictorial* between the Autumn of 1884 and the Spring of 1886. The original letters were well received and gave rise to a 'large amount of correspondence' and new patients. Anna wrote:

> No lady possessing any scientific qualifications, has, hitherto, so far as I am aware, interested herself specially in the study of the 'cosmetic arts,' or attempted to instruct her sex on matters connected with the improvement and preservation of physical grace and good looks. Yet the demand for such instruction is universal, and, obviously, one who is both a woman and a doctor, competent to understand at once what is required, and the most efficient of supplying it, is, from every point of view, the fittest exponent of the subject.

A partial list of chapter headings gives an indication of the scope of the book: On Obesity; On Leanness; On the Complexion; On the Hair; On the Figure; On the Teeth; On Perfumes; On 'Baby'; On the Culture of Beauty, Grace and Health in Youth (nine chapters); and On the Hygiene and Cuisine of the Sick-Room (five chapters). Any impression that Anna was an impractical mystic lost in a world of unreality is quickly dispelled by a perusal of this book. Her advice covering a wide range of topics is eminently practical, and she obviously enjoyed writing these letters to impart her knowledge. Anna gave a number of recipes for the making of skin lotions, hair washes and tonics, and toothpaste to promote the health of her readers. This lighter writing gave Anna opportunities to express her sense of humour. For example, referring to tight lacing she wrote: '…girls are greatly mistaken if they imagine that by deliberately abandoning the form of a human creature to assume that of an insect they are commending themselves to male admiration.'[7]

Anna spent some time at the vicarage, and although she was reluctant to leave, Maitland persuaded her to seek a more favourable climate. After staying for a few days with the Kenealys at Watford, Anna departed to the Continent with Maitland. Their next stop was Ostende in Belgium to meet Mme Blavatsky. Maitland wrote they spent three 'most enjoyable ' days – 5 to 8 October – with Mme Blavatsky and her secretary and friend the Countess Wachtmeister.[8] The Countess told of the meetings between Anna and Mme Blavatsky:

> Both ladies were usually occupied with their respective work during the day, but in the evenings delightful conversations ensued, and it was interesting to me to hear different points of The Secret Doctrine discussed from the Eastern and Western standpoints of occultism. The powerful intellects of these two gifted women would be engaged in animated discussions, starting from apparently two opposite poles. Gradually the threads of their conversation would seem to approach each other, until at last they would merge in unity. Fresh topics would then arise which would be grappled with in the same masterly way. But these delightful evenings soon drew to a close, for Mrs Kingsford became very ill and was not able to leave her room, and Mr Maitland thought it expedient to take her to a warmer climate.[9]

Anna and Maitland next visited Antwerp, Bruges, and Ghent before going on to Brussels, from where Anna wrote to Lady Caithness on 12 October:

> I am so grieved to hear of your suffering. I know well how distracting a thing facial neuralgia is, having suffered from it terribly myself, both at Atcham and Ostende, where I had to go to bed in consequence and put on hot poultices. We shall remain here until we hear from you; and as I told my husband to forward letters, etc., to your care, perhaps you will keep them until we call for them, which we will do at once, if we do not become your guests. Pray do not think of undergoing any inconvenience if not well enough to receive us, for we can easily find shelter elsewhere. Miss Dawson will take me in. While at Ostende we stayed nearly three days with Madame Blavatsky, at her urgent request. She was very genial and hospitable, and we got on together admirably. She is hard at work on *The Secret Doctrine*, which promises to be a larger book than even *Isis*. I trust most earnestly to see a letter in your own handwriting in a day or two announcing your recovery from the sad pain you have been so long enduring. How is it you did not mention to us before this that you were suffering? We should not then have ventured to think of trespassing on you.—Yours always most affectionately, A.K.

When in Paris, Anna continued her task of exposing to the world Pasteur's cruelty to animals in his experiments. However, her activities were soon to be cut short by an occurrence which had tragic consequences. Anna related the events in a letter to Florence Miller. It reads in part:

> One horribly wet day, November 17 [1886] last, I took into my head to visit M. Pasteur's laboratory. I waded across Paris in the sleet and mud, and stood a long time in wet boots and clothes, and got back at last after about five hours, soaked to the skin. Result, severe neuralgia and inflammation of the lungs. Inflammation did not dry up as it should, but got 'cheesy,' and, after I had been in bed a month, I began to spit blood. I had a cough that was almost incessant, and, after many doctors had debated over me, I was informed that my best chance was the Riviera. Husband came over, and we started.[10]

Notes

1. Dworkin, 303.
2. Atwood, 596.
3. *Life and Work of Thomas Hardy,* 185.
4. Alice Meynell (1847-1922), a friend of Anna, became a Roman Cotholic in 1872. In 1877 she married the journalist Wilfrid Meynell and bore eight children. Alice 's poetry reflected her faith, and she also wrote essays.
5. Ethel Walker (1861-1951) was the daughter of Arthur Abney Walker, a Yorkshireman and a member of the firm of iron founders who built Southwark Bridge. In Ethel's late twenties she studied art seriously and became the leading woman painter of her generation. Her paintings of women were particularly admired. She corresponded with Dr Elizabeth Blackwell in the 1890s. Ethel also took an interest in Theosophy and donated two of her visionary paintings, the 'Zone of Love ' and the 'Zone of Hate,' to the Tate gallery in 1946. She was a small active woman with a 'deep husky voice ' and an 'extremely interesting personality.' In 1943 she was created a Dame.
6. Russell, 281.
7. Kingsford 1886, 93.
8. Countess Constance Georgina Louise Wachtmeister (1838-1910). In 1863 she married her cousin, Count Karl Wachtmeister (1823-1871), a Scandinavian diplomat. In 1879 she investigated spiritualism, but found it unsatisfactory. In 1881 Countess Wachtmeister joined the Theosophical Society and first met Mme Blavatsky in London in April 1884. She became a close friend of Mme Blavatsky and worked tirelessly for the Society.
9. Wachtmeister, 58.
10. Letter from Anna to Florence Miller dated April 1887, reprinted in Florence 's obituary of Anna in the *Lady's Pictorial.*

Chapter - 16

Dying is a Very Slow Process

Anna was now seriously ill, so she took a course of action many people in her condition followed in the nineteenth century: she headed for the south of France and Italy, seeking a beneficial climate. On 13 December, 1886 Anna moved to the Dawsons' place in Paris, where Eadith was staying. The Burtons arrived in Paris from London on 13 January 1887 and visited Anna, who 'cheered up a little ' at seeing them. Sir Richard Burton, perceiving Anna's parlous state, wrote in his journal, 'Here we parted with my wife 's friend and colleague in philanthropy, Anna Kingsford, M.D. She was in the last stage of consumption, suffering from mind and soul, distressed at the sight and sound connected with vivisection. Her sensitive organisation braved these horrors in order to serve and succour, but both she and my wife could not help feeling that their efforts were in vain.'1 Burton advised Maitland he favoured Tenerife as the best place for Anna.

However, Anna and Maitland decided to follow the advice of Dr Lutaud, whom Anna knew from her crusade against Pasteur. He recommended Saint Raphael in the French Riviera, and on 15 February she and Maitland were on their way, accompanied by Algernon, who had joined them in Paris. The doctors said Anna's left lung was too far gone, and she had only a few weeks or months to live. Meanwhile, 'thanks to her indomitable will,' Anna kept up her weekly medical letter, and her answers to readers, for the *Lady's Pictorial,* and also her monthly article for an American magazine.

On arriving at Marseilles Anna relayed her news to Lady Caithness at her Winter home in Nice:

> By the time this reaches you we shall be at St Raphael, Hôtel Beau Rivage. My husband is with me. We came on Tuesday 15th, in

wagonsalon, and arrived here today at[1] am, more dead than alive – at least I was. Mr M. has been passing most of his time with Baron Spedalieri, and will spend the evening with him.[2] I want my husband to go over to Nice and see the next Battle of the Flowers, but I fear he won't like to leave me, which is a pity, for he won't have another chance. We find the weather bitterly cold, and not at all what we expected. Lady Burton is at Cannes.[3]

On 20 February 1887 Anna wrote to Lady Caithness about how she froze to the bone in St Raphael:

My husband thanks you for your kind invitation, which, however, he could not accept because of the sore throat given him by the bitter cold. Today he is quite laid up, and has written to decline Mrs Thursby Pelham's invitation to lunch with her on Monday and see the Battle of the Flowers. I never felt such cold; it is glacial. We shiver all day, and can only get warm in bed. We have very nice rooms, all en suite, full south. Looking over the sea, but at present I have seen little of the beauties of the place, as I dare not leave the hotel. Lady Burton, at Cannes, writes that she is also laid up with cold, as are other friends of ours at Beaulieu; so that altogether the slings and arrows of this wintrytime seem to have done fell work!

Since I wrote the first page of this letter we have been out for our first walk together. As it is my first walk since the beginning of my illness on 17 November, you may suppose it has been quite an event. We only went a very little way along the shore, but still it is a beginning. I am hoping now that before this week is over we may be able to take a trip to Nice, though I fear we shall see nothing of the Carnival.

After my husband has gone home to England, Mr M[aitland] and I think of going on to Naples, and then spending Easter in Rome. I have always longed so much to see Rome, and especially at Easter.

You must let me know how your ball went off. Send me a paper about it. St Raphael knows nothing of the Carnival; it is as quiet as you please. My doctor (Lutaud) comes this week, and, I expect, will come to see me whether tomorrow or the next day. He is the editor of the *Journal de Medécine*, and is Pasteur's bitterest enemy. Hence we are already quiet comrades. I should like to get a sight of Nice in the season. When I saw it the Promenade de Anglais was quite desolate. Moreover, I want to see your beautiful house, about which I have heard so much.

I am trying out find out whether I can make the journey to Nice and back in the same day.

Always your loving Nina.[4]

Although Anna and Maitland found the scenery of St Raphael 'charming,' the sun was intense and the wind bitterly cold. Early in the morning on 23 February a severe earthquake struck the Riviera. Algernon and Anna pounded on Maitland's door asking what they should do. He advised they go back to bed and wait it out. On hearing the subterranean rumbles which preceded each shock they called out to each other, 'Here comes another.' Luckily they were not injured, but considerable damage occurred over a large area and there were numerous casualties.

After seeing Algernon off on his return to England, Anna and Maitland arrived at Nice on the evening of 8 March. Their lodgings in Nice were badly damaged by the earthquake, so they didn't go to bed, but spent the whole night pacing their rooms, burning stramonium (Jimson weed) for Anna's asthma, sipping hot coffee, and fighting off swarms of mosquitoes. Next day when they informed Lady Caithness of their predicament, she sent her carriage round to take them to the Hôtel Cosmopolitan, which they found to be entirely satisfactory. In the afternoon they called on Lady Caithness in her beautiful home, the Palais Tiranty. Maitland wanted to hurry on to Naples, but Anna was reluctant to leave her friend so soon. Besides, having invited Baron Spedalieri to their hotel, they spent three satisfying days with him conversing on Hermetic topics of mutual interest.

Anna particularly enjoyed the scenic drives she took with Lady Caithness, and the popular Battle of the Flowers. This was a parade of carriages decorated with flowers which drove up and down the Promenade des Anglais while the occupants tossed bouquets to one another. It was instituted by the festival committee in 1876 to attract and entertain the Winter visitors.[5] Maitland wrote about this occasion and the change in Anna:

> The scene was bright and animated in the extreme, and Mary enjoyed it vastly, showing a gaiety and vivacity which made for me the most vivid and saddening contrast with her actual state, only too plainly visible to me, as I sat opposite her [in the carriage], in the lines of her wan and wasted face, which were so strongly brought out by the brilliant sunlight as to confirm the worst anticipations of the results of her malady. But, as was characteristic of her, excitement lifted her into another sphere, where all consciousness of the lower was lost, and

> even the apprehensions expressed by me of the danger of her exposure to the keen wind that was blowing seemed to her unfounded.[6]

Anna and Maitland left Nice on 20 March for Genoa, heading for Rome. They cancelled Naples from their itinerary as Anna had heard animals in the streets were cruelly treated. As arranged, they met her brother General Joseph Bonus at Genoa, and also the owners of a flat in Kensington they were planning to lease. In Pisa, while Maitland was inspecting an hotel, Anna saw from the carriage where she was waiting a boy ill-treating a dog. She rushed to the other side of the piazza and shook the offender vigorously, forcing him to release the poor animal. When the boy called out to a man who appeared to be his father, she beat a hasty retreat into the hotel. She showed Maitland her broken parasol and said 'if she was to stay in Rome, she must get her a stout stick to carry, as she could not keep her hands off ruffians who illtreated animals.'[7]

In April Maitland sent a circular to members of the Hermetic Society informing them of Anna's illness and the impossibility of holding a session that year. It was too early to return to England as Anna's new home would not be available until July. Maitland summoned John Bonus to join them, which was a 'vast relief ' to Maitland and a 'great comfort' to Anna. They left Rome on 21 May and visited in turn Siena, Florence, Parma, Milan, Turin, Chambery, Clermont-Ferrand, and Royat, reaching La Bourboule in central France on 17 June. At Florence Anna and Maitland called on a stroke afflicted Dr Gryzanowski and his wife. They were much saddened to see their 'venerated friend' in such an enfeebled condition.

Anna's brother John left her and Maitland at the health resort of Bourboule-les-Bains where Anna wrote despairingly in her diary on 5 July 1887:

> Not cured yet! No, nor even mended, were it but a little. Still the cough, still the afternoon fever, still the weakness, still the neuralgia. From November to July the same continual malady and enforced idleness. Where now are all the projects I had formed for this year, the book I had to write on the Creed, the novel, the stories, the essays? I have past a year of bitterest suffering, of weariness of spirit and torment of body. My left lung is in caverns, they say; my right is inflamed chronically. My voice is broken and gone, with which I had hoped to speak from platforms; wreck and ruin is made of all my expectancies. Can a miracle yet be wrought? Can will accomplish what medicine fails to perform? The hard thing is that I cannot will heartily, for lack of knowing what I ought to desire. Is it better for me to live or to die? Unless I can be

> restored to the possibility of public life, it is useless for me to live. Dying, I may the sooner obtain a fresh incarnation and return to do my work more completely.[8]

Anna returned to London and took up residence at 15 Wynnstay Gardens on 15 July 1887. Her maid was already there, and Algernon speedily joined them, visiting whenever he could spare time away from his parish. Electric bells were installed in the rooms to ensure Anna could summon assistance whenever required. She was placed under the charge of Dr William Henry White, an old friend of Algernon's, who did not charge a fee for treating a fellow doctor.[9] 'It was clear from the first that he considered the case hopeless,' wrote Maitland.

Anna was philosophical about her condition when she wrote in her diary on 3 August:

> Dying is a very slow process. Save that I am a little weaker, a little thinner, and my cough a little more frequent, I am in the same state as when I made my last memoranda at La Bourbuole. It does not appear to me possible now that I should recover. I expect to die this autumn; for I am sure I will not survive the first frosts:
>
> O Death, rock me to sleep!
>
> Give me my rest!
>
> Let pass my weary ghost
>
> Out of my breast.
>
> Life is a fever; death is convalescence. Life is a fury and a brawl; Death is sweet peace and quietness. It is a black and hateful planet on which I am now incarnate, and to be away and rid of its abominations will be all for joy. I shall go to the Gods; I shall see my Master, Hermes, the Teacher and queenly Athena and their holy Angels.

On 14 August Maitland wrote that Anna was feeling 'extraordinarily low' due 'partly to a chill caught when out in a wheel-chair in Kensington Gardens on Friday last, but mostly to the fatigue of seeing some visitors on Saturday, one of whom stayed a long time and affected her very disagreeably by reason of the uncongenial nature of his magnetic aura.'

On 16 August 1887 Anna made her will, appointing as executors Algernon, her brother in law the Rev. Edward Gilliat, and George Butler Lloyd of Shrewsbury. The last sentence of her will reads, 'I hereby declare that I am the person commonly known in the Medical profession as Anna

Kingsford.' She signed her name 'Annie Kingsford.' The will was witnessed by Lady Caithness and her son. George Lloyd (1853-1930), a good friend of Algernon, was mayor of Shrewsbury in 1887 and 1889, and an MP from 1913 to 1922.

Despite her pain, Anna was most distressed by her inactivity, as her diary entry of 23 August shows:

> When the Feast of the Assumption came round this year, I was too ill to write even my customary prayers for little Rufus. But I thought of him, and prayed for him in my heart. I wish I knew whether I am to recover or not. It seems, judging from physical signs, as if I could not live long; but then strange things happen where prophetesses are concerned! I am so sure that the prophecy is not finished, and that a vast amount of work remains to do which must be done by me, or not at all, that I cannot but think the Gods will restore me in time. Meanwhile the suffering and exhaustion are very bad indeed to bear. Of all my pains, the enforced idleness is the worst. To rise at eleven; to crawl – not dressed, but only wrapped up in a loose gown – from the bedroom to the drawing-room; to sink wearily into an easy-chair, and to lie there all day – hour after hour – with idle hands and nothing to mark the progress of the time except the coming on of the afternoon fever and its slow departure; to creep wearily back to bed at night, and lie propped up with pillows and racked with cough all the dreary night – this now represents the routine of my life, and this is now the eleventh month of my illness.
>
> And all the while my spirit is alive and beating its wings like a caged wild-bird against the bars of this body of death, longing to be away, out yonder in the clear high blue of the supernal height, longing to break forth as of old into song – into song, and to search out the secrets of the Lords of Dawn. O sweet, sharp wind blowing between the turfy spaces of the hills, laden with bean and clover scents, I feel you on my face! I greet you. You are full of health and comfort. Deep, deep dome of holy sky, up there above the fir trees, I look towards reverently. I know you are the bosom of the Father wherein the Son, our Lord, dwelleth. But upon the glory of his face I cannot look, I shade my eyes. I salute the beautiful dappled lights of it, lying here and there under the trees along the woodland pathway.

It was not until September that Anna ceased writing for the *Lady's Pictorial*, forced at last to 'confess herself beaten.' Maitland wrote in the last year of her life she earned nearly one thousand pounds from all sources connected with her profession. Still fighting for the animals, she wrote her last letter to the press, the *Pall Mall Gazette,* on 14 September, 1887:

> Fur And Feathers
>
> Sir,
>
> Mr Punch's lines against the massacre of birds for dress, reprinted in your issue for this evening, are very pretty, and their sentiment very sound. But, alas! the birds are not the only or the worst sufferers in the interests of our fine ladies. The horrors of the seal-fishery are infinitely worse in their heart-rendering details than anything Mr Punch has depicted. It is some years that I satisfied myself that the fur trade, and the sealskin trade in particular, were incompatible with the gentle life it should be the aim of civilised beings to lead, and since that time there have been no furs in my wardrobe. There are, however, certain feathers which are obtainable without slaughter, and, I am assured, without cruelty – ostrich-feathers, the plumes being cut yearly from the birds, which are kept in large numbers for the purpose and well treated. Ostrich-feather muffs, boas, and trimmings are extremely pretty, warm, and more hygienic than furs, because they are permeable to the air and do not shut in the transpiration of the skin as furs do.
>
> Your obedient servant.
>
> Anna Kingsford, M.D.

In her *Autobiography* Florence Fenwick Miller wrote sadly of her last meeting with Anna in November 1887:

> Her beauty seemed hardly faded, and she made a charming picture, dressed in a long black satin gown and using a large red fan, as she lay on the couch in her drawing-room. She had no grey hairs, no perceptible wrinkles, and her complexion was still lovely! Yet it was to me a painful interview; for I was but too well instructed in the delusive bloom and the hopefulness which are characteristic, indeed pathognomic, signs of advanced consumption in many cases. She said to me:
>
> 'Medically speaking, I know I am dying, but I cannot believe it. My mind, my soul, all that makes *me*, is as alive as ever, and I cannot realize that it is finished.'
>
> Yet though she knew that I should be only too well aware how her case stood, she could not refrain from presently asking me if I thought she

> might be able to resume her work at Christmas? It was with a lump in my throat that I replied that she must wait for the Spring and its warmer weather for that – knowing that it could never be.

In her obituary of Anna, Florence also wrote about her last visit to her friend:

> She was terribly ill, but her gay spirits and her beauty of face were almost undiminished. 'I think my face eats on its own account,' she said, 'it absorbs the cold cream I give it. My arms are thin enough!' She knew, reasonably speaking, how very ill she was, and that her recovery was impossible. 'But, I cannot feel that I am going to die,' she declared, 'life, all that makes me, my intellect, my feelings are so keen – as acute as they ever were; how can I believe that it is all over with me.' She said it cheerfully – nay, stoically, but it was a painful moment. With the extraordinary hopefulness of consumption, she then began to talk about beginning some new literary work 'at Christmas.' She asked me to find her a lady to read Greek and Latin poets with her,'for I may as well make use of my involuntary leisure,' she added.

The last entry Anna made in her diary was on 26 December 1887, 'In the night or early morning of this day – Christmas night – Piggy died. She had suffered a long time.' Piggy number two had been Anna's guinea pig since 1885. Anna was much relieved, because she had not been able to find a suitable home for the creature. Maitland noted,' "I am so thankful Piggy has gone first," she more than once remarked.'

On 2 January 1888, when Anna rallied briefly, Dr White called in Sir Andrew Clark for the second time. Sir Andrew, born in 1827 in Scotland, was a specialist in consumption and lung diseases. Anna asked her Catholic friend Mrs Alice Meynell if she could find her a nurse, and a nun was dispatched. According to Maitland, the nun was more interested in claiming Anna for the Church than helping her. Without permission, the nun called in a priest to give Anna the last rites, which she accepted just for the sake of the experience.[10]

Anna decided against cremation to spare possible difficulties for Algernon, in particular 'offending the prejudices of the rustic population of his parish, who would inevitably visit their disapprobation on A… "I see now," she remarked, "cremation is the best plan in itself, and for the generality; but it is not best for me, placed as I am in regard to others, and it would be selfish in me to persist." '[11] Anna wished to be buried in a 'spot in the Atcham Churchyard, on the edge of the Severn's bank, above the reach of floods, in view of the vicarage windows, and where she had been wont to stroll, gathering herbs for her pets, or watching the sunset gleaming on the river.'

Maitland wrote, 'As is characteristic of consumption, the approach of the end was marked by increased hopefulness on the part of the sufferer, leading her to fancy she was actually mending, and might yet recover, even though at death's door.' At times Anna would 'forget her pains and be even blithe and cheerful, especially when the sister had retired to rest.' Maitland would wheel her into the parlour to sit beside him at his meals, and she told him of her conversations with the sister. Anna still received 'glorious' illuminations; '"But," she would add tearfully, "I am too weak now to retain the particulars so as to tell you, or to write them down." '

Release was a long time coming, but it came at last. Anna Kingsford's immortal soul left its earthen vessel in the small hours of 22 February 1888. Her age was forty one years and five months.

One of the first friends to pay her respects was Mme de Steiger, who gave a graphic description of what she saw:

> One day I received a telegram, when I was living at Bedford Park, asking me to go to Wynnstay Mansions without delay, as Mrs Kingsford had died during the night. I knew she was ill, but periods of illness came and went, so I was taken by surprise. I was met at the door of their flat by Mr Maitland and Mr Kingsford (the nurse was in the background), *both* with streaming eyes and truly woebegone faces. They had also somehow been taken by surprise. Did *they* think she could not die? I fear so, but do not know for certain. In any case we mourned without a shadow of any other feeling but that she was actually gone from earth. We loved her dear and beautiful presence. When they took me to the bedside where she lay I was indeed startled by what I saw. I expected to see a lovely ivory-hued goddess-like body with a smile of beatific happiness at having escaped from the imprisonment of a suffering body, but instead I saw a tiny doll-like form, a small, yellow, shrivelled effigy, not Mrs Kingsford, but 'her remains.' I put the veil back, laid my wreath at her feet and retreated, and my tears seemed dried up. I said to the men, 'She was never completely alive physically in this world. We never had her!'
>
> It seemed to me that her spiritual body was only able to be half incarnate – beautiful and suitable though her physical body was. But truly her corpse seemed to me very much like that of the famous

> sorceress 'She,' when she suddenly resumed her old body at the fire.[12] It was a shock to me and a stern reminder of the small value of material things.

Towards the end of her reminiscences Mme de Steiger wrote of Anna:

> She had indeed found her place in Valhalla, and could not therefore remain long with us, but she will stand out by her writing as a type of lovable and most exquisite soul; the kind of woman who, while one felt she was not in this world, yet had the on ne sait quoi in her nature which raised one 's interest in this world to the highest point. She at once put one, along with herself, on a high platform of thought, for which one ever after felt

The cause of death on Anna's death certificate reads 'Pulmonary Phthisis several years, Asthenia Certified by W. H. White, M.D.' The entry under occupation reads, 'Wife of Algernon Godfrey Kingsford, Clerk in Holy Orders.' This reflects the social attitudes of the day, for despite her profession as a doctor, Anna was considered first and foremost to be a 'wife.' Algernon G. Kingsford was the informant and it is stated he was 'In attendance.' His residence was given as 15 Wynnstay Gardens, that is, Anna's flat. This indicates he must have been staying with Anna in London for some time.

Anna's funeral took place at Atcham on Wednesday 29 February, 1888. It was fully reported in the *Salopian Shreds and Patches* 14 March 1888:

> FUNERAL OF THE LATE DR ANNA KINGSFORD
>
> The remains of Dr Anna Kingsford were interred in Atcham churchyard, on Wednesday, the proceedings being exceedingly simple, yet none the less impressive. The coffin, which was of polished oak, with brass furniture, was borne from the rectory to the church by some half-dozen men belonging to the village, and was followed by the Rev. A.G. Kingsford (husband of the deceased lady), Mr John Bonus, Mr Henry Bonus, Major-General Joseph Bonus and Mr Schroder Bonus (brothers), Mr Maitland (London), Mr G.B. Lloyd (Shrewsbury), Mr Burton (Longner), &c. As the procession entered the church the 'Dead March' in Saul was played, and the funeral service commenced with the hymn 'The radiant morn hath passed away' and concluded with 'Now the labourer's work is o'er,' both being feelingly sung by the choir. The officiating clergyman was the Rev. Edward Bonus, rector of

Bucklandwith- Hulcote, Bucks. The coffin was lowered into its last resting place – an ordinary grave – in the midst of a heavy snowstorm, and in the presence of perhaps not more than a score of spectators.

Very beautiful wreaths, or crosses, were sent by the following: – the 'Victoria Street and International Society for the protection of animals from vivisection: With sincere condolences;' 'From the London Anti-Vivisection Society, as a small token of very heartfelt gratitude for very many years of earnest devotion to the cause of poor animals;' 'With kind sympathy: From Mr and Mrs G.B. Lloyd;' 'With deep sympathy: Mrs E.M. James, 10 Pelham Place, South Kensington;' 'In ever-loving memory : From Ethelind Bonus;'[14] 'To Annie's dear memory: From Emily;' 'To my dear mother: With her sorrowing daughter's deepest love;' 'From Lady Eleanor Harbord.'[15] Lady Mount-Temple also sent a splendid wreath composed of violets.

Later a cross was erected over the grave, bearing the inscription on the top two of three base stones:

In Loving Memory of

ANNIE KINGSFORD, M.D.

WHO DIED

February 22nd 1888

After Anna died the Catholic papers *The Weekly Register* and *The Tablet* falsely claimed Anna returned to the Church on her deathbed. Both Algernon and Maitland wrote letters to the papers forcefully refuting this claim.[16]

Maitland, on returning to the flat in Kensington, received a number of letters of condolence from friends. Lady Caithness wrote with compassion from Nice on 25 February:

Your sad news reached me this morning, and has naturally affected me very much; though I knew how *very, very* ill she was, yet I always fancied she would recover. I thought she was an instrument in the hands of those who would be powerful to protect her for their work. I fancy that they must be as deeply grieved as we are that she should be called away from earth just when she seems, *to us* at least, to be the most wanted. Of course we are but short-sighted mortals; and, after all, her withdrawal *may* ultimately prove to be for the advantage of the great cause in which she was the foremost worker. I shall not be at all surprised to hear before long that you will *feel* her presence, and that she will be able to accomplish much more through you than she could have done henceforward *with* you. Perhaps she had to go first that she might thus work through you, instead of having to seek for another; and to this hope I now cling.

But, my poor friend, my heart bleeds for you in your loneliness. What will you ever do without her glorious companionship, to which you have now been accustomed so many years. And at Atcham! in that lonely little study, without her bright presence, what will you do?

Oh! It is too sad to think of you thus all alone, and with no sympathetic nature with whom to share your thought; and then to see that sad grave! Still, perhaps, she can come sooner to you there than anywhere else; for you will be surrounded by her *aura* and influence. Every book on the shelves will seem to you part of herself. I am so glad I have been at Atcham, and can see you there, but always with her! Poor Mrs Kingsford! And Eadith too! My poor, darling, sweet, lovely friend, it seems impossible I shall never see her again, or receive her beautiful letters. I shall always keep her portrait before me. I thought as long as I kept the little one where she is in the same frame with you, and the Holy spirit in the shape of a Dove between you, that she would live on; but there it is before me, and you are alone! I am going to write to the Mount-Temples to tell them the sad news. Let me hear from you as often as you can. And oh! Pray remember that I feel deeply for you, and sympathise most affectionately in your grief.

Your affectionate old friend, Marie Caithness.

Lady Mount-Temple also expressed her deep feelings:

Cirniez, 25 February, 1888

Dear Mr Maitland,

What a blow! I thought she would be restored to us. What will you do? Can you live without her? *Where* is she? Is she near you? I have told Broadlands to send a wreath. Will you lay it over her beautiful body, with love in every leaf? I long to pour it out warm and living from my heart over her, noble, lovely creature, the friend of God, woman, and the lowest creatures! What a dreadful loss to poor Earth! Dear Mr Maitland, tell me some time that you are not in despair. Tell me if I can do anything for you. Count me your friend to the end of the chapter—and *beyond,* I hope.

Yours ever, and *hers,* Georgina Mt.-Temple.

Lady Wilde sent a card inscribed, 'With deep grief for the loss of one of the noblest and most gifted of Englishwomen.' She later penned these perceptive remarks about Anna to Maitland:

> Reading her writings, I at once appreciate the deep thought, vivid imagination, and great learning displayed in them. Truly she was a great light in the world, gifted beyond her sex, with strange insight for the deep and mystic things of the spirit. Much of her nature is now a revelation to me. I wish I had known her better while she was present here. She was but half-understood by all of us. Her queenly social graces were so striking that we rested there in admiration, while the inspired prophet-nature within her was not recognized as it merited, nor her ceaseless efforts in all she wrote to lift the Human to the divine.

Elma Stuart, a writer and friend of the novelist George Eliot, sent her commiserations to Maitland from Montreux:

> …I tenderly love her and with my whole heart and soul admired her – even for me there is a blank that can never be filled. The world will not now know its loss, *but it is very great.* She was a Power for good in it. Ah! who is left like her at all? And what is in her place?…Even now I can hardly realise it, hardly believe it. It seems too dreadful. We are all bereaved – all robbed of something that made life better and higher, more worth living, more lovely.

The *London World* published an obituary which was reprinted in *The New York Times* of 18 March 1888:

> The death was announced a few days ago of Mrs Anna Kingsford, M.D. of Paris, one of Pasteur's determined opponents in this country. Mrs Kingsford was a clever woman in many ways. She spoke once at a meeting of the Hermetic society, of which she was president, and she seemed both clear and logical in her remarks, and, indeed, the only intelligible remarks made at the meeting were made by her. She was a vegetarian for some 16 years or more before her death, but whether it was wise for a woman with diseased lungs to give up meat and wine is a question. She had the most perfectly bloodless complexion, and was under 40 [*sic*]. Delicate vegetarian women had better take warning by her death.

John Bonus sprang to the defence of his maligned sister with a letter to the *London World*:

> You appear to have seen, in my sister, Mrs Kingsford's death, a moral against Vegetarianism. As I was responsible for her adoption of that regimen, I beg to say that my sister was herself convinced it had been of the greatest advantage to her health and to the increase of her physical powers. In recognition of its value to her in the pursuit of her successful studies, she inscribed to me the original edition of her wellknown dissertation. This conviction of hers was fully shared by my brother Kingsford (himself not a Vegetarian), and by all those competent to form one on the subject.
>
> Mrs Kingsford died of phthisis supervening on severe pneumonia, which she brought upon herself by getting drenched in the rain on her way to M. Pasteur's laboratory, in the winter of last year, and by remaining there several hours in her wet clothes, letting them dry upon her body. I have known several persons killed in precisely the same way who were not Vegetarians. Had she *not* been a Vegetarian, she would, in all likelihood, have succumbed to the primary inflammation at once. The martyr-spirit was never a prudent frame of mind from the more usual point of view, and she died a martyr to the scrupulous conscientiousness with which she followed M. Pasteur's experiments and processes, the fallacies of which, as she considered them to be, she was desirous to make patent to all, as is well known in the scientific world.
>
> There is no man, I conceive, sir, less likely than you to wish to give currency to a misrepresentation of facts, and so you will gladly give insertion, I think, to this short letter.
>
> John Bonus
>
> Felixstowe, 6 March [1888]
>
> P.S. The description of Mrs Kingsford's complexion as 'perfectly bloodless' is quite inaccurate. She had the normal complexion of a refined and beautiful woman of her type.[17]

The journalist and spiritualist William T. Stead (1849-1912) recorded his vivid impressions of Anna in his review of her biography by Maitland:

> I remember Anna Kingsford. Who that ever met her can forget that marvelous embodiment of a burning flame in the form of a woman. Divinely tall and not less divinely fair! I think it is just about ten years since I first met her. It was at the office of the Pall Mall Gazette, which

I was editing in those days. She did not always relish the headings I put to her articles. She was as innocent as the author of *The Bothie of Toberna-Vuolich* of the necessity of labeling goods in your shop-window in such a way as to attract attention, but we were always on good terms, being united by the strong tie of common antipathies. I saw her once at her own place, when, I remember, she wore a bright red flower – I thought it was a great gladiolus, but it may have been a cactus, which lay athwart her breast like a sword of flame.

Her movements had somewhat of the grace and majesty that we associate with the Greek gods; and, as for her speech – well, I have talked to many of the men and women who have in this generation had the greatest repute as conversationalists, but I never in my life met Anna Kingsford's equal. From her silver tongue as in a stream, 'strong without wrath, without o'erflowing full,' her sentences flowed in one unending flood. She talked literature. Had an endless phonograph been fitted up before her so as to be constantly in action, the cylinders might have been carried to the printer, and the copy set up without transcription or alteration. Never was she at a loss for a word, never did she tangle her sentences, or halt for an illustration. It was almost appalling after a time. It appeared impossible for her to run dry, for you seemed to feel that copious as was her speech, it was but as a rivulet carrying off the overflow of the ocean which lay behind. What a strange creature she was! Utterly incomprehensible, and therefore cruelly misunderstood by those who did not know her, and by some of those who thought they did. She was one of the most interesting and fascinating of the women of the Victorian era.[18]

The journalist and writer George R. Sims (1847-1922) also praised Anna:

Dr Anna Kingsford was a lovely woman, with classical features and a mass of wonderful golden hair. I think she was the most beautiful 'clever' woman I have ever known. She told me one evening at a dance at my mother's house that she would like above all things to see a rehearsal of a pantomime, and George Conquest[19] kindly gave me a box. I could see that everyone on the stage was struck by the ethereal beauty of my companion. After the rehearsal was over, when I had gone behind to speak to Conquest, he told me that whenever he had looked at the box that evening he felt as if he were entertaining an angel unawares.

And then I told him that he had been.[20]

Notes

1. Burton, 333
2. Baron Nicolas-Joseph Spedalieri (1812- d. after 1887) was born in Siciliy of an ancient family. In his twenties he became interested in magic and the esoteric and about 1842 he moved to France. On meeting Eliphas Levi in 1861 he became not only a follower but a friend. Sharing the same religious views, the Baron corresponded with Anna and Maitland.
3. *Life*, II. 301
4. Ibid., II. 303.
5. Haug, 51.
6. *Life*, II. 306.
7. Ibid., II. 308.
8. Ibid., II 322
9. Dr White (b.1849 Ireland) was a distinguished physician who received his M.D. in 1877 and his M.A. in 1879 in Dublin He became a member of the Royal College of Physicians, London in 1882. He held various posts including pathologist and assistant physician at the Royal Hospital for Diseases of the Chest in 1884.
10. *Life*, II 355
11. *Life*, II. 359
12. de Steiger, p.169. Mme de Steiger was referring to Rider Haggard's novel *She* (1887), wherein the captivating heroine Ayesha tried renew herself with fire, but something went wrong and she shriveled up and shrank to the size of a monkey before passing away. In his book The *Crystal and the Way of Light* (1993), the Tibetan Dzoghen lama, Norbu Nankhai, has related cases where advanced Tibetan lamas have shrunk to the size of a small child after death, and after seven days their bodies have disappeared. Nankhai explained that because of their advanced spiritual evolution, the bodies of these lamas did not decompose, but were absorbed into the Body of Light. This could be the explanation as to why Anna's body shrank after her soul passed on.
13. Ibid., 299.
14. Ethelind Bonus was John Bonus' daughter.
15. Lady Eleanor Harbord (c.1851-6 to1905) must have known Anna through a mutual interest in esoteric matters, for in 1893-1894 she was a member of the Golden Dawn. (Gilbert, 151) In 1900 Lady Harbord obtained a divorce from her second husband, Major Walter Harbord, on the grounds of adultery and cruelty.
16. Ralph Shirley's remarks amplify this situation: 'Perhaps in no single point does Roman Catholicism present a worse and more undesirable aspect than in the manner in which its missionaries besiege the last hours of the passing soul in the effort to induce its victims, when too weak for resistance, to say "ditto" to the formulae which their priests pretend to regard as constituting a password to the celestial realms. Certainly, in Anna Kingsford's case, the admission of a Roman Catholic sister to tend her in her last illness was productive of the worst results,

troubling her last hours with an unseemly wrangle that did not cease even after her body was consigned to its final resting place.' (*Occultists and Mystics of All Ages*, 167)

17. Forward, 123.
18. Stead wrote a nine page review of *Anna Kingsford: Her Life, Letters, Diary and Work* in *The Review of Reviews*, 15 January 1896. He observed, 'Mr Kingsford appears to have been an ideal husband for the woman whom he chose, and so absolutely devoid of jealousy.' Stead had the singular misfortune of going down with the *Titanic* in 1912.
19. George Conquest was an actor-manager who for many years staged popular pantomimes at the Grecian Theatre, London.
20. Sims, 54.

Chapter - 17

After Anna

Anna's mother survived her daughter by less than one month, passing away at her home in St Leonards on 19 March 1888. In her will she was very particular in distributing her possessions to various members of her family. All Anna's water colour drawings went to Eadith, together with a gold bracelet, and a gold brooch in which Anna's photograph was set. The gross value of the estate was a tidy £12,066, with Eadith being granted one eighth of the residue.

Anna's will was proved in Shrewsbury by Algernon and George Lloyd on 4 May 1888. The gross value of her estate was £534.10.2, the net value £423.12.1. Underneath these amounts is written, 'Resworn July 1889 £887.11.0.' (This was worth £57,906 in 2002.) Anna bequeathed to Algernon for the rest of his life the annual income from her trust fund. Eadith received her 'jewelry and trinkets of every description.' Maitland was given a life interest and share in the books they had jointly purchased, and those they had written together. She left all her unpublished manuscripts to him, and on his decease, bequeathed them to Algernon 'absolutely.' Maitland also received the monies in her account at the London and County Bank and 'all investments, securities, stock, shares and business interests and all other monies whatsoever not accruing to me under my Father's Will for his life.' In addition to this 177 generous bequest, Maitland also received Anna's furniture, fixtures and effects at 15 Wynnstay Gardens, Kensington.

In May 1888 Maitland moved into No. 1 Thurloe Square Studios, Thurloe Square, South Kensington. The studios attracted him because they were new and he favoured the 'large, lofty, and well-lit rooms.' He wanted to mend his broken health and to carry on his and Anna's work. Anna had made him 'her literary executor and trustee, and bequeathed to [him] the few hundred pounds saved of her professional earnings,' to be spent publishing her 'literary remains' and furthering their work.

During the Summer of 1888 Maitland prepared Anna's *Dreams and Dream Stories* for publication. The dreams occurred between 1876 and 1887, with the most, ten in number, occurring in 1877. In her preface Anna wrote, 'So far I have not yet met with any one in whom the dreaming faculty appears to be either so strongly or so strangely developed as in myself.' She saw an 'intelligent purpose' in her dreams which gave 'priceless insights and illuminations' into 'many difficulties and enigmas of life, and even religion.' Anna had no theory to offer to explain her dreams, and as a person with a medical education, she was familiar with the various theories put forward by 'medical experts.' She was sure that 'hysteria' and other conventional explanations of dreams did not apply to her.

Anna did not wish to explain her dreams, except to say 'the majority are obviously allegorical.' She found 'dry air, high levels, and a crisp, calm exhilarating atmosphere' favoured her dreaming faculty. She noted that fasting, in her case and among the ancients, promoted cognitive dreams. She had expanded some of her dreams into stories which were published in various magazines.

Towards the end of that year William Butler Yeats met Maitland and recorded his impressions in a letter to Katharine Tynan dated 21 December 1888:

> I met Maitland at Lady Wildes last week; he talked much of Mrs Kingsford. I could hear her name in every conversation he held. He is an old man with a shrunken chest. He praised her continuously...It was quite pathetic to watch Maitland that day at Lady Wildes. For the first time Mrs Kingsford interested me. She really must have been good to have inspired so many people with affection.

Anna appears briefly in Yeats's unfinished novel *The Speckled Bird*. In the novel, Michael is at a social function when an unnamed lady is pointed out to him. '"She will interest you so much," said Mrs Allingham. "She is very learned about Biblical interpretation and has quite a little following."'

Oscar Wilde wrote a review of *Dreams and Dream Stories* for *Woman's World*, February 1889, which in part stated: 'No one who had the privilege of knowing Mrs Kingsford, who was one of the brilliant women of our day, can doubt for a single moment that these tales came to her in the way she describes; but to me the result is just a little disappointing. Perhaps, however, I expect too much.'

Not surprisingly, Wilde confessed his ignorance of mysticism and the philosophical significance of allegory, therefore he could not truly appreciate the dreams. He concluded on a positive note, 'However, from a psychological point of view, these dreams are interesting, and Mrs Kingsford's book is undoubtedly a valuable addition to the literature of the mysticism of the nineteenth century.'

The reviewer in the Theosophical journal *Lucifer* had only praise for *Dreams and Dream Stories.* Part of the review reads as follows:

> To my own thinking their style is somewhat akin to that of the shorter tales of Nathaniel Hawthorne. They have his peculiar weirdness and force of expression, together with his marvelous insight into the soul of things. They thrill us by their realism, while they leave us in doubt as to the exact line between fact and fiction, and a certain delicacy of touch, indicative rather than descriptive of character, recalls at times the hand of that inimitable master. But the sentiments are strikingly Mrs Kingsford's own…To the initiated, the interest lies outside and beyond the stories.

Clothed With the Sun, compiled by Maitland, was published in 1889.[1] This is a collection of some sixty-eight illuminations Anna received, mostly in her sleep, between 1877 and 1884. The book is a significant addition to mystical literature. Anna and Maitland's 'ripe mystical friend,' the Rev. Dr John Pulsford, expressed his appreciation of the book to Maitland on 31 January 1890:

> I cannot tell you with what thankfulness and pleasure I have read *Clothed With the Sun.* Sincerely and very much I congratulate you as the editor and collaborator of the Seeress. It is impossible for a spiritually AFTER ANNA 179 intelligent person to doubt that these teachings were received from within the astral veil. They are full of the concentrated and compact wisdom of the Holy Heavens and of God. If Christians knew their own religion they would find in these priceless records our Lord Christ and his vital process abundantly illustrated confirmed.
>
> The regret is that so few will be able to read the book, or, reading it, to be aware of the tithe of its pearls. But that such communications are possible, and are permitted to be given to the world, is a most promising

sign of our age. The editing and the added notes, together with the appendix, are beyond all praise.

It is no little joy to me to feel that, through these illuminations, I am so much more in sympathy with God's daughter, the Seeress, than I supposed. The testimony is so clearly above, and distinct from, the degraded and degrading species of Theosophism derived from the occult powers of the universe rather than from the Supreme Spirit, and Father-Mother of our Spirits.

Now let us expect Evah and her Seed – the coming of her kingdom of the fourth dimension. Psyche, who is within and before Ether, shall yet be the flower and crown of Ether.

In the holy covenant and joy of her Love, John Pulsford.

The reviewer in *Lucifer* found a number of parallels to Theosophical teachings in *Clothed With the Sun.* The review concluded, '...of the work itself we cannot speak too highly. It will remain a worthy companion to the "Perfect Way," as a lasting monument to the genius, the intellect, the lofty and penetrating insight and the great spirituality of Dr Anna Kingsford.' In his preface to Mme de Steiger's memoirs, the mystic Arthur Edward Waite wrote highly of the book, 'I shall always regard it as one of the books beautiful of the prolific Victorian age.'

In November 1891 Maitland formed The Esoteric Christian Union with the object of propagating the 'New Gospel of Interpretation,' the name he gave to his and Anna's teachings. Samuel Hopgood Hart, a London solicitor who was to become the editor of Anna's and Maitland's works, joined the Union in 1894. He wrote that the Union lacked money and workers, and the members were too spread out to be effective. After Maitland joined there was never a general meeting of the members. 'For all practical purposes, Edward Maitland himself was the society,' and Maitland was busy with lectures, articles, and writing Anna's biography. In Hart's words it was 'dead through stagnation' at the time of Maitland's death in 1897.

On the second anniversary of Anna's death, 22 February 1890, a 'memorial service ' was held in Steinway Hall, London. Admission was open to those with a 'visiting card,' and Antoinette Sterling 'would favour the company' with a selection of songs. Madame Sterling, an American born contralto residing in London, took an abiding interest in spiritual matters and sang at Lady Mount Temple's gatherings at Broadlands.2 For reasons not stated, Madame Sterling did not attend the memorial. Perhaps she was ill, for advertisements in *The Times* show she had numerous engagements at the time, including a recital before Queen Victoria and other members of the royal family on 5 March. Charles Massey and George Chaney, a spiritualist, gave their scheduled speeches at the memorial.

After several years labour, Maitland finished his biography of Anna, which he had been working on for up to eighteen hours a day. *Anna Kingsford: Her Life, Letters, Diary and Work* was published by George Redway in January 1896. Later in 1896 a 'second edition' of the book was published, but it was simply a reprint of the first edition. The third edition of *Anna Kingsford: Her Life, Letters, Diary and Work* was edited by Samuel Hopgood Hart and published in 1913 by John M. Watkins. After suffering a stroke in September 1896 Maitland was moved to the home of Colonel Algernon Currie and his wife in Tonbridge, Kent, where he died on 2 October 1897.

Algernon married Mrs Catherine Burton of Longner Hall, near Shrewsbury, on 4 June 1896. In 1898 the couple changed their surname to Burton by deed poll and royal licence. Catherine Sophia, born in Pimlico, Middlesex in 1841, married Robert Linger Burton (1835-1880) of Longner Hall in 1861 and bore eight children. The estate had long been in the Burton family, with Edward Burton buried there in 1558.

Mrs Burton was an associate of the Society for Psychical Research from 1882 to 1900. In February 1883 she wrote to the Society relating her experiences of second sight which were published in *Phantasms of the Living* by Edmund Gurney and others.3 Mrs Burton possessed creative talents, for she wrote and composed a hymn, 'My Soul Cleaveth to the Dust' (London, 1886), and *Phyllis: a pastoral play in one act* (Shrewsbury: Bunny & Davies, 1887), both held in the British Library.

Algernon retired from his official positions at the age of sixty in 1905. In addition to his post as vicar, he had also been chairman of the Rural District Council, and chairman of the Atcham Board of Guardians. The new chairman of the Board warmly thanked Algernon for his service and personal qualities, which included impartiality, good humour, and common sense. 'Speaking with much emotion' in response, Algernon said the occasion of his departure was 'one of the most painful things that could happen.' He then gave statistics on improvements to the Workhouse that had been made over the years. The new chairman remarked Algernon had been a constant visitor to the workhouse and 'had taken a lively interest in the inmates and seen to their comfort and welfare.'[4]

On 10 August 1905 Algernon and his wife gave a farewell tea for upwards of 320 parishioners of Atcham. Algernon was thanked for his restoration of the church, the rebuilding and enlargement of the church organ, and the 'doubling of the schools.' The Burtons then moved to Petworth, Sussex, where Algernon was elected to the local Board of Guardians to continue his Poor Law interests.[5] Algernon died on 10 August 1913 at Overnoons, Petworth. His will, dated 11 May 1897, bequeathed his personal effects to Catherine, 'other than money or securities for money.' He left his real estate and the residue of his personal estate to Eadith. Anna's trust fund is not mentioned in his will, but most likely separate arrangements were made for its transfer to Eadith. The gross value of his estate was £2,241.

Anna's influence has lived on in various ways. On 1 March 1888, one week after Anna died, the Hermetic Order of the Golden Dawn came into being. The tarot expert and author, Mary Greer, has observed, 'The magnetic and influential Anna Kingsford was thus, in some sense, the mother of the Golden Dawn and its first magical woman.'[6] The Golden Dawn played a pivotal role in the development of esotericism in the modern era. Caitlin and John Matthews, noted proponents of the Western Mystery Tradition, have written that the Golden Dawn 'became, in the next few generations, the most prestigious organisation of its kind since the Renaissance. Most modern esoteric schools trace their descent from the Golden Dawn, and through it, knowingly or not, make contact with both the Rosicrucian impulse and the great Classical and pre-classical foundations.'[7] Two of the founders of the Golden Dawn, Samuel L. MacGregor Mathers and Dr William Wynn Westcott had known Anna and gave lectures to the Hermetic Society.

According to Mary Greer, since meeting Anna and Maitland, MacGregor Mathers had been searching for a woman to be his partner in magical projects. He found her in Mina (later Moina) Bergson (1865-1928), sister of Henri Bergson, the famous French philosopher. MacGregor Mathers met Mina in 1887 as she sketched his favourite Egyptian statues in the British Museum. After their marriage in 1890 they maintained celibacy in order to sublimate the sexual energies for magical workings.[8] The leading members of the Golden Dawn would have particularly interested Anna because of their association with the theatre. Annie Horniman (1860-1937) provided funding to allow the Abbey Theatre in Dublin to turn professional. The plays W. B. Yeats wrote during the 1890s drew upon the Celtic Mysteries for their symbolism. The actress Florence Farr (1860-1917) collaborated with Yeats in his Irish Mystery plays and the intoning of mystical texts accompanied by music of the psaltery. Moina and Macgregor Mathers devised rites of Isis which were performed in public and in private in Paris. True to form, Aleister Crowley, the notorious magician and exmember of the Golden Dawn, called Anna an immoral woman, but he still had the wit to recognize she 'did more in the religious world than any other person had done for generations.'[9]

Like Anna, Dion Fortune (1890-1946) had deep mystical and occult experiences. As a leading occultist of the twentieth century, Fortune wrote unique occult novels and various works on occult theory and practice. In her *Mystical Qabalah*, a major modern work on the subject, she mentions that Anna Kingsford, and other writers such as Eliphas Levi and Mary Atwood, can be read for instructive symbolism of Kabbalah. In his biography of Dion Fortune, Alan Richardson wrote she had 'taken up the torch of Anna Kingsford.' Before her marriage to Thomas Penry Evans in 1927, Dion Fortune led the Christian Mystic Lodge of the Theosophical Society. A year after her marriage it became the Community of the Inner Light, and later was called the Society of the Inner Light. Richardson wrote 'Community became very close in spirit during these early years to the Hermetic Society of Anna Kingsford, which espoused an occultism based upon Greek and Christian inclinations.'

Gareth Knight, prolific writer on magic and the esoteric, has observed, ...the work of Dion Fortune had developed out of the pioneering work of others – Barrett, Lytton, Kingsford, Mathers, Moriarty, Brodie-Innes and the like.' Knight wrote of Dion Fortune:

> If she could be compared to any mid-Victorian ladies it would more appropriately have been, not the literary figures of Elizabeth Barrett Browning and Emily Bronte, but the campaigning visionary, Anna Bonus Kingsford. Both she and Kingsford were champions of a Western Esoteric Tradition. Anna Kingsford aided MacGregor Mathers just as Dion Fortune helped Israel Regardie. Both had their problems with certain elements of the Theosophical Society, and both were materially assisted by a devoted older man as general factotum, Anna Kingsford by Edward Maitland, and Dion Fortune by Charles Loveday.[10]

Mohan (Mahatma) Gandhi (1869-1948) was an enthusiastic disciple of Anna and Maitland. In 1888 he met Mme Blavatsky and Annie Besant in England when he was studying law. He took an interest in Theosophy but did not join the Society. Although he grew up on a meatless diet, it was only after reading Henry Salt's *Plea for Vegetarianism* that Gandhi made a conscious choice to be a vegetarian. He also read with benefit and gratitude Anna's *The Perfect Way in Diet*. In 1893 Gandhi settled in South Africa, and through Christian friends in England he became aware of Maitland, leading to a 'prolonged' correspondence. Maitland sent him some of their works, including *The Perfect Way*. The 'independent thinking, profound morality, and the truthfulness' of *The Perfect Way* 'left an abiding impression' on Gandhi.[11] He placed notices in *The Natal Mercury* and *The Natal Advertiser* for the sale of *The Perfect Way, Clothed With the Sun,* and works by Maitland.[12]

Since the 1980s an increasing amount of attention has been paid to Anna in the fields of her accomplishments. She is honoured in histories of vegetarianism and animal welfare for her knowledge and selfless dedication to these causes. The women's movement has paid her tribute, especially regarding women in science and religion. Numerous seekers of enlightenment have been inspired by her mystical works.

Notes

1. Gladstone wrote in his diary that he read *Clothed With the Sun* on 2 July 1889. I believe some of the illuminations came from Maitland. In a footnote to 'Concerning the Divine Image, or the Vision of Adonai', the last illumination in the book, Maitland says he had the vision of Adonai before Anna had it. He then states they had joint visions, sometimes together and at other times apart. It appears to me that the visions in the book involving occult phenomena come from Maitland. In contrast, Anna's visions contain genuine spiritual insights.
2. Antoinette Sterling (1843-1904) was born in Sterlingville, New York State. As a girl she 'possessed a beautiful voice of great compass and volume.' She settled in London in 1873 and in 1875 married John MacKinlay, a Scotch American. She supported dress reform for women and never wore a corset. There is a good possibility Anna and Antoinette knew each other through their common interests in spiritual matters and humanitarian causes. Antoinette was cremated after her death, which was uncommon in those days.
3. Gurney, v.2, 427.
4. *Shrewsbury Chronicle* (21 April 1905).
5. Obituary in the Shrewsbury Chronicle (22 August 1905).This obituary notice for Algernon ends, 'His first wife was Dr Hannah [sic] Kingsford, a brilliantly clever woman who had an extraordinary career as anti-vivisectionist and Theosophist.'
6. Greer, 56.
7. Matthews, 46. New members of the Golden Dawn joined the First Order to study esoteric subjects such as astrology, tarot and Kabbalah. They worked up through grades, and when sufficiently prepared, were admitted into the Second

Order to practise ceremonial magic such as the invocation of god forms. Having realised the higher self, the ultimate aim was divine union.

8. Greer, 163.
9. Crowley, 14.
10. Knight, 16.
11. Gandhi 1948, 172.
12. Gandhi, 1958, 141.

Chapter - 18

Maitland's Biography of Anna in Question

When I began to write this biography of Anna Kingsford, Maitland's biography was no longer in print. My initial idea was to abridge his work, but I soon found inadequacies in his book, especially a serious lack of personal information on Anna's background and life. In his book Maitland assumes centre stage, and we see Anna only through his distorted lens. Florence Miller gave a significant assessment of Maitland when she remarked on his 'colossal, indeed crazy, egotism.' She wrote of his biography, 'It is about Maitland himself, rather than his professed subject. Page after page is given to the vapourings of spiritualistic media, about *his* soul, and *his* importance in the Universe!' Florence wrote that she had read many biographies, 'But the worst of all is Maitland's *Life of Anna Kingsford.*' Florence was the only contemporary of Anna to have made such criticisms of Maitland and his book. Her strong comments induced me to look at the biography with a critical eye. I went through the whole biography again, putting everything Maitland wrote under the microscope. I noticed many inconsistencies and shortcomings in the book. I saw patterns in what he wrote and did, giving me insights into his thinking and motivations. I discovered that he seriously misrepresented Anna, and these distortions
 are still being repeated today. In this chapter I expose the many lies Maitland wrote about Anna, and offer explanations for his attitudes.

Contemporary reviews of Maitland's biography of Anna were mixed or extremely negative. Florence Miller criticized Maitland in her obituary of him in her paper *The Woman's Signal*:

> Then it seemed to Mr Maitland good that he should publish a 'Life ' of her, and an account of her visions. This unhappy book appeared last

year. Alack! what a melancholy display it was. The famous 'revelations' are printed in quantities, and they are mere ravings, the wild stuff of hysterical dreams, in which it is not easy to recognize the woman who had written not only sanely, but with the most calm logic and brilliant insight upon so many important questions – diet, the position of women, vivisection – and who was also the holder of one of the best scientific degrees of the world, the M.D. of Paris.

More singular still, was poor Maitland's display in that book of egotism and vanity, a large proportion of the work being about himself, and including pages of such twaddle as what was said to him about himself by trance mediums at different stages of his career. The Anna Kingsford that I knew, the clever, intelligent woman (the most beautiful creature that I have ever seen in my life, too), was absolutely nonexistent in that book, and even those who only knew her by her work *The Perfect Way in Diet*, which is perhaps the most scientific, logical and unexaggerated presentiment yet given of the vegetarian case, must have been as bitterly disappointed by Maitland's work as were those who knew Dr Anna Kingsford personally.[1]

Arthur Edward Waite wrote a favourable review of Maitland's biography for *Light*.[2] He was convinced that Anna's illuminations were 'derived from a high transcendental source and were produced under high influence.' But he did not challenge any of the accusations Maitland made against Anna. Waite concluded his review on a positive note, welcoming 'the appearance of a most memorable book.'

An unsigned review in *The Theosophist* called Maitland's biography a 'unique and transcendental work.'[3] It said those who think Maitland 'sometimes overestimates the loftiness of his mission, can easily pardon his enthusiasm,' for he overcame 'many obstacles' in pursuing his 'noble work.' Maitland's 'monumental' works are predicted to 'mould the thought of future ages.' However, the reviewer did not mention any of Anna's achievements.

Another Theosophist, G.R.S. Mead wrote a harsh review of Maitland's biography in the Theosophy journal *Lucifer*.[4] After praising Anna for her love of animals, Mead went on to say it was an 'unbalanced' love. He was in 'entire sympathy' with her 'general programme,' but according to him she lacked the 'two things absolutely necessary' for the task. These were the 'faculty of scholarly research' and the abilities of the high initiate. However, Anna's inspiration took her far beyond the pedantic 'scholarship' which Mead demanded from her. Mead showed distinct sexist attitudes, placing the priest of olden time above the seeress, and criticising Anna's 'glorification of woman.' He said he had no time for the most widely used symbol of duality, namely 'sex symbology.' Mead concluded, 'there are so many good ideas scattered throughout the volume,' but he failed to mention them.

The Times was also scathing in its review of Maitland's biography:

> We confess to an insuperable distaste for the literature of the kind provided for us by Mr Maitland in his ANNA KINGSFORD: HER LIFE, LETTERS, DIARY AND WORK (two vols. George Redway). Mrs Kingsford, who died – or as Mr Maitland would say 'withdrew' – seven years ago, was a lady doctor well known in her day, on the one hand, for a considerable charm of person, and on the other, for her hostility to vivisection and for her very public profession of the theosophist creed, in the pursuit of which she 'collaborated' with Mr Maitland, who now writes her biography. Readers who are interested in the career of what the Americans call 'cranks,' may find some satisfaction in these two ample volumes, to describe which we may borrow the words which Mr Maitland himself applied to a book of Laurence Oliphant – 'ponderous in style and astral in character'; but to the larger and saner portion of mankind they will be found to consist of a farrago of rubbish, sometimes of malicious rubbish. The term is merited not only by the attacks upon the vivisectionists, who are well used to abuse from such quarters, but by the language applied, of all people in the world, to Miss Frances Power Cobbe, who because she declined to propose Mrs Kingsford for a ladies' club is here attacked in the most monstrous fashion. We must apologize to the Rev. Dr Townshend for placing his EDWARD HOARE, M.A., in juxtaposition to these two volumes, for a greater contrast could hardly be imagined than that between the sane and sober vicar of Tunbridge Wells and the 'astral lady' that we have just described.[5]

It would have been too much to expect *The Times* to realise the person most maligned in the biography by Maitland was Anna herself.

The medical establishment also was only too ready to disparage Anna with the ammunition supplied by Maitland, as shown in this 'review' in the *British Medical Journal*:

> RE-EMBODIED SPIRITS.
>
> We are asked to state that a book published last Saturday with the title *Anna Kingsford: Her Life, Letters, Diary and Work*, has been issued

> not only without the approval of her family, but in spite of the strongest representations on their part made to the author so soon as the family accidently became aware of his project, to induce him to renounce his intention. The book is a curious example of the mental obliquity which has characterised much of the agitation against vivisection. The author, Mr Edward Maitland, believes that Mrs Kingsford was the re-embodied spirit of Faustina, and that he himself is a re-embodiment of Marcus Aurelius. He further believes that to these two curious modern personages was divinely revealed a new kind of Christianity, and that they were charged incidentally with the duty of opposing vivisection, even, as it would seem, to the extent of compassing the death of those who practised it. The book is a perfect wilderness of nonsense, and its assertions do not appear to call for serious discussion.[6]

The following review from *Theosophy in Australia* is a further example of the damage Maitland did to Anna's reputation:

> One of the most bewildering and weirdest books published this year is Mr Maitland's *Anna Kingsford: Her Life, Letters, Diary and Work.* As a sympathiser with the movement for the enfranchisement of woman, and an apostle of a new revelation which was to spiritualise all the doctrines of Christianity, she has long been familiar to Theosophists; but as an Avenging Angel killing vivisectionists by the power of will alone, she appears in a new character to most of us.[7]

The Irish Theosophist James Cousins, however, wrote an enthusiastic review of the third edition of Maitland's biography for *Light.* He stated, 'The visions and experiences of Anna Kingsford…are of the order of Francis and Teresa.' He went on to praise her:

> …this wondrously gifted woman takes rank among the seers of all time. Whatever activity she took part in, such as the food reform and anti-vivisection movements, or the then young Theosophical Society, her vision was always turned towards 'The Day of the Woman.' She was one of the pioneers of the movement for the freedom of women, and her clear utterance in poetry and prose of its coming triumph was not a thought fathered or mothered by the wish; it was rather the splendid articulation of her vision of the Cosmic Feminism, the Divine Duality that is the necessary condition of universal existence...
>
> In the enunciation of this her gospel, Anna Kingsford adopted the Christian revelation; but she lifted it from the level of a local creed to that of a universal significator, and alternated with it an esoteric

> presentation of the Greek mythos. She paid her homage to the Virgin Maria, 'the star of the sea;' she paid equal homage sea-born Aphrodite; but to neither was her homage the idolatry given to a person; it was the reference given to the immortal personifications of spiritual powers. Hence it was that in her work for woman she worked not for woman only, but for the purifying, nurturing, regenerating power of the divine Motherhood in man as well as woman. Hence also that in her experience of deepest insight and exalted emotion, she passed beyond the limits of sex and personality, and in her supremest moment beheld the Adonai as the universal Father-Mother, One in Essence, twain in operation, whose right hand with will sends forth the stupendous Thought of the Universe, whose left hand with Love recalls it to its Divine Source.[8]

However, like most other reviewers of Maitland's biography, Cousins did not mention the contradictions in Maitland's presentation nor his animosity towards Anna.

The Roman Catholic author G.K. Chesterton made fun of Anna thanks to Maitland's biography. When it came out Chesteron was working in the publisher's bookshop. He related in his autobiography that a distraught woman rushed into the shop, described her spiritual symptoms, and asked him for suitable books. Being 'incompetent' to select for her, he pointed to the biography which was near at hand. She said no, Anna told her not to read it. Chesterton had read at least some of the book, for he concluded 'malicious' was a too mild a word for Anna, and in his opinion she was 'mad.' Obviously such ill-informed comments from a well-known writer helped tarnish Anna's reputation.

Maitland took drastic measures to ensure no one could prove him wrong about Anna. In late December 1896 Samuel Hart made his last visit to Maitland, who was physically helpless and could not speak coherently. On returning to London Hart went to Maitland's former residence seeking Anna's manuscripts, in particular those relating to her Hermetic lectures. He found nothing, and the caretaker informed him that before Maitland left for Tonbridge he 'spent three days in tearing up and burning old papers.'[9] Hart subsequently asked Colonel Currie, Algernon Burton (Kingsford) in 1906 and Eadith Kingsford in 1915, if they had manuscripts by Anna, but they all replied in the negative. Hart assumed that Maitland, due to his deteriorating condition, did not know what he was doing when he burnt all the papers. It never occurred to Hart that Maitland must have burnt her diaries and letters to hide his misrepresentations of Anna. Maitland burnt

Anna's original lectures to the Hermetic Society, and no doubt other priceless works.

Yet Maitland did not stop at concealing Anna's own thoughts. In his biography Maitland reveals a vengeful nature. He must have disliked orthodox clergymen, for he disparaged his father's beliefs, his brother the Reverend Brownlow Maitland, and Algernon Kingsford. Maitland wrote that Anna's brother, the Reverend Edward Bonus, paid her an 'unlooked-for visit' as she lay dying. He asserted Edward tried to pressure her into seeing a priest and receiving extreme unction.[10] However, the Rev. Bonus officiated at Anna's funeral, indicating there was probably no rupture in their relationship.

Maitland also disparaged Miss Cobbe, Mme Wachtmeister, and even Lady Caithness. He alleged Miss Cobbe was Anna's 'relentless enemy,' and that after annotating her copy of *The Soul and How It Found Me* with 'impure imaginings,' she circulated it among her acquaintances. Maitland also accused Miss Cobbe of refusing to sponsor Anna's application to join a women's club early in 1881. We only have Maitland's word for these dubious allegations.

The evidence indicates Maitland conceived a personal antipathy towards Mme Wachtmeister. The latter wrote that Anna and Maitland visited her and Mme Blavatsky for a fortnight at Ostende in October 1886. Maitland took this slip-up over severely, refuting her in the pages of Lucifer with his travelling notebook and hotel bills before him, stating emphatically it was only three days.[11] In his biography he isputed other minor details of the visit given by Mme Wachtmeister. Maitland claimed her memory was faulty due to the influence of 'objectionable ' entities she encountered during her mediumship days. He also accused Mme Wachtmeister of 'systematically depreciating' Anna by alleging, in conversation and letters, she was a meat-eater.[12]

In a lengthy interview she gave to *Light* in 1895, Lady Caithness mentioned she paid for the publication of *The Perfect Way* to ensure it would not be 'lost to the world.'[13] She also spoke about her long-held belief that she was in contact with the spiritual soul of Mary Queen of Scots. Therefore it greatly pained her when Maitland insisted, in correspondence, that she was only in contact with Mary's astral shell. Maitland reiterated his view in a letter in the next issue of *Light*. He also wrote that he and Anna would have sacrificed all to publish *The Perfect Way*, and they only accepted Lady Caithness's offer because they did not want to hurt her feelings by refusing. Again, Maitland showed a critical attitude that was scarcely warranted by the circumstances.

Maitland further reveals his attitude to women in his novels. The leading female character in each novel is tall, fair, and beautiful, with long golden hair. She has an otherworldly quality, and is submissive to the male character. Obviously this is a projection of Maitland's ideal type of woman which he carried in his mind. Maitland harboured the typically (Christian) male attitude of regarding woman as Madonna or whore; the idealised woman can be rapidly transformed into the whore by the sexist male when she does not live up to his preconceived ideal. In *By and By* Maitland revealed a sadistic side to his nature. In this novel, Nannie, the young wife of Christmas (Criss) Carol, told him how her sister enjoyed being beaten by her husband to control her wildness. Nannie wanted Criss to beat her to make her good, but he thought this was unreasonable. Anna was Maitland's 'ideal woman,' in all but one vital respect: he could not dominate her as he desired, therefore he turned against her and gave vent his feelings in his biography.

Maitland's sexist view is clearly expressed in this passage from England and Islam:

> The ideal woman brings herself to her male affinity as a sheet of blankest paper for him to write upon it that which he pleases. The Madonna was absolutely unselfish, in that it never occurred to her to have a wish of her own in opposition to that of her husband, or to the good of her children. In fact, she was such a one as some of us have known among our own English wives and mothers – women who have been so perfect in all the relations of their lives that they never seemed to us to want anything on their own account; but in that boundless love of which woman is the special representative on earth, subordinate themselves without effort to the good of those about them, until by sinking themselves far below the man in respect of the things of the flesh, they rise far above him in respect of those of the spirit. Who better than I, who am doubly son of such a one, should know how to describe them?[14]

Maitland began his misrepresentations of Anna on the very first page of his biography; he wrote Anna was 'descended from a great Italian Family.' He claimed a John Bonus was the architect of the Vatican, but there is no evidence for this assertion. Maitland also wrote that one ancestor was the founder of Venice, one was a cardinal of the church, and another was a noted alchemist and occultist. In the absence of further details, we must question Maitland's veracity on these'ancestors.' He claimed that from a very early age Anna had second sight, namely, a capacity to foretell the death of a person. There is no evidence outside Maitland that Anna had second sight, and she never mentioned it in her writings.

Maitland claimed that Anna went fox hunting in the period between leaving school and getting married. He wrote she told him she found a 'savage joy' in seeing the dogs tear the fox to pieces. He claimed she stopped hunting through pity for the fox and a feeling that if man was the superior being he should not harm other creatures. The words Maitland quotes are written in his style rather than Anna's. It does not ring true that Anna ever hunted foxes, for she was an extremely sensitive, religious and imaginative girl, not the sort to partake in brutal sports. Anna was a truthful person, and her own words in *Health,, Beauty and the Toilet* run counter to Maitland's claims:

> I am not an advocate of hunting for women. It is a dangerous pastime, especially for the sex that rides across country encumbered with drapery, and liable, should a fall occur, to be found hopelessly pinned down to the saddle by a third pommel, or inextricably mixed up, by means of a tight habit-skirt, among the hoofs of a floundering horse. Moreover, the sport itself is hardly one in which refined and womanly women will be able to take much pleasure; the spectacle of the 'death,' even when Reynard is concerned, ought not to inspire of joy in the hearts of English girls, and when poor 'pussy' is the victim the aspect of the thing is, to my mind at least, wholly revolting and contemptible. No doubt the actual chase is exhilarating; but its purpose – that of deliberately running to death an innocent and sensitive creature, and making pastime of its bitter fear and physical distress – has always seemed to me a cowardly and unworthy game for Christian ladies and gentleman. I would never encourage any son or daughter of mine to find delight in such an amusement; and I think the time is not far distant when the view I take of the matter will become pretty general.[15]

If Anna had ever hunted foxes, she would have mentioned it in the above as a salutary warning to her readers.

Maitland claimed Anna was introduced to spiritualism by Florence J. Theobald in Hastings in December 1867. Miss Theobald was an active spiritualist and wrote books on the subject. Here Maitland contradicted himself, for in *The Soul and How It Found Me,* written in 1876-77, he wrote, '...for although sharing my convictions respecting the nature of my book, [Anna] was as yet no believer in the current "spiritualism."'[16] Maitland wrote he and Anna regularly contacted spirits via automatic writing and use of the planchette, even at the vicarage. Anna was never a spiritualist, that is, a person who seeks contact with disembodied spirits such as ghosts and entities on the astral plane. When Anna believed in a cause, she put all her energies into promoting it. She never joined a spiritualist group, nor spoke or wrote for spiritualism. Quite the contrary, for in 1882 she spoke to the British National Association of Spiritualists, urging them to forsake the mere ghosts of the seance room and follow a truly spiritual path in life.[17]

Maitland gave mixed messages on his own attitude to spiritualism. He wrote some letters to *Light* criticising spiritualism, and in his writings he questioned the practice. However, he also attended various séances and mediums over many years, giving in his biography long accounts of spirit messages he received. Maitland especially liked to hear spirits tell him he was chosen for a great purpose. For example, in October and November 1880 he visited a medium in London twentyfour times to investigate the spirits. Maitland claimed the spirits were 'bogus' because they did not read his thoughts about them being bogus! However, he did not object when the spirits said he was 'to be their instrument for the new manifestation of the Christ.'[18]

I also believe Maitland exaggerated Anna's health problems throughout her life. His novels show that he liked his woman companion to have poor health so that he could be in charge and she would have to rely on him. In his biography he presents Anna as being almost continuously in poor health. On the first page Maitland says that when she was born it was thought she was dead, so she was wrapped up and put to one side. Also Maitland alleged that Miss Theobald wrote when she met Anna she was 'just recovering from a severe illness, during which all her lovely hair had been shaven off.' According to Maitland Anna's honeymoon was drastically terminated when Anna had a life-threatening asthma attack the day after her wedding night. He wrote Anna speedily went to her mother's place until Eadith was born, 'suffering constantly and severely,' but he did not specify the nature of this constant illness. Anna's health in 1868 must not have been in such dire straits, for she wrote a long pamphlet on women's suffrage, part of a novel, and helped organize the ill-fated Ladies' Secular Club.

Maitland wrote that sometimes Anna would feel faint and fall unconscious to the floor or ground. He stated, 'rarely did a week pass without some acute and prolonged access of pain, of prostration, or of insensibility' affect her. Although her health was not robust, Anna achieved an extraordinary amount in her short life. A person with the poor health Maitland presents could not have matched Anna's achievements.

Maitland's account of his first visit to the vicarage in February 1874 has elements of dubious veracity. His sense of self importance comes through in the first sentence of his narration, where he states the welcome accorded to him 'was more than cordial; it was eager, as if they had been already impressed with a sense of results to follow from my visit no less desirable than important.' He wrote, 'Once assured of her auditor's sympathy and appreciation, her self-revelations were unrestrained. And it soon became clear to me that one at least of the functions I was expected to fulfil was that of interpreter; she herself being both the propounder and the subject of the enigma to be solved, the Sphinx for whose benefit I was to enact the part of Oedipus.' In the course of this visit, Maitland claimed Anna opened her soul to him. He wrote, 'Suspicion and distrust were ingrained in her, and nothing but her intense ambition for high achievement withheld her from seeking refuge either in a convent or suicide.'[19] Nothing in Anna's life or writings indicates she had such a pessimistic outlook on life.

As he returned home Maitland pledged himself to the development of Anna's nature, for otherwise she 'was as surely destined to disaster and wreck as a ship set adrift on the ocean without rudder, compass, or helmsman. So strong was my sense of her need of assistance to enable her to possess and master her ideas instead of being possessed and mastered by them.' It is a constant theme by Maitland in the biography that Anna needed him, and was lost without him.

It would have been news to Anna just what was on Maitland's mind after he left the vicarage:

> My visit to the rectory resulted in an intimacy which made me to such an extent a member of the family as to remove all obstacles to the collaboration required of us. It was soon made evident that not only our association, but her design of seeking a medical education was for both of us an indispensable element in our preparation for our now recognised joint-mission.[20]

Throughout his biography Maitland stated he had a oneness with Anna, which he claimed she reciprocated. Maitland claimed Anna wrote to him from Paris in May 1877, 'I cannot do real, worthy, and valuable work apart from you. I think your magnetism imparts a vigour to my brain which nothing else gives me...You must detach yourself from your present world. You must be one with me.'[21] Maitland wrote of an evening in November 1877 when he was writing in his lodgings, two miles from Anna's place. At 11.30pm he had a blockage and could not write further. Next day when he saw Anna, she said she had felt an urge to write at 11.30pm the previous night. According to Maitland she had written down the very ideas that Maitland had been trying to express. In the context of Maitland's attitude to their relationship, this can only be his invention. In August 1879 Maitland was in poor health, with his pulse ranging from 110 to 120 beats per minute. He had severe tinnitus due to disease of the auditory nerve. He pondered, 'What if it should become chronic! It was more than my life and reason that were at stake – it was our work; it was she! To lose me would, I was assured, be her ruin for this life, for I was to her as a tether to hold her to her centre.' Referring to May 1880 Maitland wrote he 'was placed as the guardian of Mary.' Maitland also thought he was the superior partner, for he wrote, 'I learnt to see in her a soul of surpassing luminousness and variousness, who had been entrusted to my charge expressly in order that by my study of her I might recover for the world's benefit the long-lost knowledge of the soul's being, nature, and history.'[22] As further evidence of their 'oneness,' Maitland claimed Anna's genius was red and his was blue, and they mysteriously fused to form the royal colour purple.

One of the most bizarre incidents occurring to Anna, as recorded by Maitland, was that her mind was taken over by a black magician. Maitland wrote that Anna became seriously ill and depressed in mid 1877. In this weakened state she was subject to psychic attack by a black magician whom he called 'Apollyon' or 'Monsieur O.,' a fellow medical student. Maitland claimed Monsieur O. took over Anna's mind by projecting himself into her dreams. Maitland said he had a battle of wills with the malfeasant before finally conquering him. Anna, Maitland claimed, gave up her spiritual views and high ideals and adopted the materialistic views of Monsieur O. He wrote she even agreed to leave him and join Monsieur O. On returning to Paris they found out that Monsieur O. had conveniently succumbed to 'an attack of brain-fever,' and was never heard of again.

It's impossible to believe this episode ever happened, for Anna had a mind of her own and made her own decisions. She defied her family to marry Algernon and stood up to her professors, refusing to attend any classes where vivisection was conducted. Maitland himself wrote of her regarding her study of medicine, 'The courage, perseverance, and resourcefulness with which she faced and overcame obstacles which would have daunted anyone of weaker will or meaner purpose were altogether admirable.' Maitland wrote of the 'indomitable will' that enabled Anna to continue writing her weekly medical letter to the *Lady's Pictorial* early in 1887 when she was ill.[23] In his telling of the alleged episode Maitland never showed compassion for Anna, nor did he do the obvious thing of telling Monsieur O. to his face to cease his unwanted advances.

Maitland's accounts of séances in *The Soul and How It Found Me* drew the ridicule of reviewers upon him. For example, he told that on one occasion at the planchette with Anna, some writing appeared. A spirit informed them that the spirit of a dog was trying to write. Although the 'dog' claimed he was not a dog, the other spirit knew he was. Then the dog wrote, 'Me no baby!' This story is repeated in Maitland's biography, except the profound words of the dog are omitted. One reviewer took Maitland to task for writing that a spirit told him not to wear flannel next to his skin, and to take castor oil as a purge after eating lobster.[24]

According to Maitland, Miss Cobbe spread rumours about him and Anna after *The Soul and How It Found Me* was published. He claimed this caused Anna such distress she turned against the book, after having agreed beforehand to its publication. Maitland then purchased all copies for destruction. This did not concern him unduly, for he stated he could use the material in his biography, which to a large extent he did, knowing it was against Anna's wishes. He claimed that at a séance in 1889 Anna's spirit came through and said he was right and she was wrong over the issue, as he had predicted she would one day. Maitland had used this ploy before, for he wrote that though he and his father disagreed over religion, after his father died, his spirit came to Maitland and indicated he now supported Maitland's beliefs. Maitland did not use Anna's real name in *The Soul and How It Found Me,* he called her 'The Seeress' throughout. Such was his portrayal of Anna that the reviewer called her his 'hysterical female friend.' It is no wonder Anna opposed the book, for it misrepresented her as a credulous spiritualist who attended séances and unquestioningly accepted dubious occult phenomenon.

Maitland made the far-fetched allegation against Anna that she contemplated offering herself for vivisection in December 1877. Maitland wrote she was particularly upset about vivisection at the time, and 'became fascinated with the idea of offering herself to the *Faculté* for experimentation' if they would henceforth cease the practice.[25] Maitland said he persuaded her not to persist with this impractical idea.

It's inconceivable that an intelligent woman like Anna would contemplate such an idea for one second. The allegation fits the pattern of Maitland's vicious and desperate attacks on Anna.

We now come to the most serious accusation by Maitland against Anna, namely that she killed two French vivisectors. On 11 February 1878 Anna and Maitland had occasion to visit the *École Médecine*. On arrival they found it was closed and a notice on the gate informed them that Professor Claude Bernard, the notorious vivisector, had died on the previous day. On learning this news, Maitland claimed Anna kept repeating 'Claude Bernard dead!' She nearly collapsed and needed his assistance to sit on the steps. She buried her face in her hands, overcome with emotion. She then told him she had put a curse on Bernard during the previous December.[26] Maitland also claimed Anna killed Paul Bert in the same manner in November 1886.

After Maitland's biography appeared, *Light* published a number of letters discussing his claim that Anna had killed the two French vivisectors. Maitland wrote a letter claiming the Gods acted through Anna to kill the vivisectors.[27] This contrasts with his allegation in his biography that Anna herself was directly responsible. He claimed she wrote in her diary on 12 November 1886 these words, '…I have killed Paul Bert, as I killed Claude Bernard; as I will kill Louis Pasteur, and after him the whole tribe of vivisectors, if I live long enough. Courage: it is a magnificent power to have, and one that transcends all other vulgar methods of dealing out justice to tyrants.'[28] Such a bloodthirsty attitude is totally against Anna's character and beliefs, indicating it is a fabrication by Maitland.

Harming anyone, let alone committing murder, was completely against Anna's principles. She stated her position quite clearly in her lecture '" Violationism," or Sorcery in Science:'

> For, to be an adept in this, it is indispensable to be pure of heart, clear of conscience, and just in action. A divine intention presupposes a divine method. As it is forbidden to man to enrich himself by theft, or to free himself by murder, so also it is forbidden him to acquire knowledge by unlawful means – to fight even the battles of heaven with the weapons of hell. It is impossible to serve humanity by the sacrifice of that which alone constitutes humanity – justice and its eternal principles...All the triumphs of civilisation have been gained by civilised methods: it is the Divine law that so it should be, and whoever affirms the contrary is either an imbecile or a hypocrite.[29]

By accusing Anna of killing vivisectors, Maitland put her on the same level as those cruel and unfeeling men.

I suggest Maitland could have put curses on the vivisectors himself, or at least he fantasised about doing so. In his novels *Higher Law* and *By and By* he showed he wanted to be a power behind the scenes. He wrote in October 1882 that he and Anna were discussing her will (testament) in the presence of Eadith. He was successful, he said, in preventing Eadith from understanding their conversation by use of his mind power upon her. There is further evidence of Maitland's vengeful nature in that wrote he prophesied the 'doom' of the International Association for the Total Suppression of Vivisection and the Reverend H. Oxenham (1829-1888).[30] He related with scarcely veiled satisfaction that later the Association ceased to exist and Oxenham died.

Maitland claimed that when he and Anna visited Mme Blavatsky at Ostende in October 1886, Anna spoke to Countess Wachtmeister about black and white magic. He reproduced three pages discussing black and white magic which he stated came from Anna's diary.[31] He claimed Anna wrote, 'The subject arises out of a controversy between Countess Wachtmeister and myself as to whether it is or is not justifiable to "will" the destruction of evil men.'

The document states that black magic is performed by the lower self for purely personal gain. White magic is exercised by the higher self for positive ends. God is justified in using human agents to kill evil men, because the latter 'have forfeited their manhood.' This so-called diary entry must have been written by Maitland, for it contains Maitland's ideas, and is written in his style. It is dated 17 November 1886, the day of her fateful visit to Pasteur's laboratory. Also on that day her brother General Joseph Bonus and one of his sons came to see her. She surely had other things on her mind than writing long entries in her diary on that dreadful day. Further, Maitland claimed that while at Ostende Anna proposed to Mme Blavatsky they gather a number of occultists to destroy vivisectors by using their will power. Countess Wachtmeister does not mention this in her account of the meeting. Maitland reproduced a letter dated 29 November 1886 which he claimed Mme Blavatsky sent to Anna. It stated the Master disapproved of Anna's method of opposing vivisectors.[32] This alleged letter does not appear in Mme Blavatsky writings, and neither it nor the alleged meeting are mentioned outside Maitland's biography.

Writings on sorcery tell us that effective spells traditionally involve physical contact with the victim, such as a piece of hair, clothing, or a nail clipping. In voodoo a doll is made in the rough likeness of the victim. There is no reliable evidence that one can kill others by mind power alone. This further indicates Maitland fabricated Anna's participation in the deaths.

Maitland claimed Anna was a number of famous women in past lives, the best known being Mary Magdalen, Faustina, Joan of Arc, and Anne Boleyn. Anna believed in reincarnation, but in her writings she never mentioned that she was a specific person in a past life. The evidence Maitland presents for her famous past live comes mostly from dubious spirits.

Maitland had his reasons for claiming certain past lives for Anna. He believed he was with her in the past, and would be with her again in future lives. He thought he was John the Apostle in a past life, and therefore with Anna who was Mary Magdalen. Maitland believed he was once the Roman emperor Marcus Aurelius, the husband of Faustina. In the popular mind both these women are seen as leading immoral lives, thus by using them Maitland attacked Anna's reputation. Joan of Arc and Anne Boleyn suffered gruesome deaths. It appears Maitland chose them to indulge his sadistic attitudes for revenge against Anna. His claim that she offered herself for vivisection also fits into his pattern of a sadistic attitude to women.

Other past lives Maitland claimed for himself were Daniel, John the Evangelist, a mahatma in Tibet, the Renaissance philosopher Pico della Mirandola, and the Swedish mystic Emanuel Swedenborg. For a long time he suspected that he was John in a past life, but it is significant he never told Anna. He wrote he would leave it up to their 'illuminators' to inform her, but this they never did. In fact, in his biography he never spoke to Anna about any of his supposed past lives, indicating she would not have believed him if he raised the subject with her.

Maitland alleged Anna wrote in her diary that on the night of 14 January 1881 she had a visitation from the spirit of William Lilly, who explained her horoscope to her. Lilly (1602-1681) was the leading astrologer of his day, and accurately predicted the 1666 Great Fire of London.

Maitland wrote, 'She declared of her horoscope that it perfectly explained her to herself, and she had no difficulty in accepting the whole of it. Nor was I able to take exception to it even in respect of the disagreeable personal liabilities ascribed to her.' The horoscope allegedly showed she was destined to lead a life of harlotry and luxury. Her sufferings in this life were because she did not follow this destiny. Maitland wrote they learnt about karma from Lilly's visitation. However, the doctrine of karma is not fatalistic, for it teaches we are punished by past 'sins,' not *for* them. Karma gives the opportunity to learn from our mistakes and lead a better life. Karma does not punish any one for being virtuous. The alleged horoscope is no horoscope at all, for the technical details of a horoscope which any astrologer would include are absent. Maitland showed little comprehension of astrology in his biography. For example, several times he stated Anna was born under Libra, but this was not the case; her Sun was in Virgo, her Moon in Leo, and Aquarius was on the ascendant.

Also, Maitland did not live with Anna as often as he claimed. For example, he wrote that he resided with her at 11 Chapel Street, London, from October 1880 for twenty one months, yet the 1881 census provides the telling evidence he was only a visitor. At times Maitland did not specify Anna's address, but gave the impression he was living with her. Maitland played down Algernon's contact with Anna by failing to mention various occasions when he was with her in London. Anna and Maitland most probably lived under the same roof only when he visited the vicarage, when traveling together, and in the last months of Anna's life.

Even in death Maitland misrepresented Anna. According to him, around six p.m. on Tuesday 21 February 1888, Anna moved from her bed into a large easy chair to facilitate her breathing. She rested her head on a pillow placed on a small table before her. During the night she motioned him to come close and she rested her head on his shoulder as he knelt on a cushion. Towards dawn she asked Maitland to telegraph Algernon to come by the first train from Shrewsbury. She asked for the doctor who came about ten a.m. At around eleven a.m. she again rested her head on his shoulder and clasped his hand. Maitland felt he could read her mind, and she was thinking of withdrawing from her body. He wrote, 'we had been accustomed to read each other's thoughts in a manner that often startled us.' At noon Maitland stood up and steadied Anna's face with his hands while she 'exhaled out her life in one long breath.' Maitland observed she had made a rapid and complete withdrawal from her body. He reported Algernon arrived some two hours later.

In her memoirs Isabelle de Steiger gave a markedly different account of Anna's death. She received a 'telegraph' on 22 February stating Anna had died in the night, and would she go around without delay. When she arrived she found both Algernon and Maitland present. Although Maitland wrote that Algernon 'passed with her as much of his time as could be spared from his clerical duties,' he did not give one instance of Algernon being there before her death.

Anna's death certificate helps refute Maitland's misinformation about Algernon's presence during her last months and her last hours. On the certificate in the informant section it is stated that Algernon G. Kingsford was 'In attendance,' and his residence was '15 Wynnstay Gardens.' The fact that Maitland made no mention of the visit to Anna by Florence Fenwick Miller in late November 1887 is further evidence of his unreliability. Indeed, he told of no visits to Anna by her relatives and friends in her last months.

After Anna's funeral Maitland went back to London. He wrote, 'the tension on the spiritual bond between us was so extreme as to require all my force of will to avoid being drawn over to the other side where now my colleague was.' He decided now Anna was free of her body she could continue working with him from the other side. Maitland wrote that from May 1888 onwards he visited a number of mediums in attempts to contact Anna. He claimed a Mrs and Miss W. contacted her spirit which said she had risen too far beyond the earth sphere to contact Maitland directly.

On 28 September 1888 Maitland went to a clairvoyant called Mrs H., who told him what he wanted to hear:

> Her function in our joint work, Mrs H. added, was essentially reflective. She [Anna] was given to me to be a mirror to reflect to me the universe and man. To my parting expressions of affection it was responded that there was no need for us to give our love to each other; for that is a perpetual possession between us – a fixed, unalterable fact, recognised by both, and not needing words. For it dates from long ages past, as we had been together in the closest union in many lives, and shall be hereafter.

In the last week of October 1888, Maitland went to the vicarage at Atcham. He visited Anna's grave daily in the churchyard, beside the River Severn. A number of times he silently projected his wish to contact her, and on his last attempt he was convinced he had established a line of communication to her. He claimed that on 4 November he received a letter from Miss M.H.E., a young Scottish woman who allegedly had corresponded with Anna but had never met her. The letter, he alleged, was in Anna's handwriting, and gave the location in her study of her preface to *Dreams and Dream Stories*. Algernon, he said, also received a copy of the letter. William B. Yeats mentions this episode in a letter he wrote to Katherine Tynan. In creating this story it is likely Maitland was thinking about the 'mahatma letters' of Theosophy. At various times Sinnett and other

Theosophists received letters which appeared out of thin air, allegedly from the masters. It seems that Maitland did not want to be outdone in experiencing occult phenomena, so he invented supernatural letters for himself. Once when writing about Sinnett's claim to be in contact with the mahatmas, Maitland went one better and said he himself was a mahatma in a past life.[33]

At a seance on 5 June 1889 a Mrs H. gave Maitland a message, allegedly from Anna, saying that 'some members of her family may object on conventional grounds' to his biography. She said go on writing it, for on publication 'those who might object to it will either be sufficiently advanced to object no longer or will be removed.' The alleged message is not in Anna's style, and she would not have made a threat.

Maitland reported he attended a seance conducted by a Mrs C. on 24 June 1889. He 'was perplexed well-nigh to despair about the projected Biography.' He thought that if he mentioned Anna's previous lives her relatives would take offence. However, he wanted to 'write in full' about her. At the seance Anna allegedly wrote through the medium, 'Do not withhold anything.'

We know from the mention of it in the *British Medical Journal* that Anna's family made 'strong representation' to Maitland not to publish the biography. In view of the libels against Anna in the biography, it is strange her family took no action to suppress it, or to issue a more factual biography. The answer, I believe, is to be found in the will of Anna's brother John Bonus. Here it is revealed he had an illegitimate daughter called Ethelind, born on 13 June 1866. The mother's name is not given, and John stated Ethelind was christened without his knowledge or consent, at South Hampstead. She was raised by her father and his friend Mrs Kate Fisher Wilson at Lavender Cottage, Walton, Suffolk.

Anna's family were no doubt disturbed with the things Maitland wrote about her, but protection of John Bonus and Ethelind came first. The family must have closed ranks and made it known that they were opposed to any biography, and would not cooperate with anyone else who thought about writing one. It is likely that the family destroyed all papers and letters in their possession that would assist in the writing of a biography, for none have been located.

Samuel Hart (1865-1958) edited various works by Anna and Maitland. As a young man his dissatisfaction with the Church of England in which he was raised caused him to seek for a 'true doctrine ' elsewhere. He was contemplating joining the Theosophical Society when a friend suggested he speak to Maitland. He then met Maitland at his studio on 19 April 1894 and was impressed by the man and his ideas. He avidly read *The Perfect Way* and other works by Anna and Maitland. Hart wrote, 'I shall ever remember Edward Maitland as one of the greatest, wisest, lovable, and best of men whom it has been my privilege to know.'[34] Hart wrote that Maitland's biography of Anna '...is, and always will be, the biography *par excellence* of Anna Kingsford and Edward Maitland, and it is absolutely indispensable for those who would know all there is to be known of them and their work.'[35] 'It is written...with scrupulous adherence to truth and accuracy.'[36] It is unfortunate Hart lacked judgement regarding Maitland, for he never questioned the inaccuracies Maitland wrote about Anna. He was in a very good position to interview people who knew Anna, but he presented no new information about her. He missed an opportunity to provide new information and remedy the damage Maitland did to Anna's reputation.

In the light of Maitland's denigration of Anna in his biography, we may well ask why did she put up with him? The fact is she only put up with him to a point, and this displeased him. We have it in Maitland's own words that they had 'altercations' for a period of at least one year. Anna's opposition to *The Soul and How It Found Me* must have been a significant factor in their disagreements; and while Anna was alive Maitland was careful not to publish such a chaotic work again. We learn from his novels about the dominating relationship he desired with a woman. Wish as he might, he did not get this relationship from Anna, thus he must have built up anger against her. Everything that was bottled up inside him came out in the biography.

Knowing Anna so well and being in her confidence, Maitland was in a position to have written a classic biography of her. He had the chance to be Dr Kingsford's 'Boswell.' Instead, he was a Judas who betrayed her. His denigration of Anna in his 'biography' set back true appreciation of her for over one hundred years. Anna's reputation was sacrificed by various people for their own self interest. Anna was a prophet in the original sense of the word, that is, a person who speaks the word of God. But as often is the case, a prophet is without honour in her own country. Anna dedicated her life to bringing truth and light to a Dark Age. She did not fail, the world failed her. The people around her were human, all too human. As the untruths about her have now been exposed, her efforts to enlighten humanity can be more fully appreciated.

Notes

1. *The Woman's Signal* (14 October 1897): 248.
2. *Light* (7 March 1896): 115-117.
3. *The Theosophist* (March 1896): 374-5.
4. *Lucifer* (18 and 15 March 1896): 1-8.
5. *The Times* 23 January 1896: 8.
6. *The British Medical Journal* (25 January 1896): 253.
7. *Theosophy in Australia* (11 April 1896): 7.
8. *Light* (15 August 1914).
9. Kingsford, 1916, 62.
10. *Life*, II.326.
11. *Lucifer* (February 1894): 517.
12. *Life*, II.280.
13. *Light* (19 January 1895): 31-2.
14. *England and Islam*, 496.
15. Kingsford 1886, 36.
16. *The Soul and How It Found Me,* 125.
17. Kingsford 1916, 'The Systematisation and Application of Psychic Truth,' 170-83.
18. *Life*, I. 385.
19. *Life*, I. 47.
20. Maitland 1905, 37.
21. *Life*, I. 172.
22. Maitland 1905, 91-2.
23. Maitland's account of Anna's psychic attack further lacks conviction because he mentions no harmful after-effects upon her. A psychic attack has devastating effects upon the recipient, as shown by the occultist Dion Fortune who took ten years to fully recover from such an attack. See Fortune 2001, xviii-xxiv.
24. *The Academy* (13 October 1877).
25. *Life*, I. 249.
26. *Ibid.*, I. 250.
27. *Light* (14 March 1896): 130.
28. *Life*, II. 291.
29. Kingsford 1916, 163.
30. *Life*, II. 9.
31. *Ibid.,* II. 294- 6.
32. *Ibid.,* II. 296- 97.
33. *Ibid.,* II. 66.
34. Kingsford and Maitland 1912, 60.
35. Maitland 1905, vii.
36. *Life* I. vii.

Appendix - 1

Some features of Anna's character as revealed in her horoscope

Those with the Sun in Virgo, like Anna, are described as being discriminating, practical, kind and courteous. Purity and perfection are attributes of Virgo, so it is fitting that she published books called *The Perfect Way in Diet* and *The Perfect Way, or the Finding of Christ.* In fact, she envisioned these works as the beginning of a 'Perfect Way' series. Mercury, the planet of communication and the mind rules Virgo, and is exalted in this placement. Anna had the Sun and Mercury conjunct in Virgo, indicating an alert mind and good teaching abilities, with excellent speech and writing skills. She was a born teacher, and everything she wrote, whether it was stories, on health, or religion, had didactic intent. Mercury, or Hermes to the Greeks, was the messenger of the gods; a divinity with particular significance to Anna, as the Hermetic teachings are said to have been inspired by Hermes. Further, Anna herself brought divine wisdom to humankind.

Although Virgo is sometimes held to be critical of others, she reserves the severest criticism for herself. In a letter to *Light* in 1882 Anna mentioned the conflict between the lower and higher selves as 'the very fundamental doctrine of all religion.' She went on, 'Speaking personally, I am profoundly sensible of this conflict, and am daily 209 reminded that I am a compound personality.'[1] According to Sheila Farrant, 'Virgo has the only truly pure and holistically integrated mind in the Zodiac, the only one that forever retains its integrity.'[2] Her writings and achievements show Anna had a brilliant mind.

The goddess associated with Virgo is Artemis, a most suitable symbol for Anna. Artemis of the Silver Bow was the child of Leto the white swan and Zeus, along with her twin brother Apollo. Farrant wrote of Artemis:

> Her arrows are the arrows of the intellect, keen, swift and impersonal, and at her temple at Delphi her priestess pronounced on political, legal and moral problems as well as those to do with healing. Her priestess was called the Pythia (Serpent/snake), and was reputed to be immune to snake-bite. As Artemis of Pythia her shrine was famous throughout the Aegean, and was renowned for healing and prophecy. Her priestesses were celibate.[3]

Artemis loved pristine nature and animals, for she was the mistress of wild things. She was beholden to no male, and Zeus guaranteed her wish for freedom and independence. Artemis is portrayed as a huntress, shooting animals with her well aimed arrows. However, this must be understood in terms of its inner meaning, for in the esoteric sense, wild animals stand for our own untamed passions. The arrows represent intellect shooting down the wild beasts of our lower nature. Farrant points out that Artemis has been greatly insulted by being turned into a fertility goddess. This arose because she was confused with the many breasted Artemis of Ephesus.

Anna mentioned a liking for Pallas Athene, the Greek goddess who sprang fully formed from the head of Zeus. Though some people associate Athene with the sign Libra, Farrant mounts a persuasive case for relating her to Aquarius. As Anna had Aquarius rising, this is a factor in her attraction to Athene.

The rising sign is the sign on the eastern horizon at birth. It indicates the persona or outward personality and the manner in which one receives first impressions. Anna showed Aquarian features in her character. Aquarius is an air sign, thus the thinking function is emphasised. Aquarians often live in the mind, sometimes to the neglect of the emotions. Further, Anna had no planets in water signs, indicating a lack of contact with the emotional nature. She pursued fulfilment in the world of ideas rather than in emotional involvements. Being a fixed sign, the Aquarian has a strong will and follows her own path in life. The Aquarian often is original in her thinking and behaviour, and deliberately chooses not to follow the crowd. This was certainly true with Anna. Aquarius is the sign of friends and social groups. Anna had a wide circle of friends, though few of them are mentioned by Maitland. She was also much involved in group activity to promote her causes, an Aquarian attribute. Those with Aquarius rising have a highly charged nervous system which needs much activity and creative outlets to prevent the 'blowing of a fuse.'

Anna's Moon in Sagittarius indicates a questing, restless person who loves to roam about. She moved constantly between the vicarage, London, St Leonards and the Continent. It also signifies a teacher who can inspire others. The Sagittarian Moon is apt to find fulfilment in spiritual pursuits rather than in family life. Her Moon in the ninth house shows a person whose dreams and visions can be of great significance. This placement indicates seer-ship and a mind that is receptive toward the super-conscious realms.

Various planetary aspects in Anna's chart shed further light on her personality. With her Moon square to Saturn, the mother had a contracting and negative influence. Anna has Venus and Pluto in opposition, showing that the love and power drives were entangled. Anna's Venus and Uranus are in opposition, indicating a desire for emotional freedom with no restrictions. These aspects are indicative of her karma, for she was not cut out to be a conventional wife and mother but sought achievement outside the home.

Anna's Moon is trine with Uranus, an aspect which gives an original mind with strong intuitive powers. A highly creative and inspirational person with genius potential. A unique personality with changing experiences. In an advanced soul like Anna, this aspect gives healing abilities.

Her Mars is trine with the Sun, showing will and action were in good combination for constructive achievement. In past lives the lower self had been tamed by the will. The father was an inspirational role model. Mars and Mercury are trine, showing an alert and courageous mind which enjoys the exchange of ideas. She was totally committed to her beliefs. She was most active in the public arena, conveying her ideas by speech and the written word.

Notes

1. Kingsford 1916, 192.
2. Farrant, 130.
3. Ibid., 134.

Appendix - 2

Some features of Maitland's horoscope

Maitland's Sun was in Scorpio, showing a person with a strong will, much determination, and an intense desire nature. Scorpio is a fixed sign, and he can be the most stubborn sign in the zodiac. The Scorpio personality may pursue his personal desires beyond all reason to extreme lengths. Maitland showed this in his 'biography' of Anna, the bulk of which is pure fantasy: his fantasies about Anna, and fantasies of his own self aggrandizement. Scorpio is well known for being extremely secretive. Maitland kept his real feelings about Anna secret while she was alive, but after she died he poured them all out in the 'biography.' As the time of his birth is unknown, we cannot be certain of his rising sign. However, a solar chart, drawn up for sunrise or noon, can give significant data which delineates character.

Maitland's Moon was in the sign of Capricorn, showing strong ambition and a power complex. The Capricorn Moon wants recognition as an important and powerful person. Maitland showed in his novels that he saw himself as a power behind the scenes, combining Capricorn and Scorpio characteristics. Capricorn is ruled by Saturn, the planet of limitation. The Moon in this sign has trouble expressing the emotions because they are rigid and crystalised. He was not a demonstrative man and his emotional side was certainly repressed. In his writings he expressed his feelings and an intense fantasy life.

Certain planetary aspects shed light on prominent personality traits in Maitland. Jupiter is square to the Sun, indicating an inflated ego. Neptune conjunct the Moon and Uranus shows an openness to the astral plane and psychic phenomena. He paid many visits to mediums to receive spirit messages and, by his own account, he had various direct psychic experiences himself. His psychic messages came from low level spirits or 'astrals,' and were highly coloured by his obsessive imagination. Neptune dissolves boundaries, and being close to the Moon gives a desire to merge with others. This helps explains Maitland's feeling of oneness with Anna, intensified by his strong Scorpio desire nature. Mars in Sagittarius indicates an impulsive person who scatters his energies. There is an interest in sports, gambling, religion and philosophy. Maitland said he won the champions trophy in archery, and he enjoyed swimming and ice skating. Moon square Pluto indicates a powerful and controlling mother, resulting in a tendency to deny one's negative emotions. His Mars square Pluto indicates an extremely wilful person with anti-social tendencies and violent feelings under the surface. Together with aggressive Mars in Anna's tenth house of public reputation, this helps explain his denigration of Anna in his biography.

Appendix - 3

The fate of Eadith Kingsford

Eadith Kingsford is recorded in the census of 1901, with her first name spelt 'Edith.' She was living in Hencairn, a boarding house in picturesque Barmouth, a town on the west coast of Wales. No doubt Eadith's love of the sea came from her young days at St Leonards. Eadith's age is given as 29, but she was 32 at the time. The only other boarder mentioned in the establishment is Conradine Roschel, a 39 year old German born spinster. Samuel Hopgood Hart met Eadith 'for the first time,' in July 1915, in connection with his search for Anna's manuscripts. Eadith and the Harts must have kept in touch, for in her will she calls Hart and his wife Elizabeth her friends. If Eadith talked to Hart about Anna, he did not publish any new information about her.

Eadith died on 31 March 1955, aged 86, at The Old Manor, Salisbury, Wiltshire. Her will, drawn up in 1936, gives previously unknown information about her life and activities. She owned a house called 'Fyning Cottage' on Marine Parade, Lee-on-Solent, Hampshire. For many years she lived with her maid, Elizabeth Mary Voak, to whom she bequeathed one year's salary and £650 cash. Eadith also instructed £3,000 be invested and the interest paid to Elizabeth for the rest of her life.

Eadith revealed in her will the intriguing information that she wrote a 'book' called 'Desolation,' the manuscript, papers and notes of which she bequeathed to the Society for Psychical Research. The archivist of the Society has informed me they have nothing by Eadith, nor any record of receiving anything. She also left a typed copy of the first part of 'Desolation' to Constance Hinton (nee Lingen Burton), wife of Dr Hammond Tooke Hinton, whose will, if any, has not been located.

Eadith must have done a certain amount of writing, for she left to her cousin Charles Bernard Goodrich Dick, 6 Elsworthy Terrace, Primrose Hill, London, 'all my books, manuscripts, letters and correspondence.' He died, and in 1951 she made a codicil replacing him as a benefactor with his son, John Bernard Goodrich Dick. John Dick died on 24 July 1953, aged 71, at 1 Neville Court, Grove End Road, London. He left all his estate to his wife, Mary Blanche Dick, but made no mention in his will of anything from Eadith.

Eadith left to her cousin Harold Leonard Bonus a number of Anna's possessions. These were her bridal veil of Honiton lace, her diploma, her portrait painted on china and framed in velvet, her miniature made into a brooch, and her album containing 'old autographs.' Harold died intestate in 1941 at the age of 52, and his estate of £710 passed to his wife, Daisy Emma Bonus, 14 Beech Road, Norbury, Croydon, Surrey. Harold was the son of Leonard Bonus (b.1855), the son of Anna's brother Albert. Eadith left to Mary Bonus (b.1858), widow of Rev. Albert Bonus, of Alphington, Exeter, Devon, items of family silverware and china plaques painted by Anna.

On 22 July 1949 Eadith appended a codicil to her will stating'although certain of the beneficiaries of my said will have died I do not consider it necessary to make any further alteration to my said will.' Maybe Eadith gave to other family members the items intended for the beneficiaries who died before her. Eadith appointed the Westminster Bank Limited, 41 Lothbury, in the City to be her executor and trustee. Now called the National Westminister Bank, it has informed me that it has no record of Eadith's will.

Bibliography

Adams, Carol J. *The Sexual Politics of Meat: a Feminist-Vegetarian Critical Theory.* New York: Continuum, 1990.

Anderson, Elizabeth Garrett. 'The Ethics of Vivisection,' *Edinburgh Review* (July 1899): 147-169.

Anderson, Nancy Fix. *Woman Against Woman in Victorian England: a Life of Eliza Lynn Linton.* Bloomington: Indiana University Press, 1987.

Asquith, Margot. *The Autobiography of Margot Asquith.* London: Thornton Butterworth, 1920.

Atwood, Mary. *A Suggestive Inquiry Into the Hermetic Mystery.* 1918. Reprint. Jacksonville, FL : Yogi Publication Society, n. d.

Auerbach, Nina. *Woman and the Demon: the Life of a Victorian Myth.* Cambridge, MA: Harvard University Press, 1982.

Australian Dictionary of Biography. Melbourne: Melbourne University Press, 1966-2000.

Avery, Jeanne. *The Rising Sign: Your Astrological Mask.* Garden City, NY: Doubleday, 1982.

Barker, Felix. *Greenwich and Blackheath Past.* London: Historical Publications, 1993.

Benn, Miriam. *Predicaments of Love.* London: Pluto Press, 1992.

Besant, Annie. *Annie Besant, an Autobiography.* London: Fisher Unwin, 1893.

Blake, Catriona. *The Charge of the Parasols: Women's Entry to the Medical Profession.* London: The Women's Press, 1990.

Blake, William. *Collected Works.* Edited by Geoffrey Keynes. London: Oxford University Press, 1972.

Blavatsky, Helena P. *Collected Writings.* Adyar: Theosophical Publishing House, 1958-1966.

— *The Letters of H.P.Blavatsky to A.P.Sinnett and Other Miscellaneous Letters.* London: T. Fisher Unwin, 1925.

Bonner, Thomas Neville. *To the End's of the Earth: Women's Search for Education in Medicine.* Cambridge, MA: Harvard University Press, 1992.

Bonus, John. *Shadows of the Rood; or, Types of Our Suffering Redeemer Jesus Christ Occurring in the Book of Genesis.* London: Printed for the Author, 1856.

— *Thoughts in Verse For My Friends*. London: Longmans, 1914.

— *The Ideal in Diet.* Richard J. James: London, 1915

Briggs, Lynn. Compiler. *A Shropshire Christmas.* Far Thrupp: Alan Sutton, 1993.

Bryan, Benjamin. Editor. *The Vivisectors' Directory.* London: Victoria Street Society, 1884.

Burfield, Diana. 'Theosophy and Feminism: Some Explorations in Nineteenth-Century Biography.'In Pat Holden, editor. *Women's Religious Experience.* London: Croom Helm, 1983: 27-55.

Butt, G. Baseden. *Madame Blavatsky.* London: Rider, 1930.

Caine, Barbara. *Victorian Feminists.* Oxford: Oxford University Press, 1992.

Carpenter, Edward. *My Days and Dreams: Being Autobiographical Notes.* London: George Allen & Unwin, 1916.

Chesterton, G.K. *Autobiography*. London: Burns & Washbourne, 1936.

Cleather, Alice Leighton. *H.P. Blavatsky as I Knew Her: With an Addendum by Basil Crump.* Calcutta: Thacker, Spink, 1923.

Clifford, Edward. *Broadlands As It Was.* London, 1890.

Cobbe, Frances Power. *Life of Frances Power Cobbe by Herself.* London: Richard Bentley, 1894.

— 'The Scientific Spirit of the Age,' *Contemporary Review* 54 (1888): 126-139.

Coleman, William Emmette. *Blavatsky Unveiled.* Bombay, 1892.

Cooter, Roger, editor. *Studies in the History of Alternative Medicine.* Oxford: Macmillan Press, 1988.

Crawford, Elizabeth. *The Women's Suffrage Movement: a Reference Guide 1866-1928.* London: UCL Press, 1999.

Crow, Duncan. *The Victorian Woman.* London: George Allen & Unwin, 1971.

Crowley, Aleister. *Book 4*. York Beach, ME: Samuel Weiser, 1980.

Davies, Charles Maurice. *Heterodox London: or, Phases of Free Thought in the Metropolis.* 2v. London: Tinsley Brothers, 1874.

Dictionary of National Biography. London: Oxford University Press, 1917-1990.

Dijkstra, Bram. *Idols of Perversity: Fantasies of Feminine Evil in the Fin-de- Siecle Culture.* Oxford: Oxford University Press, 1986.

Dworkin, Andrea. *Pornography: Men Possessing Women.* London: Women's Press, 1981.

Ehrenreich, Barbara & Deirdre English. *Witches, Widwives, and Nurses: a History of Women Healers.* Old Westbury, N.Y.: Feminist Press, 1972.

Eliot, George. *Daniel Deronda.* 1876. London: Zodiac Press, 1971.

Ellis, Havelock. *My Life.* London: Neville Spearman, 1967.

Farrant, Sheila. *Symbols for Women: a Feminist Guide to the Zodiac.* London: Mandala, 1989.

Fawcett, Millicent Garrett. 'The Future of Englishwomen: a Reply,' *The Nineteenth Century* (August 1878): 347-357.

— *What I Remember.* 1925. Reprint. Westport: Hyperion Press, 1976.

Feinman, Clarice. *Women in the Criminal Justice System.* Westport, CT:Praeger, 1994.

Ferrante, Joan. *Woman as Image in Medieval Literature.* New York: Columbia University Press, 1975.

Fortune, Dion. *The Mystical Qabalah.* London: Aquarian Press, 1987.

— *Psychic Self-Defense.* York Beach: Weiser Books, 2001.

Foster, Joseph. *Alumni Oxonienses.* Nendeln: Kraus Reprint, 1968.

Foster, Michael. *Claude Bernard.* London: T. Fisher Unwin, 1899.

Foster, R. F. *W.B. Yeats: a Life, I: the Apprentice Mage 1865-1914.* Oxford: Oxford University Press, 1997.

French, Richard D. *Antivisection and Medical Science in Victorian Society.* Princeton: Princeton University Press, 1975.

Gandhi, M. Gandhi's *Autobiography: the Story of My Experiments With Truth.* Washington: Public Affairs Press, 1948.

— *The Collected Works of Mahatma Gandhi* v.1. Delhi: Ministry of Education and Broadcasting, 1958.

[Garrigues, John?] *The Theosophical Movement 1875-1925.* New York: E. P. Dutton, 1925.

Gates, Barbara. *In Nature's Name: an Anthology of Women's Writing and Illustration, 1780-1930.* Chicago: University of Chicago Press, 2002.

Gelling, Margaret. *The Place Names of Shropshire.* Pt. 1. Liverpool: English Place Name Society, 1990.

Gilbert, Edmund W. *Brighton: Old Ocean's Bauble.* London: Methuen, 1954.

Godwin, Joscelyn. 'Lady Caithness and her Connection with Theosophy,' *Theosophical History* 7, no. 4 (October 2000): 127-146.

— *The Theosophical Enlightenment.* Albany: State University of New York Press, 1994.

Goldfarb, Russell M. & Clare R. *Spiritualism and Nineteenth-Century Letters.* Cranbury, NJ: Associated University Press, 1978.

Golub, Edward S. *The Limits of Medicine: How Science Shapes Our Hope for the Cure.* New York: Times Books, 1994.

Gomes, Michael. *Creating the New Age: Theosophy's Origins in the British Isles.* London: Theosophical Publishing House, 2000.

Greer, Mary. *Women of the Golden Dawn: Rebels and Priestesses.* Rochester, VT: Park Street Press, 1995.

Gurney, Edmund, Frederic Myers and Frank Podmore. *Phantasms of the Living.* 2v. 1886. Reprint. Gainsville, FL: Scholar's Facsimiles and Reprints, 1970.

Hackwood, Frederick William. *Staffordshire Customs, Superstitions and Folklore.*

1924. Reprint. East Ardsley: EP Publishing, 1974.

Haig, Alan. *The Victorian Clergy.* London: Croom Helm, 1984.

Harrison, Brian. *Separate Spheres: the Opposition to Women's Suffrage in Britain.* London: Croom Helm, 1978.

Harvie, Christopher & H.C.G. Matthew. *Nineteenth-Century Britain.* Oxford University Press, 2000.

Haskins, Susan. *Mary Magdalen: Myth and Metaphor.* London: HarperCollins, 1993.

Haug, C. James. *Leisure and Urbanism in Nineteenth Century Nice.* Lawrence: The Regents Press of Kansas, 1982.

Hedrick, Joan D. *Harriet Beecher Stowe, a Life*. Oxford: Oxford University Press, 1994.

Hellerstein, Erna. Editor. *Victorian Women: a Documentary Account of* Women's Lives in Nineteenth-Century England, France and the United *States*. Stanford: Stanford University Press, 1981.

Henderson, Archibald. *George Bernard Shaw: Man of the Century*. New York: Appleton-Century-Crofts, 1956.

Herber, Mark D. *Ancestral Trails: the Complete Guide to British Genealogy and Family History*. Baltimore, MD: Genealogical Publishing Company, 1998.

Hirsh, Pam. *Barbara Leigh Smith Bodichon 1827-1891: Feminist, Artist and Rebel*. London: Chatto & Windus, 1998.

Horn, Pamela. *The Changing Countryside in Victorian and Edwardian England and Wales*. London: Athlone Press, 1984.

Howe, Ellic. *The Magicians of the Golden Dawn*. York Beach: Samuel Weiser, 1978.

Hutch, Richard A. 'Helena Blavatsky Unveiled,' *Journal of Religious History* 11, no. 2 (1980): 320-341.

Inman, E.C. *History of Lichfield Theological College*. Lichfield: Lomax's Successors, 1928.

Jalland, Pat. *Women, Marriage and Politics 1860-1914*. Oxford: Clarendon Press, 1986.

Jeffries, Richard. *The Open Air*. 1885. Reprint. London: Eyre and Spottiswoode, 1948.

Jex-Blake, Sophia. *Medical Women: a Thesis and a History*. 1886. Reprint. New York: Source Book Press, 1970.

Johansson, Sheila Ryan. 'Sex and Death in Victorian England.' In *A Widening Sphere: Changing Roles of Victorian Women*. Edited by Martha Vicinus. Bloomington: Indiana University Press, 1977:163-181.

Kean, Hilda. *Animal Rights: Political and Social Change in Britain since 1800*.London: Reaktion Books, 1998.

Kingsford, Anna. 'Address of the President: October 21st 1883 To the London Lodge of The Theosophical Society,' *Theosophical History* (July 1987): 82-85.

— *Addresses and Essays on Vegetarianism*. 1912. Reprint. Kila, MT: Kessinger Publishing, 1997.

— *Beatrice, a Tale of the Early Christians*. London, 1863.

— *"Clothed With the Sun" Being the Book of the Illuminations of Anna (Bonus) Kingsford.* Edited by Edward Maitland. 1937. Reprint. Third edition. Edited by Samuel Hopgood Hart. Santa Fe, NM: Sun Books, 1993.

— *The Credo of Christendom and Other Addresses and Essays on Esoteric Christianity.* Edited by Samuel H. Hart.1916. Reprint. Kila, MT: Kessinger Publishing, 1997.

— *An Essay on the Admission of Women to the Parliamentary Franchise.* London: Trubner & Co., 1868.

— *The Perfect Way in Diet.* 1881. Reprint. Kila, MT: Kessinger Publishing, 1997.

— 'Recent Researches into Hydrophobia,' *The Science Monthly* 2 (1884): 1-4; 78-82.

— *River Reeds.* London: Joseph Masters, 1863.

— *Rosamunda the Princess, an Historical Romance of the Sixth Century and other Tales.* London: James Parker, 1875.

— *The Virgin of the World.* 1885. Reprint. Wizards Book Shelf: Minneapolis, 1977.

— 'Unscientific Science.' In William Colville, *Spiritual Therapeutics,* 1890. Reprint. Kila, MT: Kessinger, 2003: 292-308.

— 'The Uselessness of Vivisection,' *The Nineteenth Century* (February 1882): 171-183.

Kingsford, Anna (Bonus) and Edward Maitland. *Addresses and Essays on Vegetarianism.* Edited by Samuel Hopgood Hart.1912. Reprint. Kila, MT: Kessinger, 1997.

— *The Perfect Way, or the Finding of Christ.* Seventh Edition. Santa Fe, NM: Sun Books, 1996.

— *Reply to the 'Observations' of Mr T. Subba Row.* London: National Press Agency, 1884.

Knight, Gareth. *Dion Fortune & The Inner Light.* Loughborough: Thoth Publications, 2000.

Kuhn, Alvin Boyd. *The Lost Light: An Interpretation of Ancient Scriptures.* 1940. Reprint. Kila, MT: Kessinger, 1997.

Lansbury, Coral. 'Gynaecology, Pornography, and the Antivivisection Movement,' *Victorian Studies* 28 (Spring 1985): 413-437.

Leadbeater, Charles. W. *How Theosophy Came to Me.* Adyar: Theosphical Publishing House, 1930.

Levine, Philippa. *Feminist Lives in Victorian England: Private Roles and Public Commitment.* Oxford: Basil Blackwell, 1990.

Lewis, Jane, ed. *Before the Vote Was Won: Arguments For and Against Women's Suffrage.* London: Routlegde and Kegan Paul, 1987.

Life and Work of Thomas Hardy. Edited by Michael Millgate. Athens, GA: University of Georgia Press, 1985.

Lilly, W.S. 'The New Naturalism,' *The Forthightly Review* 38 (1885): 240-256.

Lonsdale, Margaret. 'Platform Women,' *The Nineteenth Century* 15, no. 85 (March 1884): 409-415.

Maitland, Edward. *Anna Kingsford: Her Life, Letters, Diary and Work.* Third edition. Edited by Samuel H. Hart. London: John M. Watkins, 1913.

— *By and By: an Historical Romance of the Future.* 1873. Reprint. Boston: Gregg Press, 1997.

— *England and Islam.* 1877. Reprint. Kila, MT: Kessinger Publishing, 2003.

— *Higher Law: a Romance.* Revised edition. London: Tinsley Brothers, 1871.

— *How the World Came to an End in 1888.* London: Field & Tuer, 1884.

— *The Keys of the Creeds.* London: Trubner, 1875.

— *The Pilgrim and the Shrine.* London: Tinsley Brothers, 1872.

— *The Soul and How It Found Me. Being a Narrative of Phenomena Connected With the Production of England and Islam.* London: Tinsley Brothers, 1877.

— *The Story of Anna Kingsford and Edward Maitland and the New Gospel of Interpretation.* Third edition. Birmingham : Ruskin Press, 1905.

Manton, Jo. *Elizabeth Garrett Anderson.* New York: E.P. Dutton, 1965.

Matthews, Caitlin and John. *The Western Way: a Practical Guide to the Western Mystery Tradition. Vol. II The Hermetic Tradition.* London: Arkana, 1986.

Mee, Arthur. Editor. *Shropshire: County of the Western Hills.* London: Hodder & Stoughton, 1939.

Merchant, Peter. 'Double Blessedness: Anna Kingsford and *Beatrice*.' In Women of Faith in Victorian Culture: Reassessing the Angel in the House. Edited by Anne Hogan and Andrew Bradstock. London: Macmillan, 1998.

Meynell, Viola. *Alice Meynell, a Memoir.* London: Jonathan Cape, 1947.

Miller, Florence Fenwick. *Autobiography 'An Uncommon Girlhood'* [London] c.1920s-30s. Unpublished manuscript, Wellcome Library, London. — 'Woman: Her Position and Her Prospects, Her Duties and Her Doings,' [Obituary of Dr Anna Kingsford] *Lady's Pictorial* (3 March 1888): 216.

Millett, Kate. *Sexual Politics.* London: Rupert Hart-Davis, 1970.

Millgate, Michael. *Thomas Hardy: A Biography.* Oxford: Oxford University Press, 1982.

Muirhead, Findlay and Marcel Monmarche, editors. *Paris and Its Environs.* London: Macmillan, 1927.

Nairn, Ian and Nikolaus Pevsner. *Sussex.* Harmondsworth: Penguin, 1965.

Neff, Mary K. *How Theosophy Came to Australia and New Zealand.* Sydney: Australian Section Theosophical Society, 1943.

Olcott, Henry S. *Old Diary Leaves. Third Series 1883-1887.* Adyar: Theosophical Publishing House, 1929.

Oppenheim, Janet. *The Other World: Spiritualism and Psychical Research in England, 1850-1914.* Cambridge: Cambridge University Press, 1985.

Owen, Alex. *The Darkened Room: Women, Power and Spiritualism in Late Nineteenth Century England.* London: Virago, 1989.

— *The Place of Enchantment: British Occultism and the Culture of the Modern.* Chicago: University of Chicago Press, 2004.

Patmore, Coventry. *The Angel in the House.* London: Cassell, 1889. Perkin, Joan. *Victorian Women.* New York: New York University Press, 1995.

Pevsner, Nikolaus. *Shropshire.* Harmondsworth: Penguin, 1958.

— *Staffordshire.* Harmondsworth: Penguin, 1974.

Pomeroy, Sarah B. *Goddesses, Whores, Wives and Slaves: Women in Classical Antiquity.* London: Robert Hale and Company, 1975.

Richardson, Alan. *The Magical Life of Dion Fortune: Priestess of the 20th Century.* London: Aquarian Press, 1991.

Roe, Jill. *Beyond Belief: Theosophy in Australia 1879-1939.* Kensington, NSW: New South Wales University Press, 1986.

Ruskin, John. *Sesame and Lilies.* London: Macmillan, 1910.

Russell, George W. E. *Portraits of the Seventies.* London: Unwin, 1916.

Salt, Henry. *Seventy Years Among Savages.* London: George Allen & Unwin, 1921.

Selvidge, Marla J. *Notorious Voices: Feminist Biblical Interpretation, 1500-1920.* New York: Continuum, 1996.

Sharpe, Robert. *The Cruel Deception: the Use of Animals in Medical Research.* Wellingborough: Thorsons Publishing Group, 1988.

Shirley, Ralph. *Occultists and Mystics of All Ages.* London: William Rider, 1920.

Sinnett, Alfred P. Editor. *The Early Days of Theosophy in Europe.* London: Theosophical Publishing House, 1922

— *Incidents in the Life of Madame Blavatsky.* New York: Arno Press, 1976.

— *Autobiography of Alfred Percy Sinnett* (1840-1921) London: Theosophical History Centre, 1986.

Stanfeld, James. 'Medical Women,' *The Nineteenth Century* (July 1877): 888- 901.

Steiger, Isabelle de. *Memorabilia: Reminiscences of a Woman Artist and Writer.* London: Rider, 1927.

Stetson, Dorothy M. *A Woman's Issue: the Politics of Family Law Reform in England.* Westport, CT; Greenwood Press, 1982.

Symonds, John. *Madame Blavatsky.* London: Odhams Press, 1959.

Taylor, A.E. 'Dreams and Sleep,' *Encyclopaedia of Religion and Ethics.* Vol 5.

Edited by James Hastings. Edinburgh: T. & T. Clark, 1976. Vol. 5: 30

Trollope, Anthony. *Clergymen of the Church of England.* 1866. Leicester: Leicester University Press, 1974.

Turner, Barry. *Equality for Some: the Story of Girls' Education.* London: Ward Lock Educational, 1974.

Underwood, Eric. *Brighton.* London: B.T. Batsford, 1978.

VanArsdel, Rosemary T. *Florence Fenwick Miller: Victorian Feminist, Journalist, and Educator.* Aldershot: Ashgate, 2001.

Venn, J.A., compiler. *Alumni Cantabrigienses.* Cambridge: Cambridge University Press, 1951.

Victoria. *The Girlhood of Queen Victoria: a Selection from her Majesty's Diaries Between th e Years 1832 and 1840. Vol.* 1.Edited by Viscount Esher. London: John Murray, 1912.

Victoria Street Society. *The Vivisection Controversy; a Selection of Speeches and Articles.* London: Victoria Street Society, 1883.

Victorian Women: a Documentary Account of Women's Lives in Nineteenth-*Century England France and the United States.* Edited by Erna Hellerstein et al. Stanford: Stanford University Press, 1981.

Vyvyan, John. *In Pity and In Anger: a Study of the Use of Animals in Science.* London: Michael Joseph, 1969.

Wachtmeister, Countess Constance. *Reminiscences of H.P. Blavatsky and The Secret Doctrine.* Wheaton: Quest, 1976.

Walters, Kerry S. and Lisa Portmess. Editors. *Ethical Vegetarianism: From Pythagoras to Peter Singer.* Albany: State University of New York Press, 1999.

Weinreb, Ben and Christopher Hibbert, editors. *The London Encyclopaedia.* London: Macmillan, 1983.

West, Geoffrey. *The Life of Annie Besant.* London: Gerald Howe, 1929.

Wilde, Oscar. *First Collected Edition of the Works of Oscar Wilde 1908-1922:*

Reviews. 1908. Reprint. London: Dawsons of Pall Mall, 1969.

Wordsworth, Elizabeth. *Glimpses of the Past.* London: A.R. Mowbray, 1913

Index

A

Alexandrian school, 142
Allinson, Thomas R., 157
Anderson, Elizabeth Garrett, 37, 65, 89
Arnold, Edwin, 156, 160-61
Astrology, 142
Atcham, 43, 69, 96, 133, 154
Atcham House, 44, 45
Atheism, 100, 133, 167
Atwood, Mary, 164, 171, 199

B

Bernard, Claude, 215
Bert, Paul, 215
Besant, Annie, 93, 102, 199
Black magic, 100, 23, 216
Blackheath, 15, 33
Blackwell, Elizabeth, 65
Blake, William, 12, 101
Blavatsky, H.P., 91, 117-42, 173, 216
  criticises Anna, 232
Boehme, Jacob, 83
Bonus, Elizabeth, mother, 13, 26
Bonus, Emily, sister, 14, 33, 91
Bonus, Ethelind, 122, 185, 220
Bonus, John, father, 9, 13, 26
Bonus, John, brother, 44, 122, 125, 178, 220
  illegitimate daughter, 220
Bonus, Joseph, 178, 184, 216
Bradlaugh, Charles, 40, 93, 133, 139
Bradlaugh advertisement, 134
Bright, Jacob, 48, 49
Brighton, 9, 18, 33, 49, 63
British Theosophical Society, 91, 113, 133
Buddha, 136, 156, 160
Burton, Catherine, 197
Burton, Isabel, 19, 63, 77, 218
Burton, Sir Richard, 175

C

Cactus, 90, 189
Caithness, Lady, 10, 83, 94, 104, 140, 208
Campbell, Lady, 160
Carpenter, Edward, 18Chatterjee, Mohini, 146, 150, 168
Chesterton, G. K., 207
Children's Hospital, Great Ormond Street, 72
Christ, 44, 76, 96, 211
Christian fathers, 142
Christianity, 44, 104, 135, 149, 202
Cobbe, Frances Power, 19, 47, 205
Collins, Mabel, 77, 78, 164
Cousins, James, 206
Crowley, Aleister, 199

D

Dreams, 75, 141, 194

Drysdale, Charles, 53
Drysdale, George, 38, 53
Dworkin, Andrea, 164

E

Eckhart, Meister, 12, 142
Esoteric Buddhism (Sinnett), 10, 115, 135, 138

F

Faithfull, Emily, 39
Farr, Florence, 198
Fawcett, Millicent, 103
Fortune, Dion, 12, 106, 199

G

Gandhi, Mahatma, 12, 133, 199
Ginsburg, Christian, 117
Girton, College, 108
Greer, Mary, 10, 198
Grysanowski, Ernest, 109
Guibert, Cardinal, 83
Gull, Sir William, 100

H

Hardy, Thomas, 33, 77, 168
Hart, Samuel H., 196, 197, 220
Health in society, 93
Hermetic Lodge, 145-48
Hermetic Order of the Golden Dawn, 10, 12, 106, 198
Hermetic Society, 10, 12, 145, 148, 154, 165, 178, 187
Hopkins, Gerard Manley, 24
Horniman, Annie, 198
Hugo, Victor, 113

I

Iamblichus, 141
Incomes, middle class, 26
Initiation, 89
International Health Exhibition, 155

K

Kenealy, Arabella, 110, 146
Kenealy, Mrs Elizabeth, 110
Kiddle incident, 133-34
Kingsford, Algernon
birth, 9; curate of Atcham, 43; rector of Pontesbury, 9, 55; retires, 136, 183; vicar of Atcham, 10, 43, 96
Kingsford, Anna
altercations with Maitland, 85, 215; appearance of, 165, 204; archery, 25, 26; attitudes to, 106, 203, 217; birth, 9, 14; birth of daughter, 9; Blavatsky, attitude to, 209; Blavatsky, meets at Ostende, 173, 216; boots, 62, 156; buys *Lady's Own Paper*, 9, 11; Chapel Street residence, 89, 218; consumption, 11, 64, 108, 156, 175; court case, 39; cremation considered, 182; death of, 52, 163; dreams, 75, 140, 219; elected president of British Theosophy, 113; elopement, 33; esoteric sources, 106; family, 9; family opposes biography, 199, 208; fatal illness, 176; final home, 10; funeral, 184, 219; ice skating, 85; illuminations, 75, 80, 89, 141, 194; impact on people, 58; inheritance, 26; influence of, 85, 106, 208; lampooned by *Punch*, 155, 181; lecture tours, 10; lecturing attitudes, 12, 102, 160; London Lodge, 90, 114, 117, 133, 145; marriage, 28, 31; medical graduation, 81; medical practice, 12, 89, 109, 157 medical studies begin, 11, 53, 61, 79; meets Maitland, 10, 57, 75; memorial for, 196-97; names of, 6; Olcott, letter to, 145; 'Perfect Way' lectures, 10, 92; resigns from London Lodge, 133; Roman Catholic Church, 9, 43, 44; schooling, 18-19, 160; seaside holidays, 16; short stories, 11, 28, 79; Sinnett, 105, 114-22, 133; vegetarian meal, 77; vegetarianism,

10, 11, 87, 96, 101, 111, 154, 200; vivisection, 10, 19, 45, 70, 83, 90, 93; votes for women, 36, 48, 103; wilderness, 116, 169, 206; woodcut stamp, 94; writes husband's sermons, 56; works, *An Essay on the Admission of Women*, 36, 66, 87; *Beatrice, a Tale of the Early Christians*, 9, 16, 17; *Clothed With the Sun*, 10, 195-96, 110; *Dreams and Dream Stories*, 10, 75, 141, 149, 194, 219; *For Richer, For Poorer*, 34; *Health,Beauty and the Toilet*, 10, 16, 18, 155, 171, 210; *In My Lady's Chamber*, 47, 51, 52; *Lady's Own Paper*, 9, 11, 45, 53; *Perfect Way*, 10, 11, 76, 92-109, 135, 158, 166, 196, 204, 221; *Perfect Way in Diet*, 10, 96, 140, 223; *River Reeds*, 9, 20-23; *Rosamunda The Princess*, 9, 28, 66, 68

Kingsford, Eadith, 11, 33, 57, 58, 78, 79, 186, 207

Kingsley, Mrs Henry, 49

Kirby, William F., 148

Knight, Gareth, 199

L

Ladies' Secular Club, 39, 209

Lansbury, Coral, 164

Leadbeater, Charles, 145, 146

Levi, Eliphas, 83, 199

Lichfield, 9, 32, 39, 45, 97

Light of Asia, 156, 160, 162

Lloyd, Francis, 148

Lloyd, George, 180, 193

London School of Medicine, 69, 110

Louise, Princess, 49

M

MacGregor Mathers, S. L., 12, 106, 198

Maitland, Edward,

and Algernon Kingsford, 9, 10, 31, 45, 47, 59, 72, 208; attitude to women, 209, 217; biography of Anna, 12, 13, 91, 197, 203, 221; death, 187, 218; early years, 13, 199; meet Anna, 33; past lives claimed, 217; *Soul and How It Found Me*, 10, 77-79, 128, 208, 210, 214; his untruths about Anna: Anna's character, 28, 101, 215; death of, 15, 52, 83, 92, 163, 206; past lives, 12, 225; fox hunting, 210; health, 8, 108; horoscope, 217, 218, 223; killed two men, 215; living with, 32, 90, 218; offered herself for vivisection, 217; overcome by black magician, 12, 100, 213; spiritualism, 13, 83, 87, 210-11;

Married Women's Property Act, 28, 111

Mary, 13, 76, 80, 177

Massey, Charles C., 92, 146

materialism, 29, 72, 75, 95, 101, 149

Matthews, Caitlin and John, 198

Mead, G R. S., 204

Meynell, Alice, 162, 168, 182

Miller Florence, 26, 44, 49, 62, 64, 89, 103, 174

Mount Temple, Lady, 159, 170, 171, 196

Mysteries, 44, 104, 115, 135

N

Nature, 26, 29, 115

Newman, Francis W., 163

O

Olcott, Henry, 9, 136, 145, 148

P

Paris Medical School, 65, 87

Pasteur, Louis, 168, 215

Plato, 141, 142

Podmore, Frank, 92, 98

Public speaking, 101, 102, 103

Pulsford, John, 119, 195, 196

Pythagorean, 141, 149

R

Richardson, Alan, 199
Ronniger, M. Jane, 47

S

St Eata, 42
St George and the dragon, 148
St Leonards on Sea, 9, 25, 91
Science, 71, 84, 93, 94
Severn, River, 43, 132, 219
Shaw, George Bernard, 99
Shelley, Percy B., 96, 109
Shropshire, 9, 43, 55, 62, 148
Sims, George R., 189, 197
Sinnett, Alfred P., 119
Soul, 10, 77, 85
Spedalieri, Baron, 176, 177
Spiritualism, 13, 83, 87, 210
Stead, William, 154, 188
Steiger, Isabelle de, 63, 77, 183, 218
Sterling, Antoinette, 196
Stratford, 9, 13, 14
Subba Row, T., 140
Sunday Lecture Society, 101

T

Taylor, Clementia, 18, 39, 103
Theosophical Society founded, 9, 90, 114

V

Vegetarianism, 10, 11, 87, 96, 111, 154

W

Wachtmeister, Countess, 173, 216
Waite, A. E., 196, 204
Walker, Ethel, 170
Walker, Mary E., 39
Ward, Samuel, 142, 153
Wilde, Constance, 150
Wilde, Lady, 146, 187, 194
Wilde, Oscar, 146, 150, 194
Wyld, George, 92, 97, 113

Y

Yeats, William Butler, 12, 90, 194